ST. MARY'S COLLEGE OF MARYLAND LIBRARY
ST. MARY'S CITY, MARYLAND

W9-ASI-971

3.87-8x1 11-66 (Sweawngew)

The Politics of Socialism

BOOKS BY

R. H. S. CROSSMAN

THE POLITICS OF SOCIALISM 1965

A NATION REBORN 1960

THE CHARM OF POLITICS 1958

PALESTINE MISSION 1947

GOVERNMENT AND THE GOVERNED 1939

PLATO TODAY 1937, 1959

Editor THE GOD THAT FAILED 1950

The Politics

of Socialism

BY

R.H.S. CROSSMAN

ATHENEUM
NEW YORK 1965

'The Control of Propaganda' is reprinted from *Sykewar*, edited by Daniel Lerner, by permission of The M.I.T. Press. Copyright 1949 by George W. Stewart, Publisher, Inc.

'Loyalty', copyright 1954 by the President and Fellows of Harvard College, is reprinted by permission.

Copyright © 1950, 1963, 1965 by R. H. S. Crossman
All rights reserved
Library of Congress catalog card number 65-15925
Printed in Great Britain by
Northumberland Press Limited, Gateshead
First American Edition

18952

CONTENTS

Introduction
page vii

PART ONE

ACADEMIC PRELUDE 1938
The Theory and Practice of British Freedom
page 3

PART TWO

RE-THINKING SOCIALISM 1951-1964

v

PART THREE

INTRODUCTION

SIX years ago, I made a book out of the political criticism I had contributed over twenty years to the *New Statesman & Nation*. I was careful to limit my selection to those book reviews which I felt to be worth preserving—portraits for the most part and assessments of politicians and pundits, of soldiers and scientists and press lords. *The Charm of Politics* was about people, not ideas; and that perhaps was the reason why it had such a kind reception.

This summer, the collecting urge came upon me once again. Since the Phoney War began in the cloudless autumn of 1939, I cannot remember such a sense of strained yet detached hiatus as descended upon me when the longest and dreariest parliament of modern times went into its final recess. I do not know how my fellow politicians felt, but I was in much the same mood as when, a year or two ago, having nearly died of a haemorrhage I was sent home to spend four weeks relaxing and getting nice and strong before returning to hospital and subjecting myself to a total gastrectomy. Now once again I felt myself floating between extreme alternatives: either a dying end or a new beginning—which would liberate me from years of frustration.

There are politicians, of course, who believe that what they themselves undertake in this period of waiting will profoundly affect their chances under the electoral knife. But in these things at least I have learned to be a fatalist. Instead of disturbing my Coventry party workers during their summer holiday, I decided to wait for the election announcement and meanwhile found myself looking back over these thirteen years of opposition and reflecting on the life I had lived in the political wilderness.

Of course one must not generalise. Most of my colleagues who entered the Commons with me in 1945 have now become exclusive parliamentarians, living single-mindedly within the confines of Westminster, Whitehall and their constituencies. As for the party machine, they regard our headquarters at Transport House as alien country; and if they attend the annual party conference they do so as visitors sitting in the gallery.

I shared this exclusive parliamentary existence until the autumn of 1952 when, almost by accident, I rode into the N.E.C.[1] on a tidal wave of Bevanism which left poor Hugh Dalton and Herbert Morrison disconsolate on the beaches. Seated on the back benches until very recently, I have counted for one vote and learned that the form of loyalty with which I am likely to win the approval of the Whips is sustained silence. My real political life was lived in Smith Square.

To the uninitiated who have never studied the Labour Party's constitution, this may take some explaining. Whereas the Conservatives have evolved a highly centralised organisation, with its leader as its apex, the Labour Party is a unique elliptical organism with two almost independent centres of power. Inside Westminster lives the Parliamentary Labour Party—an autonomous body with its own officers, its own elected Executive, even its own officials. A quarter of a mile away in Smith Square sits the National Executive, deriving its powers solely from the annual conference but excluded from any control of the Parliamentary Party's decisions. What holds them together is the personality of the Leader. His role in life, in fact, is to drive a chariot pulled by a horse and a bull. However fractious the animals may be, he can only side with one against the other with disastrous consequences to all concerned. Indeed, the task of the Leader of the Labour Party—at least while in Opposition—can be compared in this respect to that of an American President: each is faced with a completely unworkable constitution, and the proof of his leadership is that he makes it work.

Constitutionally the National Executive is responsible to conference for making new policies, while the Parliamentary Party deals ad hoc with current problems. In theory this division of function is of course indefensible. Yet in practice it has worked surprisingly well. Shadow Ministers are prepared to leave to less prominent politicians policy-making jobs which require months of attendance, first at working parties, then on sub-committees of the National Executive, then at joint meetings with the T.U.C. The evolution of new policies is a cumbrous and time-absorbing procedure. The parliamentarians are often infuriated by the result. But how many of them would be willing to share in the labour?

So, while reputations were being made and unmade across the

[1] The 26-man National Executive Committee which runs the Labour Party between annual conferences.

way at Westminster, I helped to make and unmake the party policy in Transport House. In dreary committee rooms and in that acoustic monstrosity on the 8th floor, where the N.E.C. meets each month, document after document was slowly beaten out in long hours of frustration punctuated by bitter disappointments and occasionally by the triumph of solid achievement—the adoption of National Superannuation for example. Unlike the debates in Parliament, these intra-party discussions officially take place in private—though when conclusions are near and reputations involved, confidence may be undermined by leaks. But by and large—as a glance at Robert Mackenzie's *British Political Parties*[1] confirms—the secrets of how policy is made inside the party machine have been well preserved. It is when the N.E.C. thinking has been formulated for presentation to the annual conference that public attention is alerted and public controversy begins.

Since the resignation of Aneurin Bevan in the summer of 1951, this controversy has been primarily a matter of re-thinking the philosophy and the policies worked out in the 1930s—for the most part by small groups of the Fabians—and put into practice during the early years of the Attlee Government. In the course of this re-thinking, the production of books and pamphlets was very small: a foreign observer anxious to write a doctoral thesis would find it difficult to spend many chapters describing the theoretical basis of the debate. Very soon the traditional Left Right clash ossified into a battle of cliches and squeezed the living issues out of the debate. As always, in such ideological conflicts, principles become weapons in a struggle for personal power. Those of my colleagues who have a low opinion of ideas in politics used to complain that this method of re-thinking socialism was destroying the Labour Party and delaying its return to power. But try as I may, I can see no other way of working out a new policy for a party which desires not only to preach democracy but to practice it internally.

For eleven years the controversy continued. Then a few months before Hugh Gaitskell's death, it stopped. Parties are organisms with a strong survival instinct; and the Labour Party realised that the policy-making was finished and the time had come to win power in order to carry out the policy. For two years, the controversy has been not inside the party but between the parties. Before this book is published, we shall know which has prevailed.

[1] Heinemann, London, 1955.

During our period in the wilderness, the task of re-thinking socialism by controversy has been my main interest. It struck me, therefore, in this summer of expectancy that it might be of interest to put together in a book some of the contributions which I made —often in the form of lectures delivered from notes and then worked up for publication. When I had selected what seemed worth preserving, I realised that they were linked by a single central theme. The concern of socialism, it has always seemed to me, is not merely the raising of living standards or the achievement of equality but the enlargement of individual freedom. Socialism in fact is not an alternative to parliamentary democracy but the adaptation of it to the requirements of a modern rapidly developing industrial state. And here the socialist is confronted with an 'inherent contradiction', between the means of socialism—public ownership and centralised planning, for example—and the enlargement of individual freedom which is its end.

Long before the war I had learned from the books of R. H. Tawney and the personal example of A. D. Lindsey that this contradiction can only be resolved in practice. I thought it might be interesting therefore to combine this collection—all of which are concerned with the problems of civilising and planning freedom in national and international affairs—with an academic study which I wrote in the year of Munich when I was dividing my time between the Workers Educational Association and the Oxford City Council.

Once again, as in *The Charm of Politics*, I have refused—even where hindsight tempted me—to improve an outdated judgment. Many topical references—now unintelligible—have been excised and a number of overlapping passages curtailed to avoid tedious repetition. But basically I have left each essay as I wrote it.

Prescote, September, 1964.

ACKNOWLEDGEMENTS

Since all but one of these essays have been previously published, there are a number of acknowledgements which I am glad to make. My thanks are due to Dr. J. P. Mayer and Messrs. J. M. Dent & Sons Ltd., for their kind permission to include 'The Theory and Practice of British Freedom' (from 'Political Thought—The European Tradition', 1939); to the Fabian Society, for 'Towards a New Philosophy of Socialism' (from New Fabian Essays, published by the Turnstile Press, 1952) 'Planning for Freedom' (their pamphlet 'The New Despotism') and 'The Affluent Society' (the pamphlet 'Labour and the Affluent Society'); to the publishers of the New Statesman, for 'The Lessons of 1945' (originally 'The New Statesmen' from their Jubilee Issue of 1963) and 'Grotius on Atomic War' (their issue of 14th September 1957); to the publishers of the Political Quarterly, for 'The Cold War' (originally 'Reflections on the Cold War', from their issue of January-March 1951); to the publishers of Encounter, for 'The Clause Four Controversy' ('The Spectre of Revisionism', March 1960) and 'Scientists in Whitehall' (July 1964); to the Royal United Services Institute for 'Western Defence in the Sixties' which appeared in their journal of August 1961.

Also to the publishers of Commentary, New York, for 'Nationalism' (published in May 1950 as 'Nationalism—Ally or Enemy?') and 'Eastern Kolkhoz and Western Co-operation' ('The Polish Miracle', March 1963); to The M.I.T. Press for 'The Control of Propaganda' (which appeared as a supplementary essay to Sykewar, edited by Daniel Lerner, 1949); and to the President and Fellows of Harvard College for 'Loyalty' ('The Ethics of Loyalty'), which appeared in Confluence, 1954.

Part 1

ACADEMIC PRELUDE

1938

THE THEORY AND PRACTICE OF BRITISH FREEDOM

Written in 1938, just after I had finished my first book
'Plato Today'[1]. As Dean of New College and Leader of the
Labour Group on the Oxford City Council I was still
trying to combine the theory and practice of politics.
Before the essay was published, however, I had resigned
my fellowship, become parliamentary candidate for
Coventry, and joined the staff of the New Statesman.

1. INTRODUCTORY

PERHAPS the most common generalisation about British statesmanship is that it hates theory and prefers 'muddling through'.
It is usually made by Englishmen in a tone which blends a
mixture of condescension and self-depreciation, and is usually
employed to excuse the vagaries of foreign policy or the existence
of some glaring anomaly. We have become proud of our reputation
as practical men of affairs, but we are also uneasily aware that 'the
virtue of muddling through' is not really a virtue, and does not really
explain the paradoxes of our political conduct.

Only a moment's serious consideration is necessary in order to see
that theory and speculative thought are by no means foreign to the
British mind. In natural science and economics, to mention only two
departments, Great Britain has excelled, while in the realm of
philosophy British thinkers have been as influential as those of any
other country. In every nation the vast majority of the population are
suspicious of the thinking minority, and the politicians and business
men disregard the academics whenever they can. These are facts
common to human nature at large, not peculiar to the British people.

The true peculiarity of Englishmen consists not in their disregard
of theory but in the uses for which they employ it. Our thought, like
our language, has a deep aversion to systematisation. We have
always been unwilling to base our actions upon a philosophy of life,

[1] George Allen & Unwin.

3

indeed, we have no word to correspond to the German *Weltanschauung*. Theory, for us, is not the foundation upon which practice should be built, but an instrument to be employed in the achievement of given ends. The 'reasonable' man is the man who uses not *Vernunft* but *Verstand*, and it is again significant that the French *raison* and the German *Vernunft* have no equivalents in English. The Anglo-Saxon peoples have produced scientists, historians, and philosophers, but not one pre-eminent exponent of a systematic philosophy or theology. In short, our speculations are employed to destroy or to support a given belief, not to demonstrate the premises of belief itself.

In a very profound sense, then, British political thought is dialectical in character. It is always part of a controversy, and therefore it is only intelligible in the context of conflict which gave rise to it. Even our most academic theorists and our speculative thinkers have elaborated their theories to meet a given situation. We do not dislike theory as such, but we do suspect any theory which has no relation to immediate practical objectives.

This characteristic of our philosophy has its analogy in our institutions. Here, too, we can perceive a dislike for systematisation as such, and a tendency to graft new adjustments onto the body politic. Just as political ideas have developed in the conflict of parties and interests, so our constitution is the result of successive adaptations of the existing structure to new emergencies. We have never undergone a reconstruction of our social system based upon clear-cut principles, and we have never experienced a revolution which was not fundamentally conservative in character. Neither Cromwell's army, nor the Whig aristocrats in 1688, tried to create a new political structure: deeply though they differed in aim, both were concerned to preserve already existing liberties, or at least to persuade themselves that the liberties which they were safeguarding were really parts of an ancestral tradition.

It is a matter of indifference to our argument whether these characteristics are resultants of racial traits, or of social and economic factors, or of both. In this essay it is our aim not to explain but to classify the peculiarities of British political thought. Nevertheless it should be remembered that certain geographical and economic factors have been deeply influential in its development. That this country was insulated from the worst effects of European religious and dynastic struggles, that the development of its national unity was naturally conditioned by its insular position, that its resources of coal and iron gave it a long lead in industrial development, and lastly, that its position between Europe and America gave it a feeling of independence from its neighbours—these are all facts of inestimable importance in our political evolution. They have all tended to produce an easy-going inability to perceive the difficulties and the dilemmas which have faced most other countries fairly frequently in the course of their history. As a result, while ridiculing the excesses of others, we often fail to understand the foundations of our own social order. Busily engaged in argument about our immediate objectives, we leave unnoticed the premises on which these arguments are based; whereas other countries, such as Germany, which are not so fortunately situated, have been forced to consider those premises because they had to construct a social order instead of merely adapting it to change.

This contrast is well illustrated by the problem of nationalism and nationality. The German people found no easy ready-made solution to it. For them, in Luther's time, as to-day, state and nation were separate, even contradictory, terms. National unity had to be achieved, not within, but in spite of, political institutions. They were faced by the questions: What is the German people? What parts of that people shall be included in the German national State? Which (if any) Germany dynasty shall wear the imperial crown? How can national frontiers be reconciled with strategic and economic needs? Thus throughout German history the practical problems of every-day statesmanship necessitated a consideration of the fundamental postulates of the nation-state. There is no necessity to assume that the Germans are racially or hereditarily more profound thinkers than we. Man seldom thinks unless he has to: his most abstract chains of speculation originate usually in some immediate practical need. The fact that, ever since the break-up of the feudal system, Germans have been compelled to solve for themselves problems solved for us by geography is sufficient to account for the difference. But to account for it is not to remove it, and the difference, once made, has influenced the language, the institutions, and the ethics of both nations.

A similar conclusion will be reached by a comparison of France and England. Here, however, it is the problem of internal and not external freedom which we must examine. The foundations of a political order, which secured freedom for a privileged class, had been laid in this country by the Glorious Revolution; and a system of representative institutions had come into existence one hundred years before the period of economic revolution which was to open the way for democracy. The ideas of personal freedom and political responsibility had time to develop in England before they were fully actualised in democratic government. The privileged aristocracy, even in the hey-day of Tory reaction, neither held undisputed power, nor were they, as in France, the useless appendages of a centralised bureaucracy. They were not a ruling caste, but a responsible ruling class, which had not only evolved the system of cabinet government to replace the royal executive (thereby avoiding the perils of autocratic centralism) but was also willing to open its ranks to any individual members of the *nouveaux riches* who would accept its traditions.

The Industrial Revolution, therefore, found a political system elastic enough to adapt itself to the new conditions. Capitalism could develop within it and modify its detail without any violent change; and, more important still, the middle classes, instead of ousting the landed aristocracy from power, learnt from it the traditions of responsibility and social conservatism which were to soften the cruelty of class struggle. Indeed we may go further. As Halévy has shown so brilliantly, the Industrial Revolution in Great Britain should not be considered as a sudden and devastating break with tradition occurring at the end of the eighteenth century, but as a slow process of transformation begun in the fifteenth century and still unfinished to-day. The economic structure of British society was wellnigh complete before the inventions occurred which were to revolutionise the technique of production, and for this reason their political effects were not so disturbing. From the fourteenth century on, the landed interests mixed with the commercial interests of the cities, and the emancipation of the middle classes was accelerated, not begun, by the introduction of machinery and of the factory system. Everywhere in our history we find this softening of the effects of change, which is therefore so gradual and so gentle that it is difficult to analyse it into periods without distorting it.

How striking the contrast is when we turn to eighteenth-century France, and find an ossified political system, within which the landed aristocracy held no responsible position! The economic problems of the country could easily have been rectified and there were men at the disposal of the Government competent to carry through the necessary reforms. The French Revolution occurred, not only because of the overwhelming pressure of economic hardship, but because the middle classes could feel no loyalty to an autocracy which denied them the share in government which their self-respect demanded. It was, in fact, a democratic revolution: the French *bourgeoisie*, unlike the English, at the end of the eighteenth century had to use that right of revolution which Locke had praised, and so democracy came not by a peaceful extension of privilege but by the destruction of a system of government. Here again we observe that political theory is the product of conflict and its instrument too. In the fifty years before the Revolution, France had been forced by the logic of fact to consider the theory of popular sovereignty. Faced by a sovereign monarch, the people made the claim, not to abolish absolute sovereignty as Locke had wished, but to assert its own sovereign power, as the Americans had done. Thus the theory of democracy was evolved both in France and America as the instrument for the attack on irresponsible power. No other idea had the dynamic power to create a revolutionary spirit and to overthrow a system. In the hands of Rousseau and Tom Paine, Locke's cool and reasonable defence of natural rights against the encroachments of James II became a flaming sword to destroy all limitations of the popular will. In short, democratic theory was needed in France to achieve freedom, in Great Britain it was not.

Yet a third illustration of this contrast may be found in the relations of Church and State. In almost every country in the world, the Reformation brought a conflict between Church and State which was the cause of merciless religious wars. Scarcely a people in the world avoided that fundamental dilemma which the competing loyalties of the spiritual and temporal power, of ecumenical Rome and national monarchy occasioned. And this dilemma forced every thinking person to ask himself the questions: What are the rights of the State? Is it the supreme lord and protector of morality? Or is there set against it another institution more holy though less powerful than it? England by a miracle avoided this sharp dilemma. A monarch, claiming divine right, instituted a national church which was neither Protestant nor Catholic, but a blend of both. The whole people was united by a rising tide of nationalism in throwing off the yoke of Rome. They would be divided upon the questions of divine right, the character of the national Church, and the right of dissent. They would persecute and pillage and finally fight out a civil war. But all these conflicts would take place upon the basis of national unity: they would be problems posed to the individual in his relation to the nation-state, never problems which endangered the existence of the nation-state itself.

Our case can be rounded off by a consideration of the fourth great problem of modern political theory. We have seen that the concepts of national unity, political responsibility, and religious freedom were never evolved by Englishmen in their complete revolutionary logic, because there was no need to do so. It remains only to indicate that the problem of economic freedom has been blurred in a similar way. British socialism has never become a systematic body of doctrine based on a scientific analysis of the economic structure; and the British Labour movement has at no period in its history, with the possible exception of Chartism, been a class party determined to monopolise for itself the privileges of power. The elasticity of the social system, the rising standard of living which characterised the last half of the nineteenth century, and, above all, the fact that the co-operative and trade union organisations preceded and conditioned the nature of the political movement—all these factors have prevented the growth in the British mind of any clear-cut theory of economic justice or of economic freedom. Just as the British capitalist found himself evolving a system of monopoly and of imperialism without fully understanding what he was about, so the Labour movement at the end of the nineteenth and the beginning of the twentieth century built up its organisation unaware of the laws of its development, uncertain of its philosophy, and attentive only to the immediate ends in view. It never experienced the martyrdom of Bismarckian persecution, and for this reason never felt in its political actuality the full force of the class war. Inspired largely by the social ideals of nonconformity, it could hardly believe that religion was the opium of the people; and, drawing profit, at least in part, from the prosperity of the export trade and from the social services which the foreign investments of a prosperous *rentier* class could comfortably afford, it could not easily believe in the law of increasing misery which continental scientists conscientiously demonstrated. Thus it inevitably conceived its role as an actor upon the traditional and firmly constructed stage of national politics. British Labour, try as it might, could never seriously believe that parliamentary institutions were a 'superstructure' (the executive committee of the ruling class) which it must first destroy before it erected a brand-new stage precisely suited to its own performance. No! Parliament and local government were its stage; and upon that stage, in collaboration with other parties—and with the monarchy as well—it has been fully satisfied to work out the drama of democratic evolutionary legislation.

2. HOBBES AND LOCKE

Clearly it is somewhat unreasonable for us to claim a greater measure of common sense than our neighbours, or to suggest that 'muddling through' is a peculiar characteristic of the British mind. We are neither more practical than the rest of the world, nor less speculative; but we have been faced by political problems whose solution did not demand speculation. We can no longer pretend, as I suggested at the beginning of this essay, that we, unlike others, are specially devoted to immediate objectives, but we must see that our immediate objectives, unlike those of others, did not usually necessitate drastic reconstruction. For clear-cut theory and profound speculation are not the result of academic tranquillity and cloistered ease: on the contrary, tranquillity produces a mood of easy-going moralising. Urgent and deeply practical necessity is the soil in which philosophic systems, which are always either revolutionary or counter-revolutionary, are grown. Plato, Calvin, Hegel, Marx were not philosophers of peace, but thinkers who realized that drastic discipline, and with it rigorous theory, were necessary to heal the wounds of a stricken society. Such rigour and such discipline are alien to the British mind, not because British common sense disowned them, but because British good fortune did not feel the necessity for them.

How true this is may be seen by a consideration of the one truly systematic political philosopher whom England has produced. Thomas Hobbes is the exception which proves our rule. The *Leviathan* was the monstrous creature of a mind fearful of civil war. Strangely remote from considerations of immediate policy, it offended all parties and pleased none. Hobbes, unlike most of his successors, was faced by a profound dilemma. The new nation-state, thrown up by the convulsions of the Reformation, had been inspired by conflicting motives. In the first place, the old world order in which the local temporal power was sanctified by a Universal Church had been shattered. The wishes of an individual monarch and the will of a people had flouted ecumenical authority, and, with the doctrine of the divine right of kings, had established sovereignty within the nation. This change involved the centralization of power, both in the temporal and in the spiritual sphere. The will of the Tudor Monarch could now be limited by no external force, and would permit no rival within the State itself. But with the breaking of all its external and spiritual chains, the new sovereign had unloosed a new spirit soon to limit his despotic authority. The shattering of the Catholic dogma produced a spirit of individualism in diametrical opposition to 'divine right.' Once the Bible had become the fountainhead of truth, the right of individual interpretation was bound to be claimed by the religious conscience. If a Tudor quoted scripture, so could the meanest of his subjects, and the new Anglican Church found itself between the devil of Rome and the deep sea of nonconformity. Out of these conflicts sprang the claim to religious freedom which was to become one of the motive forces of British Liberalism during the next four hundred years.

Closely connected with this liberation of the individual conscience there rises a new movement of scientific thought. Not only conscience, but reason, had been freed and began to claim undisputed sway over the policies of men. This movement turns not to the Bible but to the classics as its authority. Aristotle, previously formalised into the theology of Aquinas, becomes a new revolutionary force. The Elizabethan, despising the barbaric mysteries of Gothic architecture, adopts the rational, clear-cut lines of Greece and Rome. The Reformation coincides with the Renaissance, and the new theology allies itself with the new rationalism in its attack on the old feudal order.

This is an epoch of ruthless individual self-assertion; it is therefore a violent epoch, in which the excesses of self-willed monarchs are equalled by the turbulence of their subjects. The divine right of kings ferociously asserts its authority over those two other divine rights of conscience and of reason. But the more the monarch manifests his own individual will and reason, the more his subjects perceive that they too, no less than he, are equipped with similar faculties. And all the time these three new forces are united in their determination (unsuccessful, as it happens) to eradicate every vestige of the old medieval world system. Out of this tumult a new social order is forged and a new economic basis of society is painfully constructed. But here, too, Mercantilism is based on a fundamental contradiction. The landholder, enriched by the spoliation of the monasteries, looks for fresh fields of capital exploitation and sometimes finds them in the new worlds discovered by the explorers: and the new order blesses economic individualism and private enterprise, protecting them with a paternal system of State control. But already there is latent a conflict between the interests of a prosperous privileged class of landowners and merchants and the interests of a sovereign monarch asserting manfully the divine right of kings. Who shall delimit the rights of property over against the rights of the sovereign power?

The divine right of kings and the rights of conscience, reason, and property: these are the four conflicting motives out of which the nation-state was born. How to reconcile them within a stable social order was the problem facing Thomas Hobbes, who lived through the convulsions of the Civil War and the Protectorate, only to see a Stuart once more upon the throne.

The *Leviathan* is an un-English book because its author really grapples with the deepest problems of the State. It is un-English also in that it gives a solution as ingenious as it is absurd. Determined to retain absolute sovereignty, Hobbes strips it of that divine right which is its only justification; determined at all costs to provide security for the individual, he removes the right of revolution by which security alone can be achieved. Basing his whole argument on a cool application of scientific reason, he denies to reason that freedom which is vital to its life. Bitterly critical of the pretensions of individual conscience, he finds the justification of sovereignty in a contract whose binding force conscience alone can feel. The four motives are stretched upon a Procrustean bed which cracks the joints of every one of them. For it analyses not the rights of the established sovereign, but the reasons which lead the individual with property and privilege to accept dictatorship: and portrays the fears, the selfishness, and the cynicism of a mind which refused to accept law from on high, and yet feared to listen to the dictates of the people below. The *Leviathan* is the first great justification of dictatorship, but its doctrine can be accepted by no dictator. It is in brief the democratic argument for dictatorship, and as such, in spite of the rigour of its logic, it is based upon a fundamental contradiction. As Locke put it, 'as if when Men, quitting the state of Nature, entered into society, they agreed that all of them but one should be under the restraint of Laws; but that he should still retain all the liberty of the state of Nature, increased with power and made licentious by

impunity. This is to think that men are so foolish that they take
care to avoid what mischiefs may be done them by polecats or
foxes, but are content, nay, think it safety, to be devoured by
lions.'

Critics of Hobbes have perhaps paid too much attention to his
personal peculiarities. He has been treated as a freakish example of
intellectual perversity, and the *Leviathan* has served as a contrast
to the sanity and common sense of *Civil Government*. As a result,
one of the greatest critical thinkers is chiefly remembered for a few
malevolent aphorisms. That later generations should have so mis-
understood him is only an illustration of our argument that British
theorists have rarely been faced by the profound problems of the
State. Alone of our classical thinkers Hobbes lived through an epoch
of chaos in which the stability of the social structure was in imminent
danger of dissolution. His confusions and contradictions are not due
to any flaws in his logic—no thinker has been more ruthlessly consistent—but to the actual conflicts in the society in which he lived.
Granted his premises, granted the elements which he held to be
necessary to any civilised society, no consistent theory was open to
him, since absolute sovereignty was incompatible with the temper
and the interests both of the property-owner and of the religious
mind. The *Leviathan* is therefore an illustration in the realm of
theory of the incompatibilities which produced the Civil War. Taking
his world precisely as he found it, Hobbes found nothing that could
reasonably be expected to hold it together. Both the incoherence and
the unpopularity of his conclusions showed that some new unknown element was necessary to bring stability back to England.
A political theorist can only analyse the data which he is given:
Hobbes cannot be blamed for failing to prophesy that this other
element would soon be available.

When we turn to the pleasant, almost sentimental, delicacies of
Locke's *Treatises of Government*, we feel ourselves at last in friendly
country. Here is the 'typical English thinker,' rational but not
rationalistic, moral but carefully unenthusiastic, shrewd but uncritical of basic principles. Locke is rightly extolled as the first theorist
of representative government, but his admirers often go on quite
wrongly to assert that he was the spokesman of democracy. No
misrepresentation could be more absurd. *Civil Government* is the
philosophy of a privileged class, jealous of its rights and sensitive to
its responsibilities. It avoids the contradiction of the *Leviathan* not

because Locke was more consistent than Hobbes—he was not—but because the propertied classes of England had developed an economic and social cohesion which rendered centralised despotism an anachronism. The upheaval of the Reformation was over: the convulsive death pangs of medievalism were stilled, and England could dispose of a tactless Stuart by a Glorious—and bloodless—Revolution. Whigs and Tories disagreed profoundly, but their deep-seated community of economic interests prevented either party from plunging the country into civil war. Hobbes had believed that the Leviathan must be imposed, artificially and from above, to create and to maintain social stability. Locke, writing after 1688, found that social stability ready made; and it becomes not the central problem but the central assumption of his theory.

We have only to glance at his theory of natural rights and at his picture of the state of nature to appreciate this difference. For Hobbes the State was an escape from anarchy, for Locke it is an instrument for improving the social order inherent in the nature of man. His natural man is a gentleman of rural England, with a comfortable property, and a respect for the property of others. In the everyday life of the country, with its traditional tables of rights and duties, he sees around him a society which in no sense owes its stability to a despotic Leviathan issuing its commands from London. And so he portrays the peace and prosperity of rural England as a natural state, whose intrinsic cohesion needs only the barest minimum of centralised government to preserve it from unnatural cupidity and ambition. Hobbes had tried, by the enforcement of despotism, to curb the war of competing rights: Locke is above all else concerned to protect the natural harmony of natural rights from the encroachments of despotism. The sovereign Leviathan is degraded to a mere servant of the representatives of property. Sovereignty is in fact abolished, and in its place is established the principle of the division of power. In a country of honourable landowners, imbued with a sense of the responsibilities which privilege brings, Locke believed that every conflict can be solved by discussion and compromise, and every one of the representatives, who reluctantly leave their homes and drive up to Westminster, will be united in the determination to preserve the natural peace and order of the shires from the tyranny and extravagance of a royal executive. An executive there must be to maintain the army and conduct foreign policy, but this executive will be jealously watched by a Parliament suspicious of its vaulting ambition. Thus the legislature, in Locke's view, has as its chief task, not the promotion of beneficial legislation but the suppression of undue government activity.

Though political theories are conditioned by historic facts, they are not 'true' reflections of them. *Civil Government* is no more a picture of England after 1688, than the *Leviathan* is of England during and after the Civil Wars. For both are logical structures based upon generalisations and hopes and fears occasioned by real situations, and elaborated by individual minds. But once a theory has been worked out and published, it becomes itself a historical factor: and whether it is influential or not depends on the special conditions in any particular country. It is noteworthy that the *Leviathan* has affected pure theory more profoundly than politics. As a theory of practical application it was still-born, whereas Locke's *Treatises*, adapted as they were to the spirit of the new age, became the standard justification both of the Whigs in England and of the revolutionaries in America. For this reason, we tend to think of Locke as a typically English thinker, whereas we should be more accurate if we said that Locke's temper and conclusions were well suited to his age; and later, when conditions changed, became an important obstacle in the way of adapting British policy and British institutions to a new environment.

We have noticed already the basic assumption of his philosophy that the rights claimed by individuals are harmonious, and that, for this reason, what we need are political institutions designed to prevent despotic power. Locke therefore makes his civil government both the protector of natural rights and the expression of the general will, and he assumes that no conflict can arise between them: the minority will accept majority decisions because they too have rights to be protected. He never considers the possibility of the majority wishing, for instance, to attack property and thereby jeopardising the harmony of rights. Nor does he conceive that the people might desire institutions adapted not to the prevention of despotism, but to the achievement of positive good. Nor, lastly, does he believe that the populace will be continually active in its influence on the representatives. His is a theory of government, not by the people, or through the people, but for the people, and, once the government is constituted, the people have no right to interfere, except in the last extremity and by direct action.

3. GOVERNMENT BY CONSENT, PRESCRIPTION, AND STATUS

This principle has been maintained ever since Locke. Even after the development of democracy, government in England has remained the privilege of the few : the people choose their representatives, but do not rule themselves, and the general will in this country is not sovereign, but a check on government. The growth of the cabinet system, of the civil service, and of highly organised political parties has only deepened this sense of the indirect influence of public opinion, both in local and in national government. Englishmen are not political animals in the sense that they all wish to be politicians : on the contrary, they prefer to enjoy their private lives under a system of free institutions which hands over to an élite the control of policy and of administration. Unlike other western democracies, we have never preached or practised the sovereignty of the general will, nor sought to direct governmental policy by popular mandate. Instead, we have always retained, as our last defence against the misuse of government, the right to direct action which is manifested in the strike, the riot, or the public demonstration. But such direct action is considered not as a part of government, nor as a regular practice, but as a sudden gesture of impatience, unpolitical, spon-taneous, and abrupt, a reminder to our rulers that there are limits beyond which they must not try us. The General Strike was just such a movement. It was not a subversive plot of anarcho-syndicalists, nor yet was it an attempt to reshape the Government : on the contrary it was a non-political expression of sympathy with the miners, an effort by the people, not to throw off the shackles of government, but to indicate to the Government the deep dissatisfaction of the industrial workers. It is typical of British political thought and practice that the deepest dissatisfactions are voiced not through the parliamentary opposition or the normal channels of constitutional government, but through a non-parliamentary and non-political movement. The same inclination is to be found so long ago as in the days of the Anti-Corn Law League, so lately as in the Peace Ballot.[1] In each case it was a non-party voluntary association which roused the people against the policy of Government, and in both cases the people were true not to the theories of constitutional democracy but to the principles of *Civil Government*.

[1] Or, in the 1960s, C.N.D.

For this reason Britain has always been a mystery to foreign observers. The French and American democrats are at a loss to understand how a country so deeply imbued with social snobbery, and so little interested in problems of government, could call itself a democracy. They observe a people cleft by profound class divisions, in which the contrasts of riches and poverty, of culture and illiteracy are unpleasantly obvious; they see, in fact, the economic and social conditions of class war which yet fail to produce a consciousness of class war; and they see, too, democratic institutions which run smoothly because the people rarely employ them for an attack upon privilege and inequality. If, however, they conclude that the English people are therefore subservient, they are sadly wrong. In no country is the intrinsic equality of human personality more deeply felt than in the north of England, in Scotland, and in Wales. The British industrial worker is not servile or obsequious to the ruling class, and yet he leaves to that ruling class, without demur, the privilege of power. On the whole he neither demands nor feels the need of either political or economic equality. Confirmed in his status, jealous of the privileges which that status gives him, and ever on the alert to defend his local liberties, he does not conceive of comparing his position with that of other classes far beyond the boundaries of his communal life. The scope of his ambition (and after all the ideals of political and economic equality spring chiefly from this motive) is limited to immediate practical objectives.

Both the stability and the elasticity of social classes in this country have contributed to this. Stability has made them homogeneous and compact and given to each grade its sense of social position and social prestige. The vast majority in any one class remain contentedly within that class and aspire higher only for their children. This contentment makes the class take on the qualities of status. Elasticity, on the other hand, removes the feeling of caste divisions and so softens the stings of social injustice. The ladder can be and is often climbed. Social divisions are therefore not merely economic divisions, though they are largely conditioned by financial considerations. The worker recognises the class difference between himself and a member of the upper classes, though wage and salary may be the same. He recognises a difference in status on the same economic level and accepts it as a proper part of the social system.

No wonder the Frenchman or the American is puzzled. Here is a democracy which, in its social life, disregards the principles of equality, a peaceful community which admits within itself a whole scale of class-divisions, a contented nation which still permits political, economic, and financial power to be the privilege of a few. Naturally he concludes that British democracy is a sham, a façade, behind which lies an oligarchy of wealth and birth; and triumphantly he points to the 'Public school and private school system' as the clear proof that he is right. Whatever your democratic philosophers may say, whatever your political institutions may be,' he will argue, 'England remains true to the principles and the sentiments of Edmund Burke. Tom Paine was the inspiration of America and of France, but his own country has firmly refused to listen to his democratic message. Instead it has absorbed the grandiloquent, inconsistent, and somewhat mystical gospel of the greatest opponent whom democracy has had to face.'

There is truth is this paradox. No writer felt the life of this country and experienced it more fully than Burke: and in his controversy with Paine we can see the struggle between political democracy and the social habits which still persists in English life. Paine tried to adapt the Lockeian spirit to the new ideal of the General Will: to assert that the people should no longer consent to government from above, but claim sovereignty for itself. Burke rightly perceived that such a claim was fatal to the compromise by which Locke had solved the Hobbesian dilemma. If government was to be based on the harmony of natural rights, it could not derive authority from the majority of votes. The majority for him was fictitious and a pernicious concept, since it denied that complex system of status and of social classes in which each citizen felt that his true being lay. When in his *Appeal from the New Whigs to the Old* Burke maintained that the revolution of 1688 was not a democratic revolution, he was completely correct. And because England had, in the course of one hundred years, evolved a political system of free institutions compatible with the preservation of inequality and privilege, he was able to clothe the lucid reasonableness of Locke's thought in the gorgeous robes of sentiment and of tradition. The businesslike compromise of 1688 had become by 1790 an eternal verity of British justice, blessed with the benevolent approval of God on High.

The spirit of Burke still permeates British political thought and practice, and prevents the institutions of political democracy from bringing with them the spirit of social democracy. The gradual extension of the suffrage between the years 1832 and 1928 has not been accompanied by any real revolt against the hierarchy of social classes. The bourgeoisie did not destroy the aristocratic tradition; on the contrary, it was influenced by it, as deeply as it made its influence felt. The tyranny of the illiterate masses, which J. S. Mill feared in the sixties, did not result from the grant of votes to the industrial worker. On the contrary, each new class, when admitted to political privilege, ranged itself dutifully in the ranks of the older parties, changing them, it is true, but permitting them to retain an unbroken continuity of tradition. And, finally, the growth of the Labour movement was accompanied by the growth of a labour and trade-union hierarchy as complex in its rules of precedence as the older aristocracy of birth and wealth. Burke is not the philosopher of British conservatism, but of British political life from Right to Left. His spirit informs the progressive movement as much as it informs the Conservative party. Gladstone, Ramsay MacDonald, and Lansbury, to name only three examples, were all of them thinkers who accepted without question the deep organic conservatism of British *social* life. Each may have passionately advocated certain economic or political reforms, and denounced certain flagrant social evils, as Burke denounced them; but, at bottom, none of them wished to abolish the structure of British society, but merely to eradicate the blemishes which marred it. None of them would have wished that this country should substitute the fierce warfare which characterises democracy in France or America for the peaceful friendship between classes which predominates within their own country. In a very real sense, British political thought is pacifist through and through. Where it sees friendliness and kindliness and co-operation, it cannot really denounce them, even though these sentiments are based on fundamental inequality and injustice. Where human feeling can join men of incompatible interests, the British politician seldom prefers the ruthless pursuit of justice to a kindly compromise. In their preference for kindliness over principle, Baldwin and Lansbury are not far apart, and it is significant that they are the two living statesmen who have aroused the highest respect and affection of their countrymen. Their actions are based, not only on political principles, but on simple sentiments of social morality, and these sentiments are only possible to men and women who accept the fundamental goodness of the social order, and the divisions of status which it implies.

Here, then, is the peculiar contribution of Britain to the problems of freedom. It has up till now been able to retain a really unequalitarian class-system in spite of the introduction of formal political democracy; and by so doing it has preserved a ruling class with a continuity of tradition and a fluidity of membership, easily able to adapt itself to the constant changes of political and economic environment. The sense of moral responsibility which inspires that élite is the factor upon which British justice and liberty depend, while the sense of security of the mass of citizens enables the élite to exert its authority without undue compulsion. The system depends, in short, upon the mutual confidence which exists between the unpolitical masses and the ruling hierarchy, whether in industry, in politics, or in the Labour movement. Given this mutual confidence, and this adherence to traditional status, democratic institutions can be operated with a minimum of risk. Contrariwise, given the democratic institutions, the masses can feel (whether rightly or wrongly) that they are free, if they so wish, at any moment to indicate to their rulers any disapproval of policy which they may feel, or even to throw them out; while the system of alternating party government enables this discontent to be expressed with the minimum of disturbance to a continuous governmental policy.

Thus, in a very real sense, British political thought is based on morality and works through custom. The constitution is impossible to analyse fully because it is a medley of traditions and statutes and institutions integrated only by instinctive obedience to 'the rules of the game.' It is only because, or in so far as, the rulers are willing to work it that it works, and this willingness is motivated by a respect for taboo as complex as that in any Melanesian tribe. Whether we examine local government or national government, the trade unions, or the churches, we find the same phenomena. Institutions of inconceivable complexity, often cumbrous and inefficient, are retained and worked by respect for 'correct behaviour' and 'fair play'. The ceremonies of the French court of 1780 are as nothing to the intricacies of the British social system. It hangs suspended, not by a single hair, but by a tortuous network of airy threads which could be severed by one violent stroke of economic or international adversity.

Most typical of this British preference for the fragile bonds of moral obligation is the present situation of the empire, in which the Crown remains the one political unit to hold it together. This sentimental bond has been preferred to any formal constitution or rational plan. Its strength is known to no one, the obligations it imposes are obscure and deliberately unexplored. It seems almost as if the statesmen were saying: 'Ask no questions; undue curiosity will destroy the delicate framework of our imperial unity.'

The refusal to ask questions, and the belief in the natural growth of tradition as the surest foundation of authority, have produced an exuberant growth of governmental, semi-governmental, and voluntary organisations. Education, trade unionism, and medical services are only three examples of a universal tendency. In all are to be seen the results of the haphazard development of voluntary organisations, co-ordinated only at a late stage of their maturity. In each case respect for tradition and the jealous retention of useless privileges have resulted in an organisation deprived of much of its social utility; on the other hand, by the sacrifice of social utility, the services have developed with a minimum of social disturbance. If they are often useless, and even harmful to the people whom they are supposed to serve, they are at least accepted as natural phenomena; and an Englishman prefers what is 'natural' to what is useful, unless the shoe pinches very hard.

Nothing else will explain the survival of the British system of law. Its division of barristers and solicitors, its recondite disregard of social utility, its unintelligibility, and its expense have been denounced by sensible men since Bentham and *Bleak House*. Derided by the onlooker, cursed by the litigant, it continues serene on its elusive way; and it continues precisely because its structure, in all its perversity, corresponds with and has grown up with the social and political institutions of the country. A country which prefers the subtle bonds of tradition, sentiment, and morality to the authority of interest and reason cannot expect to develop a rational system of law. Drastic legal reform is only necessary if reform of local government, of friendly societies, of education, are also undertaken. Where institutions survive their social utility and are still regarded with affection, it is unlikely that the Law will be anything but a complex confusion of precedents. The business man or the trade unionist who curses it will find the cause of its evils in his own industry and his own union. A Burkeian respect for status and prescription may produce a political system based on morality; but never one which is rational, simple, or (in the French sense) democratic.

When Locke described the state of nature as precedent to civil government, or when later idealists distinguished society from the State and justified the latter in terms of the former, they were indicating this fact in a highly misleading way. For there is no such thing as British society, if by society is meant a single integrated unit; nor do its members possess natural rights, if by 'natural rights' we mean a clearly articulated body of reasonable claims. Though the State is considered as a necessary evil, tolerated only for the sake of the social life which it protects and from which it is sharply distinguished, yet that social life is not the life of equal and rational human beings. Indeed, the State is there to preserve the inequalities, the intricacies, and the injustices which haphazard growth and group loyalty has produced. Progress is permitted only where it does not violate too deeply the luxuriant growth of non-political institutions and traditions, and the Englishmen's 'political' activity and ideals express themselves naturally, not in 'politics', but in the club and chapel, the 'pub' and the 'pool'. It is here in the organisation and administration of voluntary groups that the Englishman's political talent is displayed, his loyalty and idealism aroused, and his capacity for partisanship most unexpectedly exhibited. Those who would study the politics of an English town, if they use the word 'politics' in a full Aristotelian sense, must look outside the town hall and turn their attention to the countless social groups which jostle one another in their competition for the working man's time. Each has its own traditions and habits and taboos, and most of them are genuine examples of democratic co-operation and spontaneous self-government. But their life and being is self-contained and non-political: they do not challenge but make tolerable the inequality and injustice of the political and economic order. Again, we observe the same phenomenon: the English, with an unrivalled faculty for self-government and toleration, a strong sense of group loyalty, and hatred of 'the boss', dissipate all these talents in social organisations remote from the political field. And so, when they come to politics, they cease for the most part to be democrats and are content to consent to the benevolent despotism of a ruling class equally undemocratic and equally unwilling, for the sake of political and economic efficiency, to disturb the jungle of social anomalies of which this country's life is composed. In short, while they are democratic within their own social group, they have never tried to apply democratic principles to the interrelation of those social groups and classes in which they live. And, since it is only through State action that such a task could be properly tackled, we can justifiably maintain that the English have never seriously considered the political implications of social democracy.

PS

C

4. UTILITARIANS AND IDEALISTS

If we have correctly described the essential characteristics of British institutions and British thought, we must admit that these characteristics are rarely mirrored in the writings of our theorists and pamphleteers. Apart from Burke and Disraeli, there is hardly one of them who has not denounced the system which we have described. Not till academic lecturers had the good fortune to read Hegel could a philosophy be discovered obscure enough to justify it, and to persuade rational men that obedience to an irrational process of development was the supreme manifestation of reason. The British idealists, however, accomplished this task, and in the works of Bradley, Green, and Bosanquet an aura of philosophic profundity was cast round the superstitious sanctifications of existing institutions and 'the law of their development'.

Apart from this aberration, which is fortunately past, British thinkers have been notoriously rationalist, free-thinking, and utilitarian. Hobbes, Locke, Paine, Hume, Bentham, Mill, and Bagehot form a continuous chain of intellectual development, fundamentally at variance with the British tradition as I have described it. Their philosophies differ profoundly, but they all agree in this—that acceptance of traditional forms is not sufficient, that government is only defensible if it can be justified in terms of human need, and that custom, prescription, and status are often self-righteous cloaks for sinister interests and unjust privileges.

This uniformity of outlook is remarkable, and its reason is clear. Political thinkers, from Locke to Bentham, were always in revolt against the inconveniences of a stable social system. In their theories they picked out for praise precisely those elements which were lacking in the practice of their country, and omitted others so basic that they could pass unnoticed. To a people bound by ties of status and sentiment, they preached that mankind is individualistic and equal; to a nation of deeply Christian tradition, that religion is a myth based on utility; to monarchists, that royalty is a useful figment for the canalisation of emotion. For a strong sense of national unity they substituted a social contract, or the common interest of isolated individuals. Thus the picture given by British political theorists of 'man the political animal' belies at every point the British political animal. The former is a cool and calculating hedonist, bound by no ties which self-interest cannot justify; the latter is a sentimentalist, content to accept ancestral institutions and modify them to existing circumstances according to the mysterious canons of fair play. Democratic thought in this country has been fiercely businesslike precisely because it was fighting against a dead weight of tradition and a chaos of anachronistic institutions.

This tendency is seen very clearly in the Utilitarians. They are typical of English theory because they are so hard-headed, so one-sided, so essentially controversial in character. Not one of them was a philosopher or a scientist who really faced the essential problems of government: they were all pamphleteers inveighing against social evils, and, in the course of their attack, discovering a theory of government as a by-product of their political activity. Bentham became a democrat almost by accident through the failure of his proposals for legal reform; J. S. Mill a Socialist through his observation of how capitalism was operating. But neither Bentham nor Mill elaborated a theory of the new gospel they preached, nor recognised the one-sidedness of their point of view. This is equally true of their economics, which are better suited for pamphleteering than for serious scientific analysis. Here, too, we can feel that we are confronted by a theory useful as an antidote to prevalent habits of mind, but singularly ill-adapted to be the basis of a detached study of wealth and its exchange. The contrast with Adam Smith is remarkable. *The Wealth of Nations*, perhaps the most influential book written by an Englishman in the eighteenth century, had world-wide influence just because it was not so narrowly conditioned by the political necessities of a party or of an interest. Vulgarising Smith, the Utilitarians destroyed his universal validity, or rather pretended that their own special pleading was as firmly based on science as his cool speculations. Had British Liberals paid close attention to the master they pretended to revere, they would have discovered in his ethical philosophy, as well as in his severe limitation of the scope of *laissez-faire*, a statesmanship and an understanding of human nature to counterbalance the extravagance of their own polemics. Political economy, in fact, would have remained political economy and would not have degenerated into a false psychology and a barren economic theory which denied the existence or at least the relevance of any other science to the analysis of modern society. Adam Smith had a clear vision of human nature and of human society, but the Utilitarians neither presented a true picture of the landed aristocracy they

denounced, nor of the middle classes whose spokesmen they pur-
ported to be, nor of the capitalistic system which they so heartily
advocated. Instead, they portrayed, by an easy process of abstraction,
the working of certain simple principles which they quite improperly
assumed without examination to be the fundamental principles of
current politics. Consider the following passage from James Mill's
Essay on Government:

> We have already observed, that the reason for which Govern-
> ment exists is, that one man, if stronger than another, will take
> from him whatever that other possesses and he desires. But if
> one man will do this, so will several. And if powers are put into
> the hands of a comparatively small number, called an Aristocracy,
> powers which make them stronger than the rest of the com-
> munity, they will take from the rest of the community as much
> as they please of the objects of desire. They will, thus, defeat
> the very end for which Government was instituted. The unfitness,
> therefore, of an Aristocracy to be entrusted with the powers of
> Government, rests on demonstration. . . . If Government is
> founded upon this, as a law of human nature, that a man, if
> able, will take from others any thing which they have and he
> desires, it is sufficiently evident that when a man is called a
> King, it does not change his nature; so that when he has got
> power to enable him to take from every man what he pleases,
> he will take whatever he pleases. To suppose that he will not,
> is to affirm that Government is unnecessary; and that human
> beings will abstain from injuring one another of their own
> accord.
>
> It is very evident that this reasoning extends to every modifica-
> tion of the smallest number. Whenever the powers of Govern-
> ment are placed in any hands other than those of the community,
> whether those of one man, of a few, or of several, those principles
> of human nature which imply that Government is at all necessary,
> imply that those persons will make use of them to defeat the
> very end for which Government exists.

Could anything be more pig-headed than this? As a sober elucida-
tion of political problems it is laughable; as science, beneath contempt. And yet, given the atmosphere of the time, and the prejudices
against which he was fighting, it may well be that Mill's type of
reasoning served a useful purpose by giving philosophic arguments to

the practical advocates of reform. Be that as it may, it is certain that the theorists of freedom from Locke to Mill felt themselves to be a minority who chief task was the denunciation of tradition and the propagation of a cool and narrow self-interest quite foreign to the British temper. Their function was that of the Socratic gadfly, not of the sober architect of a democratic constitution.

Moreover, their theories were only acceptable to the classes of which they were the protagonists for one reason, because they defended the interests of business and of property. Their individualism was that of the shopkeeper and the merchant, and their view of political institutions sprang from a belief that it was the job of Government to protect and encourage the production of wealth. Democrats and rationalists up to the time of J. S. Mill were the champions of property against central authority, and in this sense Cromwell was the true forbear of Jeremy Bentham. Here again we note a characteristic peculiar to English thought and possible only in the historical environment of the English people. The interests of property can only challenge central authority, religion, and tradition in a country where national unity is assured, and where national security is only a secondary issue. The democrat could be antinomian only because of the overwhelming orthodoxy of his country; his individualism flourished behind her wooden walls; his advocacy of free trade convinced business men, because he and his English competitors enjoyed a monopoly of world trade. It was these factors which caused the sharp divorce between private business interests and State activity which is so characteristic of British Liberal theory. Assuming, and therefore disregarding all those vital forces which bound his country together, he was able to describe the British business man as a *pure* business man, and to advocate a State designed simply to promote the anarchic competition of private enterprise. And he was able to do this without harm, simply because the programme would by no conceivable possibility be fully realised. Utilitarian rationalism did not shock the religious susceptibilities and patriotism of the middle classes, because it was dealing with those political problems which those very classes considered to be business—and therefore materialist—problems.

That British life could be so neatly divided into compartments was highly convenient, but it did not stimulate profound political thought. The Liberal theories of democracy evolved between 1790 and 1830 became relatively uninfluential as soon as the immediate objectives of the business community had been achieved. Utility, a powerful weapon in the attack upon privilege and sinister interest, gave no answer to the problems of government, as soon as power had been attained. 'The greatest good of the greatest number' could be used to denounce aristocracy but it was useless as a guide to the administration of a State. The middle classes in the middle of the nineteenth century had won the battle, only to find themselves disconsolately searching for a positive philosophy of popular government. They found it, but in so doing they divorced themselves both from the life of the people and from the principles of democracy, and so the end of the nineteenth century saw the dawn not of political democracy but of a new era of free institutions under the capable control of a new ruling class. This change was mirrored in the revival of Oxford as the home of political theory.

The British idealists mark an important stage of development—the divorce between political theory and political practice in this country. While the problems of imperialism, Home Rule, and trade union rights dominated practical politics, Oxford witnessed the growth of a philosophy too sublime to relate itself to such mundane matters. Flourishing between 1870 and 1914, its advocates elaborated a system of *metapolitics* by which they demonstrated the place occupied by the State in the essential nature of things. Their Hegelianism was combined with a Hellenism which saw in the Greek city State the prototype of all future civilised society, in Plato and Aristotle the fathers of all reputable philosophy. By merging Plato and Hegel and discarding the latter's dialectic of history, they produced a theory of political evolution purged of those conflicts which Hegel had seen to be the ingredients of all social change. In revolt against the materialism and economics of the Utilitarians, they pictured a social order unified by a single moral purpose, whose current morality was to be accepted as the provisional commandments of universal mind, and whose institutions were sanctified as the provisional optimum of historical progress. Freedom, they urged, was to be found by the individual in self-realisation within this stable order, and criticism was only justifiable provided that it was positive—i.e. accepted the general presuppositions of current morality.

The disavowal of all scientific analysis of social institutions, the contempt for economics and for the party politics of democracy, and the revival of a type of political theory as dogmatic as that of divine right, are all signs of the successful attainment of power by the middle classes; from now on they are content, up till 1914, not to struggle for freedom, but to rationalise their acceptance of an unequalitarian society and to hand over to Providence the work of attaining equal privileges for the lower orders. Their concept of the State as an instrument of positive good is the concept of a new ruling class, whose sense of moral responsibility, unlike that of the aristocracy, demands a philosophic justification for their new power. Themselves the General Will, the prime source of current morals, and the fount of public opinion, they look with pleasure on an idealised picture of the city State, and see in Plato's guardians, or Aristotle's noble citizens, their own philosophic forbears. And, with the growth of a Civil Service for the empire and for the home country, they find a form of public service which genuinely corresponds with the philosophy they praise. The State of which Bradley and Bosanquet have their conceptual visions is a great bureaucracy, ruled by an élite of moral beings educated in the new public schools, and their ideal is one of magnanimous public service which presents to the lower orders that standard of living and education of which they are worthy. Politics has become not a matter of business haggling or party strife, but of impartial administration by high-minded Athenian citizens.

The British idealists succeeded in moralising the Leviathan which Hobbes had extolled: its sovereign becomes a public servant, who expresses the general will, because he has taught the masses what the general will should be. It is not therefore fear of attack, but devotion to the single-minded purpose of the State, which binds its citizens. In the State, each individual finds his true being and realises his ends. The rationalism, the scepticism, and the fierce individualism of earlier democrats has disappeared, to be replaced by an obedience to tradition which Burke would have deeply applauded. From now on democracy must look for its advocates not to the prophets of the middle classes but elsewhere.

But while Green and Bradley and Bosanquet were thus providing the philosophical justification for breaking with the traditions of 'Manchester Liberalism,' others in the field of practical politics were moving in the same direction. A study of the life of Joseph Chamberlain would, I believe, indicate that this great statesman was facing with an impetuous and intuitive genius the self-same problems in a not dissimilar way. Chamberlain started as a middle-class leader of a radicalism pledged to oust the Whigs from the leadership of the Liberal party. A business man, a Unitarian, and a republican, he felt the need for the completion of the democratic revolution begun in 1832, and he created the modern extra-parliamentary party as an instrument by which the masses could bring their representatives to heel. For Chamberlain in his early years, Free Trade, the franchise, and education were the three rocks upon which the prosperity and freedom of his country should be built. That his attention was diverted from *laissez-faire* to the urgent need for imperial unity in the new international competition of rival empires, and that his belief in the panacea of the franchise was replaced by a vision of a 'social service State' is proof only of his amazing grasp of the actual historical changes which were soon to render Utilitarianism a meaningless anachronism. Chamberlain's quarrel with Gladstone meant that the only Liberal who was able to accommodate his theories to a changing world was forced to impose his philosophy of life upon the Tories and to give to that party a gospel without which it must soon have passed away. The new Unionist party became the true representative of British middle-class interests, and left room for a new political movement, the Labour party, to face it with a genuine conflict of interest and ideology. Between these two a Liberal party, which still refused to see what Chamberlain had the vision to predict, was only kept alive by sacrificing its principles and by the demagogic genius of Lloyd George, a statesman whose personality was equally well adapted to the philosophies of all three political factions. In this curious confusion, Chamberlain stood out as the one man who fore-saw the inevitable development of British imperialism, and the new tasks of public service which now fell upon the middle classes in home and imperial affairs. While Green conceived 'the State as an instrument of positive good,' Chamberlain was prepared to break two political parties in order to carry this vision into action.

5. The Fabians

The year 1931 is a convenient, if arbitrary, date, which may be taken as a dividing line in the development of British political thought. It marks the close of an epoch of one hundred and fifty years during which the rate of increase in wealth, comfort, and power which this country had felt since the time of the Tudors had been vastly accelerated. Today a generation is growing up for which the idea of progress is a Utopian delusion, of peace a romantic dream, of security a dim memory of the past. The halt in economic progress which between 1900 and 1914 had caused widespread industrial unrest, and the Boer War, which first exposed to the popular mind the grim necessities of imperial power, had not been sufficient to break the nation of its belief that it could look forward to a future of inevitable, if slow, advance towards the millennium. On the contrary, the first decade of the nineteenth century saw the birth of a Labour party whose intellectuals advocated the gradual realisation of the bureaucratic vision of the British idealists, while its working-class leaders were busy turning it into a respectable institution of British social life. Even the Syndicalist dreams of G. D. H. Cole, in his Guild Socialist days, which were an attempt to evolve a British philosophy of revolution based upon trade unionism, evince a deep distaste for scientific Socialism. Nowhere in that anxious pre-War decade do we find a real advance of democratic theory; but only the uneasy feeling that all is not well which is reflected in the social novelists of the time, in Wells and Bennett, Chesterton, Shaw, and Belloc. Among these gifted amateurs, Graham Wallas stands out as a lonely scientist trying to look below the smug rationalisations of 'political theory' to the realities of political practice beneath. It may be said that he laid the foundations for a new theory upon which no one has yet begun to build.

The reason for this collapse of the rationalist tradition of British democracy is not far to seek. The cool self-interest and atomic individualism which our theorists had preached was the gospel of intelligent opposition to the lethargy and blindness of a strong national tradition; it was effective precisely as long as the class of property owners felt that tradition and centralised authority were an obstacle to the fulfilment of their plans. But when in the middle of the nineteenth century the centralised State became a necessary function of the new industrial system, and the industrialist himself won his way to the seats of privilege, both Locke and Bentham became at once outmoded. Nor could the individualist tradition pass on to the working class who were now claiming political power. Their experience had taught them that by non-political co-operation in co-operatives and in trade unions they could best lay the foundations of security and freedom; and for this reason they were naturally inclined to a theory of group loyalty and group rights such as Cole propounded before the 1914 War. Political democracy for them remained a factor of secondary importance in comparison with the defence of their own industrial organisations. Only the close connection of nonconformity with the Independent Labour Party prevented the British Labour Movement from developing a completely Syndicalist philosophy with its inevitable contempt for parliamentary democracy and political action. But Methodism was only able to evolve a crude application of Christian ethics to social problems, too vague to be the policy of a political party; and for this reason it fell to the middle-class Fabians to set their stamp on the philosophy of the Labour movement. British Socialism in their hands became not a battle for freedom against authority, but an attempt to mould the existing machinery of State to the benevolent wishes of an independent-minded middle class. It concentrated its efforts on wringing out of the existing ruling class not control, but concessions through the social services: its aim was a high standard of living, not freedom and power.

Here is the reason why in this country there has never grown up a Socialist theory of democracy on the lines of either Marxian or Anarchist philosophy: it is the reason, too, why the trade unions have maintained their control of the Labour movement. Only a Socialist party as fervent in its attack on privilege and as clear-cut in its philosophy as its Liberal predecessors could hope to dominate and shape the outlook of organized Labour. Up to 1931 such a party had failed to develop in Great Britain.

6. CONCLUSIONS

The uncertainty and lack of direction which we have noticed in democratic thought up till 1914 continued till 1931: indeed, it may be urged that it continues today. And yet I believe that 1931 was a dividing point both in England and in America. Far more thoroughly than the Great War, the Great Slump impressed on the Anglo-Saxon peoples the insecurity of the foundations on which freedom and prosperity were based, and the rise of Fascism and of Fascist imperialism has only deepened that impression. England is now a country, not, as before 1931, living blindly on the traditions of the past, but groping towards a new philosophy both of domestic and of international affairs. The post-1918 effort to apply the principles of Lockeian Liberalism to the building of a machinery of international order has failed as decisively as the Conservative struggle to return to pre-War 'normalcy'. The belief in national governmental organisation as the instrument of positive good is also undermined. In short, the economic and social conditions which rendered Liberalism so palatable have gone, and we are at last aware that they are gone. For the first time since the era of Hobbes we are faced by problems which demand a radical solution, and which cannot be shelved by kindly compromise and 'muddling through'. At last we too have reached a crisis where the only practical course open to us is to become philosophers and undertake a radical analysis of the fundamental postulates of our society. We shrink from the task, and our fear of it is reflected in our political apathy; but that apathy is also a sign of a growing recognition that statesmen and theorists alike have nothing to offer us which can satisfy our newly awakened critical powers. The prime reason why electors will not vote is because they feel dimly but surely that the true alternatives are not presented to them, and that no party offers them any satisfactory philosophy of life.

The main result of this crisis has been the growth of two new movements of thought. In the first place Liberal political theorists, of whom Laski is the chief, have suddenly discovered in Marxism the refuge from their doubts: in the second place Christians and non-political thinkers, such as Aldous Huxley, have developed a philosophy of pacifism which is basically anarchist in temper. Marxism and pacifism alone of contemporary movements seem to offer a clear and revolutionary philosophy to minds which realize that the pre-War era of security and progress is gone. But it is characteristic of the British temper that these philosophies have been accepted in their most dogmatic and least speculative forms. They have been seized upon as creeds, not assimilated as methods of thought; they have been welcomed for their final answer to all questions, not tested as lines of inquiry which could, after much research, enable us to evolve a new policy and a new direction for the democratic tradition. For this reason they are to be regarded more as emotional reactions to crisis that as positive contributions to its solution. Be that as it may, they are symptomatic of an era of painful transition more perilous than that which ushered in the industrial and democratic revolution at the beginning of the nineteenth century. For the first time for three hundred years this country is not only without a clear-cut philosophy, but in need of one. Only the future will show whether the habits of centuries will prevent its formulation.

Oxford
(1936-1938)

Part II

RE-THINKING SOCIALISM
1951-1964

TOWARDS A NEW PHILOSOPHY
OF SOCIALISM

Although published in 'New Fabian Essays' after the fall of the Labour Government, this essay, along with all the other contributions to New Fabian Essays, was virtually completed before Mr. Attlee's sudden appeal to the country in October 1951. The decision to write the New Fabian Essays was made at a weekend conference at Buscot Park, in July 1949. Discussions and conferences continued under the chairmanship of G. D. H. Cole until the outbreak of the Korean War precipitated a crisis in the Society. Feeling himself completely out of sympathy with the Labour Government's support of the United Nations armies in Korea, G. D. H. Cole suddenly resigned, and although I had taken very little part in the original discussions I found myself drafted to take his place as chairman, editor, and author of the introductory essay.

As a member of the Keep Left Group, I had been a critic since 1946 of Ernest Bevin's foreign policy as well as taking part in discussion on what, on the domestic front, should be the second stage of socialism. This essay gave me the chance to analyse what had gone wrong since 1945, and to start very cautiously and hesitantly re-thinking our socialism.

1. THE LOSS OF MOMENTUM

EVEN before the 1950 election, the impetus which brought the Labour Government to power began to fail. That impetus, despite a sharp setback in 1931, had mounted steadily during fifty years of opposition—years spent in a sustained campaign against the capitalist order. Yet, after scarcely four years in office, the Government had fulfilled its historic mission. The nationalisation of half a dozen major industries, the construction of an all-in system of social

35

security and a free health service, and the tentative application of planning to the national economy—the achievement of these reforms seemed to have exhausted the content of British socialism.

What was the cause of this loss of political momentum? Not the deadlock result of the 1950 election—far less the need for rearmament after the attack on South Korea. Even if the Labour Government in 1950 had won a large parliamentary majority, the advance to socialism would have been halted. The right wing openly advocated consolidation; the left demanded more socialism, but could only suggest those measures required to achieve it. The rearmament programme (and the defeat at the polls in 1951) came as a deliverance from indecision, not as an obstacle to action.

It would be easy to attribute this indecision to a failure of leadership. Certainly, the almost simultaneous loss of his two strong men, Sir Stafford Cripps and Mr. Bevin, grievously weakened the Prime Minister's position and revealed a dangerous rift in his Cabinet. But these personal factors were symptoms of a much more serious ailment, a failure of the sense of direction which alone can unify and sustain a great political party. The Labour Party was unsure where it was going. The familiar landmarks on the road to socialism had been left behind: it was travelling in strange country, exposed to climatic rigours it had not anticipated and against which its traditional equipment gave little protection. Buffeted and battered, it pushed ahead; but the pace slowed as it became clear that the destination would not be reached by the traditional route.

How can the Labour Party regain its sense of direction? My contention, in this essay, is that it cannot be done so long as politicians are content to rely on their 'hunch' and empirical experience. The Labour Party has lost its way not only because it lacks a map of the new country it is crossing, but because it thinks maps unnecessary for experienced travellers.

Today we can see the drawbacks as well as the advantages of this stubborn empiricism. Labour policy has always been an amalgam. It consists, first, of a number of concrete proposals and, secondly, of those ethical aspirations which constitute our socialist tradition. By 1950 most of the proposals had been implemented; and the tradition had been confused by the impact of emergency after emergency upon Government policy. Are food subsidies and price controls temporary wartime expedients, to be dispensed with as soon as we can return to the price system; or are they part of the structure of a socialist

State? Does democratic socialism involve the permanence of a mixed economy; and, if so, should profit-making in the private sector be encouraged or limited? Should wages be left to find their own level through collective bargaining, or is it the function of a Labour Government to modify the wages structure in the light of national interests and social justice? Is a centralised public corporation a more socialist method of running a public utility than municipal or co-operative ownership? Does socialist principle demand that we should receive our spectacles and dentures free, but pay for travelling on nationalised railways? Is there anything about a comprehensive school which makes it the chosen instrument of socialist secondary education as against a direct-grant school, where every place is allotted by competitive examination?

In the field of external affairs, similar questions crowd upon us. Is the object of a socialist defence policy to contain communism or to deter Russian military aggression? If it is the former, can we avoid suppressing social revolution in the colonial areas, or justify the recognition of Communist China? How can we reconcile the Labour Government's economic policy in Persia and Malaya with its avowed objective of raising the standard of living of the backward peoples? If it was right to give complete independence to India, despite the risk that she might leave the Commonwealth and even join the Russian bloc, why did we adopt the opposite policy in the Middle East? How can a socialist oppose British participation in a United Western Europe, while bowing to the American desire for a rearmed Germany?

Merely to ask these questions is to indicate the confusion which arises as soon as we seek to relate our practice to our socialist ideals. The continental Marxists certainly blunted their capacity for practical reforms by forcing their policies into conformity with a rigid doctrine. The Labour Party has gone to the other extreme. It capsulated its theory into a number of measures. Once these reforms had been accomplished, its only guide for future action was a tradition, which could be interpreted in any number of contradictory ways. The Conservatives can afford to rely on tradition and the leadership of men who are accepted as its interpreters. Indeed, conservatism can be defined as whatever the Conservative leader does or says with the consent of his party. But tradition, and the Conservative Party which is its guardian, is democracy's brake on social change. The dynamic can only be provided by a party which challenges the *status quo* on grounds of principle and uses theory to expose the inadequacy of tradition as a guide to action. We have seen, in Australia and New Zealand, what happens to other labour parties which dispense with socialism. Now we ourselves are faced with a similar danger—that our socialism may degenerate into labourism. If this happens, politics will become a matter of 'ins' and 'outs'. Soon there will be no deep difference between the two parties, and the dynamic of social change will be taken over by new and dangerous political movements.

2. Pragmatism and Philosophy

Most of the early Fabians—the one outstanding exception was George Bernard Shaw—repudiated socialist theory as dangerous Teutonic verbiage. They assumed that everyone knew the difference between justice and injustice, happiness and unhappiness, and that it was the job of the Fabian Society to show the British trade unionist— and any politician who cared to listen—the way to make Britain an efficient example of socially planned happiness. This Benthamite approach to socialism, in contrast with the Marxist theories of the Continent, had considerable advantages. It suited the anti-intellectual bias of the Labour Movement, and it faithfully reflected the conscientious objection to dogma, whether theological or political, on which our British conception of personal freedom rests. Moreover, by repudiating classical Marxism, it enabled the Labour Party, in its formative years, to welcome into its ranks all men of goodwill—the Christian Socialist, for instance, and the middle-class Liberal in search of a new vehicle of social reform—and not only the class-conscious worker. It was largely because the Party accepted this unphilosophic Fabian approach that it was able to become a national party and to assume the national responsibilities of government more easily than any Socialist Party in Europe.

It is noteworthy, however, that the Webbs, who started as the most intolerant exponents of unphilosophic Benthamism, ended as the evangelists of Soviet civilisation. Was this merely an example of senile decay? On the contrary, I believe that it was partly due to an acute apprehension of changing world conditions in the 1930s. Pragmatic social reform was sufficient so long as the balance of world power and the role of Great Britain in that balance were assumed as eternal verities. When these crumbled away, a philosophy of history became more and more necessary. The failure of the Webbs was not that they accepted this necessity in their old age, but that, trained as pragmatic social scientists, they proved themselves somewhat ingenuous students of philosophy, accepting Communist theory and practice in their old age as unreflectively as they accepted Benthamism in their youth.

The Webbs were not the only socialist intellectuals who forsook pragmatism in the 1930s. R. H. Tawney, whose philosophic training was much more thorough, had long been studying Marxism and successfully assimilated its method of historical analysis into his Christian philosophy. Harold Laski, on the other hand, like the Webbs, imposed Marxism as a superstructure on his utilitarian principles, and never succeeded in moulding the two into a consistent system. John Strachey swallowed it in a single heady draught and was the only Englishman who succeeded, not merely in translating Marx, but in re-thinking his system in Anglo-Saxon terms. It is no exaggeration to say that Tawney, Laski, Strachey and the Webbs dominated the thought of young socialists in the 1930s and deeply influenced many practical politicians in the Shadow Cabinet. The Left Book Club replaced the Fabian Society as the home of the intellectual *avant-garde*.

But this victory of Marxist theory was short-lived. Communist opposition to the war in 1939 split and ultimately destroyed the Left Book Club, and the Labour victory of 1945 brought with it a return to the old-fashioned Fabian approach. Intellectuals, who had dallied with Marx and preached class war in the 1930s, now vied with each other in picturing themselves as common-sense fellows with no time for theorising. The attention which the writings of Tawney and Laski received from the Labour Cabinet hardly encouraged anyone to follow in their philosophic footsteps.

My contention is that this absence of a theoretical basis for practical programmes of action, is the main reason why the post-war Labour Government marked the end of a century of social reform and not, as its socialist supporters had hoped, the beginning of a new epoch. To say this is not to condemn it. The development from the liberalism of 1906 to the modern Welfare State had to be completed; so did the transformation of the Empire into the Commonwealth. But neither of these processes was explicitly socialist. The principle of national self-determination, which Labour has fulfilled in its Indian policy and on which it is working in the Colonial Empire, is essentially liberal; and the planned Welfare State is really the adaptation of capitalism to the demands of modern trade unionism. The mixed economy, evolved in the decade between 1940 and 1950, has not abolished competitive free enterprise, but adapted it to meet the social and economic demands of organised labour. What was achieved by the first Labour Government was, in fact, the climax of a long process, in the course of which capitalism has been civilised and, to a large extent, reconciled with the principles of democracy. By refusing to accept the Marxist philosophy, we have almost succeeded in disproving its prophecies of inevitable conflict. This is a historic achievement, but the fact remains that, in achieving it, the Labour Party is in danger of becoming not the party of change, but the defender of the post-war *status quo*.

Philosophy begins where pragmatism fails. When the common-sense socialist has come to the end of his programme and there are no longer a number of obvious reforms which men of goodwill broadly agree should be carried out, it is time to sit back and reflect. How can this process of self-analysis best be begun? Certainly not by hurriedly borrowing a ready-made philosophy from elsewhere and forcing the facts of our history and the ideals of our movement into its rigid doctrines. That was the mistake of Laski and the Webbs, as well as of John Strachey in the 1930s. A sound philosophy of democratic socialism, as Evan Durbin realised in his sadly under-estimated *Politics of Democratic Socialism*, must be derived from an examination of our own implicit and explicit principles of action and from a fresh appraisal of the facts of the situation.

3. The Idea of Progress and the Fallacy of Materialism

Let us take the principles of action first. Do we assume that, with the usual setbacks, the world is steadily progressing towards unity and freedom; and that democratic socialism, or something like it, will eventually be the pattern of a world government? Or have we lost faith in the progress which was the almost universal belief not only of the early Fabians, but of the whole civilised world at the beginning of this century?

A simple test of this is to take two extreme points of view, those of H. G. Wells and Arnold Toynbee. Wells writes,[1]

Our history has traced a steady growth of the social and political units into which men have combined. In the brief period

[1] p. 1142 of the fifth revised edition of *The Outline of History* (Cassell and Co., London).

of ten thousand years these units have grown from the small family tribe of the early Neolithic culture to the vast united realms—vast, yet still too small and partial—of the present time. And this change in size of the state—a change manifestly incomplete—has been accompanied by profound changes in all its nature. Compulsion and servitude have given way to ideas of associated freedom, and the sovereignty that was once concentrated in an autocratic king and god has been widely diffused throughout the community.

In this passage the whole illusion of automatic progress is concisely expressed. History is the story of the evolution of society from the small unit to the large unit, and from the unit based on compulsion to the unit based on voluntary association; and this process will go on until we reach a world state, with no compulsions.

Towards the end of his life Wells began to despair, because he realised the failure of his implicit principle, that the enlargement of scientific knowledge, i.e. power to control nature and men, necessarily increases freedom. Faced by the obvious failure of rationalism to rationalise human nature, he moved very near to the pessimistic position of Arnold Toynbee.[1]

Primitive societies may be likened to people lying torpid upon a ledge on a mountain-side, with a precipice below and a precipice above; civilisations may be likened to companions of these sleepers who have just risen to their feet and have started to climb up the face of the cliff above; while we for our part may liken ourselves to observers whose field of vision is limited to the ledge and to the lower slopes of the upper precipice and who have come upon the scene at the moment when the different members of the party happen to be in these respective postures and positions. The recumbent figures, despite our first impression, cannot be paralytics in reality; for they cannot have been born on the ledge, and no human muscles except their own can have hoisted them to this halting place. On the other hand, their companions who are climbing at the moment have only just left the same ledge; and, since the next ledge is out of sight, we do not know how high or how arduous the next pitch may be. We only know that it is impossible to halt and rest.

[1] Abridged *Study of History*, (ed. Somervell) (Royal Institute of International Affairs, 1951.) p. 49.

Most of us would now agree that Toynbee's sense of direction was better than that of the early Wells. Yet until the 1930s Wells' illusions were shared by Liberals, Marxists and early Fabians; they were, indeed, the climate of all progressive public opinion.

This materialist conception of progress was based on assumptions about human behaviour which psychological research has shown to have no basis in reality, and on a theory of democratic politics which has been confuted by the facts of the last thirty years. There is neither a natural identity of interests nor yet an inherent contradiction in the economic system. The growth of science and popular education does not automatically produce an 'upward' evolution in society, if by 'upward' is meant from servile to democratic forms; and the apocalyptic assumption that, after a period of dictatorship, a proletarian revolution must achieve a free and equal society is equally invalid. The evolutionary and the revolutionary philosophies of progress have both proved false. Judging by the facts, there is far more to be said for the Christian doctrine of original sin than for Rousseau's fantasy of the noble savage, or Marx's vision of the classless society.

Our first task, therefore, is to re-define progress. In what sense can we speak of it at all? Is there, as every communist, as well as every liberal and socialist, has believed, any upward movement in human history, or is it merely a story without plot or meaning?

To begin with, we must accept the fact, that, in the strictest sense of the words, there is no such thing as moral progress. For morality consists in the decision to do good, and there is no evidence that more men decide more often to do what they believe to be their duty in a civilised society than do so in a primitive society. From the aspect of individual morality, modern civilisation merely faces men with different choices from those presented at earlier stages of our history. It enlarges the area of free choice. It enables us to cure sickness on a huge scale—and to destroy each other on a huge scale. It enables us to liberate each other on a huge scale—and to tyrannise each other on a huge scale. Men do, of course, 'behave better' to each other in a society which forbids slavery than in one which tolerates it. But, in terms of individual morality, there are just as many opportunities for a slave-owner to be a saint as for a citizen of a free democracy. Civilisation does not *make* us morally better, any more than democracy *makes* us use our liberty. The only continuous lines which we trace in human history—and even these sag sometimes for hundreds of years at a time—are (i) the social accumulation of knowledge, and (ii) the enlargement, through this accumulation, of men's power to control both nature and one another.

But both these lines of progress are morally neutral. The individual and the society that possess more knowledge and power are not necessarily better than their backward ancestors. Here is one point where Toynbee's picture is more acceptable than that of Wells or Marx—its rejection of any moral determinism in history. There is no automatic progress or improvement in human nature, but there is an almost automatic accumulation of knowledge and power, which we can use equally for self-destruction or for self-emancipation.

Of course, it would be absurd to deny the existence in history of periods of *social* progress. Athenian democracy was an advance on the Solonian system, just as our own Welfare State is an improvement on the social morality of the 1840s. The socialist measures this progress of social morality by the degree of equality and respect for individual personality expressed in the distribution of power and in the institutions of law and property within a state. This standard, indeed, is what we mean by the socialist ideal.

It is important to observe, however, that there is no evidence of any continuous upward line of social progress. Free societies, in the sense we have given to the word, have existed at various times in recorded history and probably in prehistory as well. They have grown and they have perished, to be replaced by despotism and exploitation. Once we understand the nature of human freedom, this will not seem surprising, nor will it depress us unduly. For the social accumulation of knowledge and power does not make it any *easier* for men to build a free society. Knowledge can be used to enslave much more easily than to liberate; and destruction is as natural to man as construction. T. H. Huxley was right when, in a famous essay, he compared a free society to a garden. Nature produces either a wilderness of weeds or an arid patch of ground. Left to itself, a garden runs wild, and the gardener spends far more time in rooting out weeds than in planting flowers. Social morality, freedom and equality do not grow by any law of economics or politics, but only with the most careful cultivation. So far, therefore, from viewing history as a steady advance towards freedom, we should regard exploitation and slavery as the normal state of man and view the brief epochs of liberty as tremendous achievements. They could only be preserved for a few generations by constant cultivation and they cannot be expected to become the general rule.

This is the point of departure for a modern theory of socialism. Instead of regarding social change as tending towards the enlargement of freedom, we must assume that increased concentration of power, whether in the form of technological development or social organisation will always produce exploitation, injustice and inequality in a society, unless the community possesses a social conscience strong enough to civilise them. Human institutions will always be not merely amoral but immoral, as Reinhold Niebuhr showed in his famous book, unless they are moralised by individual men and women aware of this proclivity and waging unceasing war against it. Every economic system, whether capitalist or socialist, degenerates into a system of privilege and exploitation unless it is policed by a social morality, which can only reside in a minority of citizens. Every political party degenerates into office-seeking, unless its leaders are faced by an opposition within the ranks. Every Church becomes a vested interest without its heretics, and every political system, including democracy, ossifies into an oligarchy. Freedom is always in danger, and the majority of mankind will always acquiesce in its loss, unless a minority is willing to challenge the privileges of the few and the apathy of the masses.

In the nineteenth century this challenge was the task of liberalism. Today it has fallen to socialism. But we cannot fulfil it so long as we base our policy on the materialist fallacy that material progress *makes* men either free or equal. One particularly vicious form of this fallacy is the belief that economics are the determinant factors in social change and that, if we achieve economic justice, we automatically secure human freedom.

Unfortunately, man moulds not only nature to his use, but also his fellow men: if he is a tool-using animal, as Marx declared, one of the handiest tools is his neighbour. The school, the press, the radio, the party machine, the army, the factory, are all instruments through which man, unless checked by a social conscience armed with sanctions, will exert power over the minds of his fellow men. The Political Revolution, which has concentrated coercive power and thought-control in a few hands, is just as important a historical fact as the Industrial Revolution. Yet since Graham Wallas, almost nothing has been written by socialists about the Political Revolution, although it was the techniques of thought-control and centralised coercion which frustrated the apocalyptic visions of liberals and Marxists and made possible both the modern Western democracy and the totalitarian state. Without these, it might have been possible, as the Liberals hoped, for the nation state to wither away into economic brotherhood of man, or for the Leninist dictatorship of the proletariat to develop into a peaceful anarchy, in which coercive authority was scarcely apparent. But actually those who control the media of mass communication and the means of destruction (propaganda and the armed forces) are far more powerful today than the owners of the means of production. The state is no longer the executive committee of the bourgeoisie: the bourgeoisie are becoming the managers working for the state.

Marx saw that, though capitalism was the enemy, the Industrial Revolution was 'objectively progressive', a stage in social development. Yet, as soon as capitalism reached maturity, it became a system of privilege and exploitation. Today the enemy of human freedom is the managerial society and the central coercive power which goes with it. And yet the Political Revolution has been 'objectively progressive', in the sense that the instruments of mass communication and coercion, if restrained by social morality, *can* be used to enlarge freedom. Just as capitalism *could* be civilised into the Welfare State, so the managerial society *can* be civilised into democratic socialism.

The Soviet Union is the most extreme example of managerialism, because its Stalinist rulers consciously repudiate the primacy of morality over expediency, and so destroy the possibility of an active social conscience, which could save them from the corruption of power. The capitalist class never did that, and this is why capitalist development did not fulfil the prophecies of Marx. No capitalist country was ever so theoretically and methodically capitalist as Russia is Stalinite today. This is also the reason why, judged by European standards, the U.S.A. is a better form of society than the U.S.S.R. In America, a liberal and Christian morality, and a Constitution and political tradition derived from it, have frustrated the full development of capitalism and still put up strong resistance against totalitarian tendencies. To reject America as a capitalist country and to treat the Soviet Empire as an example of socialist planning is to make nonsense of every one of our ideals. In reality, they are the two great examples of the modern managerial state, the one consciously and systematically managerial, the other moving towards the same end under the pressure of the Cold War. But

whereas, in the U.S.A., totalitarianism and aggressiveness can still
be checked by social conscience, in Russia they cannot. We can
co-operate with the Americans as allies, influencing their policies
despite their superior strength. It would be folly to expect such a
relationship with the Soviet Union. Co-existence, yes. Mutually
beneficial agreements, yes. But never co-operation.

One factor which has prevented many British socialists from
accepting this obvious fact is the belief that in some sense the Soviet
Union is a 'workers' state'. In fact, like all totalitarian states, it is an
élite society, created by a revolutionary intelligentsia, which admittedly merely used the working-class movement, such as it was, in
order to engineer its own capture of power. Indeed, the appeal of the
communist philosophy, as distinct from communist slogans, has
always been to the disillusioned intelligentsia. It offers them the
power of which they are deprived, and a theory to justify its
ruthless use; and it provides them with a scientific philosophy which
satisfies their religious cravings while permitting them to feel modern
and up-to-date.

It is noteworthy that the chief successes of communism since the
Russian Revolution have been in backward countries, where popular
education scarcely exists and a genuine working-class movement has
for that reason failed to develop. In such countries democracy must
be a sham, since power is held in a few hands and public opinion
consists of a few thousand people. The carriers of communism in
Asia are a tiny, educated minority, who form the social conscience
and who have been personally wounded by the insolence of Western
imperialism and white ascendancy. The coolie in Malaya, or for that
matter the tribesman in Nigeria, does not want either liberty, equality
and fraternity, or the dictatorship of the proletariat. He is below the
level of such political aspirations. Not so the minor civil servant, the
university professor and the lawyer. The affronts perpetrated by the
white man on this social conscience are a far more important communist lever than the economic condition of the masses. Communism enlists the conscience and idealism of this élite and offers it
a 'career open to the talents' in its totalitarian society. In the
twentieth century democracy is no longer, as it was in the period of
Marx, a *necessary* stage on the way to industrialisation. Unless
trained in the Western tradition, as the Indians were, the élite does
not desire it: and the masses do not require it, since they can be
modernised (taught to drive tractors, fly aeroplanes and worship

Stalin) without any democratic liberation. For fighting a modern war, for working on a collective farm, or for repetition work in a factory, the Chinese coolie is more malleable material and more expendable than a Western European worker, or a New England farmer. So, too, the colonial intelligentsia are more suitable members of a communist managerial class than Westerners, imbued with democratic traditions. Totalitarianism may well be the normal state of twentieth-century man, unless he has the good fortune to belong to a society which was either modernised before the century began, or indoctrinated with Western standards by a colonial power.

The recognition that progress does not necessarily bring freedom has led a considerable number of socialist intellectuals to accept defeat and to withdraw from politics into mysticism or quietism. But this is not the only conclusion which can be drawn. Facing the century of totalitarianism, we can choose between two philosophies, symbolised by the figures of Buddha and Prometheus. Buddha represents the withdrawal from the struggle for freedom. For the Oriental Buddhist or for the Western defeatist, intellectual humility is the greatest virtue; the good man is not involved, but detached; he accepts this world as a vale of woe and seeks realisation in a transcendental eternity. The other philosophy, that of the sceptical humanist, is symbolised by Prometheus, chained to his Caucasian peak, with the eagle pecking out his liver. Prometheus stole fire from the Gods in order to help his fellow men. He did not believe that any law of nature or divine purpose would automatically give them freedom and happiness. Neither God nor history was on his side. It was his duty to steal fire, in defiance of law and order, and to prefer eternal agony to the denial of truth. He was surrounded by mysteries, but he recognised that they were veils to be pierced, not divine realities to be worshipped. So too the humanist to-day knows that we are surrounded by misery and injustice, and that it is quite possible that all we have achieved in Western Europe may be destroyed. But he also knows that it is man's destiny to struggle against this natural process, and that there is no more justification for pessimism in politics than there is for a gardener to say, 'I'll give up weeding because it's a wet summer.'

By rejecting the automatism of Wells and Marx and the defeatism of Koestler or Aldous Huxley, we purify our socialist philosophy of illusions, which for many years have been sapping its strength. To realise that the socialist society is not the norm, evolved by material conditions, but the exception, imposed on immoral society by human will and social conscience, is not to emasculate our socialism, but to set ourselves a challenge.

Moreover, it shows us another difference between socialism and communism. The communist, like the Calvinist, derives his self-confidence from the sense that history is on his side and that his victory is predestined by forces largely outside his control. The democratic socialist draws his inspiration from the belief that nothing but human will and social conscience can liberate men from a historical process which, if left to itself, leads to slavery, exploitation and war. The test of communism is the statistical success of each Five Year Plan, and the size and strength of the Russian Empire. The test of socialism is the extent to which it shapes a people's institutions to the moral standards of freedom—even at the cost of a lower standard of living or the surrender of an empire.

4. THE CENTURY OF TOTALITARIANISM

With this background, let us look at our present prospects. Many socialists assume that a third world war would 'destroy civilisation'. There is no evidence for this, though it would be quite likely to destroy Europe. The fact is that two world wars have not only accelerated scientific advance, but enlarged the *possibilities* of human liberation. In the Western world, the concept of welfare economics, for instance, was largely a product of wartime exigencies. If the twentieth century had brought a long period of peace, the Western democracies would not have accepted all those responsibilities which the governments found necessary to assume in total war. The National Health Service is a by-product of the blitz; the enormous improvement in the status of the American Negro is a by-product of war mobilisation. Total war and preparation for total war, do of course, distort peacetime economies, but they may also drive towards the reluctant acceptance of fair shares and equality of opportunity as practical principles of political and industrial organisation. Despite all the pessimists, there has been an astonishing process of liberation inside the Atlantic democracies during the last forty years.

Outside the Atlantic area, the liberating effect of two world wars is still more marked. The first produced the October Revolution in Russia, the second the national and social uprising of the Far Eastern peoples. We, of course, tend to see only the threat to European civilisation which they present. But, in the perspective of the next fifty years, this is likely to look as jaundiced as Burke's view of the French Revolution. Then too, on the side of the Revolution, liberation and imperialism were inextricably bound together; in the anti-revolutionary camp the defence of established liberties was equally hopelessly involved with dynastic reaction. Social evolution was the result not of the unconditional surrender of one side to the other, but of a drawn battle. The position in the 1950s is in this respect similar. A new world order and world balance of power is in process of long-drawn-out establishment. Even if the Atlantic powers were to win an outright victory in war, they could not destroy communism, any more than the anti-Napoleonic coalition destroyed the French Revolution. Nor can the Russians destroy democracy, since a Stalinite world state, ruled from the Kremlin, would ultimately be overthrown by the national and social forces it released in climbing to power. The socialist, therefore, while prepared to join the Atlantic alliance in order to defend himself against the present threat of Soviet imperialism to Europe, must accept both intellectually and emotionally the fact that communism outside Europe is still a liberative force. He must face and overcome an acute dilemma. The throwing off of European ascendancy, however brutal the forms it takes, is a necessary phase of Asiatic and African liberation: yet, whenever the revolution is captured by the Stalinites they threaten the colonial peoples with a new imperialism, which concentrates power more terribly than its predecessor.

Let us put the same dilemma in economic terms. The whole history of Europe since the Reformation indicates that the establishment of the nation state and large-scale industrialisation are the two social techniques for liberating the masses from localised enslavement to the soil and to nature. In Europe and North America, this was achieved by the bourgeois revolution. Outside this limited area, and in this present century, the social conditions for a bourgeois revolution are not present, and this is why, in the absence of any alternative instrument of modernisation, communism often becomes the chosen instrument of history.

There was, of course, one other instrument available, but European liberalism and socialism blunted its edge. As the Webbs saw when, in their early years, they were imperialist anti-Boers, it would have been possible for the European powers to carry through the industrialisation of, say, the Middle East or India. If there had been no democratic and socialist movements protesting against imperialism, it would theoretically have been possible to imagine the ruthless economic reconstruction of Middle Eastern or Indian life under white rule and capitalist exploitation. The Germans might have created an imperial welfare state, with Slavs and Russians as second-rate citizens; and the British an Indian and African empire of the same sort; and it might all have lasted for a hundred or five hundred years. In these capitalist empires, the destruction of peasant proprietorship and the substitution of the large-scale agricultural unit (not as a collective, but as an East-Elbian estate on an enormous scale) might have produced the sort of managerial society foreseen in Jack London's *Iron Heel.*

Finally, no doubt, white imperialism would have been destroyed by its 'inherent contradictions' and by a classical Marxist revolution of the coloured proletariat against their European rulers. Indeed, what I have done in these paragraphs is merely to restate the Marxist-Leninist vision of how world history would develop. But all this did not happen. Instead, the economic basis of European ascendancy was destroyed by two world wars, and American capitalism, which has succeeded to world leadership, is most unlikely to assume the role of nineteenth-century Britain. The U.S.A. is a relatively self-sufficient economy, with an isolationist tradition; and American capitalism, after its inter-war experiences in Germany and elsewhere, has shown no inclination to undertake large-scale overseas investment. American imperialism, if it develops, will be strategically motivated.

The disintegration of the economic basis of European imperialism was accompanied by a moral disintegration as well. After 1918 Western man lost his faith in the White Man's Burden. For a generation liberals and socialists had been campaigning against the evils of imperialism. Now their ideas infected the ruling class and destroyed its own confidence in itself. Owing to its peculiar development, the U.S.A. had always been opposed to colonial empires. Now, President Wilson's naïve theory of national self-determination was accepted, in Europe as well, as the democratic solution of all political problems, including that of the relationship between the white and the colonial peoples. Far too easily, it was assumed that the march of human progress would be resumed if each oppressed people were permitted to establish its own nation state and to institute parliamentary democracy on the Western pattern.

Unfortunately there were no grounds for this assumption. Even in Western Europe, the destruction of feudalism did not take place under the forms of representative government. In the very few countries where it operates successfully, parliamentary democracy is the latest phase of a long process, which has taken place for the most part under autocratic governmental forms. Democracy, indeed, is a sophisticated and subtle form of government, which except in countries with established civil liberties and a high degree of political education, will be manipulated by the ruling groups to retard social change. It is unsuited, therefore, to societies which require to be rapidly industrialised against the opposition of the ruling oligarchy and of the illiterate masses. Wherever Western imperialism is replaced by this kind of pseudo-democracy, there is a danger that sooner or later Communism will take over the social revolution. For a centralised, one-party state, with a clear-cut if mechanical programme of modernisation, is better adapted to the requirements of a backward people than a spurious imitation of the British or American Constitution, combined with a reactionary social system. It was the understanding of this which led the Webbs to move from their support for imperialism in 1900 to their acceptance of communism in 1932.

Once again it is useful to compare our twentieth-century crisis with that of the French Revolutionary wars. Burke and Paine both tried to prove that there was a simple conflict of right and wrong; on one side stood freedom, on the other tyranny, and everyone was morally bound to make up his mind and work for the victory of the good.

We can now see that Burke and Paine were both wrong. War and revolution can never provide us with simple moral issues. The defender of law and order defends privilege as well; and the revolutionary, in his attack on antiquated social forms, threatens a settled pattern of rights and liberties. The dynamic of social change is always tyrannical and usually ends by becoming imperialist: and, under the impact of revolutionary imperialism, the defenders of liberty are driven to support counter-revolution.

Those who believe that the task of socialism is to discover a dynamic which can challenge the dynamic of communism are therefore neglecting the clear lesson of history. If we construct an anticommunist ideology, or take part in organising an anti-Cominform, we shall merely intensify the Cold War and confirm the illusion that the preservation of freedom requires the defeat of communism. In fact, if freedom is to survive, it is essential that neither the U.S.A. nor the Soviet Union should win, and that ideological passion should subside. What the Western socialist needs today is not a crusading creed, but a critical attitude to both ideologies; and the role of the British Labour Movement is to furnish an example of this critical humanism in action. Sceptical, but not cynical; detached, but not neutral; rational, but not dogmatically rationalist. The Promethean social conscience, which I have described on an earlier page, is the only force which can prevent the modern state from degenerating into a managerial society, or the East-West conflict into World War III. It exists everywhere where scientific method and critical analysis are taught (and this includes the Soviet Union as well as the U.S.A.). But in most of the world it can merely act as a brake on totalitarian forces. Only in post-imperial Western Europe, and particularly in this country, could it mould the policies of a nation.

5. SOCIALISM AND THE COLONIAL PEOPLES

Let me illustrate this critical spirit in relation to the central issue of the Cold War. We have seen that, although the Soviet Union is the supreme example of the totalitarian state, communism presents itself to many colonial peoples as a liberative force, and democracy as the defence of a corrupt oligarchy.

What should the socialist do in face of this dilemma? Should he put his trust in plans for world mutual aid, and seek to persuade the Americans that the only way to fight communism effectively is to provide dollars and technical assistance in order to raise the living standards of the backward territories?

The ideal is a noble one; and, if the Americans divert some of the resources, at present concentrated on rearmament, to its achievement, the danger of world war would be substantially reduced. For it is the unmeasured concentration on rearmament which is distorting all the Western economies and gradually creating a situation where we must either make war or collapse. To persuade the Americans, therefore, to give mutual aid a high priority would be a victory for restraint and sanity.

But it is important not to claim more for mutual aid than it can achieve and, in particular, not to fall into the materialist fallacy of assuming that economics provide the prime motive of political action. The dynamic of social revolution in Asia and Africa is not a mass demand for tractors or for bread, but the will and the social conscience of a small intelligentsia, whose aim (national liberation and modernisation) is shared neither by the ruling oligarchy nor by the masses. As we know well from our own history, a revolution is not willed by 'the people', but by a new social force with a new philosophy.

Mutual aid, therefore, even when it is combined with democracy, will not necessarily provide an antidote to communist revolutions. Parliamentary institutions retard social change by deliberately ensuring that it does not greatly injure minority groups or outpace the natural conservatism of the masses. This is why they work successfully only after civil liberties and a sound administration have been firmly established and the masses liberated, usually by undemocratic means. To impose modern democracy on a feudal or primitive social structure, therefore, merely provides the ruling groups with an instrument for preserving their privileges.

This is what has happened throughout the Middle East, as well as in, for instance, the Philippines and South Korea. In all these countries, the forms of democracy are being used to prevent popular emancipation, just as they were in the Balkan states before the war.

Economic and technical assistance provided to such 'democracies' will either be wasted or aggravate the social conflict. In any event, the new élites, which are the carriers of communism, will certainly regard it as an attempt to bolster up counter-revolution, and very often this is what it in fact will be.

The position is aggravated when the Western Powers find it necessary to keep troops in such 'democracies', or to exploit the raw materials which are usually their only source of wealth. Then both national and social aspirations are canalised against the West; Russia is regarded as a rival great power whose good offices can be used to get rid of the foreigner in present occupation; and even the ruling oligarchy has to talk nationalism in order to avert attention from the social crisis.

The socialist, therefore, who regards (i) the granting of national independence, (ii) the encouragement of parliamentary democracy, and (iii) the provision of economic aid as the complete socialist answer to communism is glossing over the real difficulty which faces us. Even if the U.S.A. (which is most unlikely) provided sufficient resources for a world-wide attack on low living standards, the result in many countries would not be to contain communism, but to create more favourable conditions for social revolution. We should still, therefore, be faced with the problem what to do when a revolutionary dictatorship, almost certainly with Russian assistance, seizes power in a backward country which we are seeking to modernise under Western patronage. Should the revolution be crushed, as the French tried to crush it in Indo-China, or tolerated, as the Labour Government tolerated the Chinese Communists? And if we recognise successful revolutions—and even assist them when they quarrel with the Kremlin—why do we continue to assert that we share the American objective of containing communism throughout the world?

Here is an unresolved contradiction, which inhibits any clear formulation of socialist policy. Is it not the lesson of the Labour Government's failure in the Middle East that it may be less dangerous to permit revolution and dictatorship (even when their motive force is hatred of ourselves) than to defend our strategic and commercial interest by a combination of military force and political fraud? The socialist must remain sceptical of plans for combating communism which really involve the suppression of national and social revolution among the colonial peoples. In the history of every Western democracy, the revolutionary war or civil war has been the first act of nationhood, just as the revolutionary army has been the first instrument of national unification and popular education. These are historical facts which the Russian Marxists have carefully studied, and from which they have drawn important conclusions. It is time that we studied them too and learnt from the French experience in Indo-China that the spread of communism may be a lesser evil than the containment of it by a ruinous colonial war.

But it is by no means certain that every social revolution will be taken over by the Kremlin, if its leaders are left free to make their own policy. Since the war Indonesia and Burma chose independence and suppressed their Communist Parties; and Tito quarrelled with the Kremlin. If the Tudeh Party in Persia, Viet-Minh in Indo-China and Mao Tse-tung are now allies of Russia, it must be admitted that Western policy did nothing to dissuade them. Social revolution in a backward country always begins as an alliance of very varied elements, among which the Stalinites are rarely the most important. Whether the Communists come to dominate the revolution depends at least as much on Western policy as on the activities of the Kremlin. Only too often strategic and economic policies, designed to contain communism, have in fact, by supporting counter-revolution, played into the hands of the Soviet Union. The American isolationist, who reacts so violently against the gigantic bill for rearmament and foreign aid,

is nearer the tradition of Americanism than the New Deal prophets
of America's world-wide responsibilities. In the past, the outstanding
virtue of American democracy has been its anti-colonial bias. Instead
of seeking to encourage the Americans to overcome this bias and
underwrite our imperial commitments, we should influence them
to revert to the moderate policies of the period of Marshall Aid, to
limit their arms programme to what they can sustain for at least
a generation, and to take the risk in Asia and Africa of leaving
unfilled the 'political vacuum' left by the dismantling of the old
European empires. An unfilled vacuum is sometimes less dangerous
than the frustration of social revolution in the name of democracy.

6. Conclusions

It is now time to return to the question with which we started. The
Labour Party, we observed, lost its sense of direction before the 1950
Election. Can we use the world picture we have sketched in order to
rediscover our bearings? We are certainly not in a position as yet to
map the new route to socialism. That will require (i) a detailed assess-
ment of the balance of world power, and in particular, of those internal
forces which mould the external policies of the U.S.A. and the Soviet
Union, and so determine the course of the Cold War; (ii) an analysis
of our strength, as measured against our commitments in a world
where colonial emancipation, combined with population pressure, has
turned the terms of trade permanently against us; and (iii) a fresh
investigation of the changes in the internal structure of this country
since 1940. These vital pieces of research have yet to be undertaken.
Meanwhile, the best we can hope to do is to ask the relevant
questions, which must be answered before the second stage of
socialism can be worked out. The first signpost is one that is already
behind us, established by the Labour Government. Although the
welfare capitalism developed since 1945 is highly unstable, what *is*
inviolable is the change in social climate, a change equal in importance with the liberal revolutions of 1832 and 1906. Its essence can be
summed up in two principles. The first states that it is the responsibility of the democratic state to provide for every citizen, as of right,
security against unemployment, sickness and old age. The second runs
that it is the function of the state to plan the use of our national
resources so as to maintain work for all and ensure fair shares of the
national income between different sections of the community.

Of course, there are many who still believe that these two principles should never have been conceded, since their full implementation must lead either to the collapse of our economy or to complete socialisation. The Conservative Party for instance, accepts them with the proviso that nothing must be done which undermines the incentives of free enterprise—that is to say, it accepts them in theory, but not in practice. But the fact remains that the social climate—and with it the categories of political controversy—was changed decisively when the Labour Government succeeded in preserving, after the war had ended, the full employment, the system of redistributive taxation, and the central planning of the economy which had previously been regarded as temporary wartime expedients.

In working out the programme for the second stage of socialism, we must start from this change of social climate. The true aim of the Labour Movement has always been not the dramatic capture of power by the working class, but the conversion of the nation to the socialist pattern of rights and values; not the violent destruction of one economic system and the substitution of another, but the voluntary acceptance of the need for socialism in order to implement in social life the values which each citizen accepts in his personal relations. Sceptical of the Marxist doctrine of inherent conflict, the Labour Party has tenaciously assumed that British people can be persuaded by an act of collective conscience to subject economic power to public authority and to civilise the conflict inherent in social change.

This belief was vindicated in the first post-war months. At that time the British people was ready to accept the peaceful socialist revolution; and if what it got was merely welfare capitalism, the fault lay with the politicians and not with the public.

Let us define precisely where welfare capitalism falls short of socialism. Under welfare capitalism: (i) Though the national income is rather more fairly distributed than before, the concentration of capital and so of economic privilege remains unchanged. (ii) Profits, wages and salaries are still determined not by any conditions of national interest or social justice, but by the traditional methods of *laisser-faire*. Under conditions of full employment, this must result in a continuous inflationary pressure, which undermines the real value of social security and small savings, as well as making our products less competitive in foreign markets and so jeopardising our capacity to maintain the standard of living. (iii) Though certain basic industries are transformed into public corporations and private industry is subject to some control, effective power remains in the hands of a small managerial and civil service élite.

There can be no advance to socialism unless each of these three problems is honestly faced. Can an unhealthy concentration of capital be prevented without a much greater extension of public ownership or, alternatively, a capital levy? Can inflation be countered, under conditions of full employment, without a national profits and wages policy? If not, how can such a policy be put into execution without some amendment by the trade unions of their cherished freedom of collective bargaining? Both these issues were avoided during the six years of Labour Government. They can be avoided no longer if the Labour Party is to face the future once again with a programme as challenging as that of 1945.

But, overshadowing these two questions is the threat of the managerial society. The planned economy and the centralisation of power are no longer socialist objectives. They are developing all over the world as the result of the Political Revolution, and the process is accelerated by the prevalence of war economy. The main task of socialism today is to prevent the concentration of power in the hands of *either* industrial management *or* the state bureaucracy—in brief, to distribute responsibility and so to enlarge freedom of choice.

This task was not even begun by the Labour Government. On the contrary, in the nationalised industries old managements were preserved almost untouched, and appointments to the national, regional and consultative boards were made as if with the express intention of affirming that no change was intended. The Government's attitude to central planning was similar. Up to 1947, no serious attempt was made to construct even a central mechanism for assessing resources and requirements of wealth and labour, and allocating them to the various needs. Not until the convertibility crisis was Sir Stafford Cripps given the task of grappling with the problem, educating the people about its nature, and developing the institutions necessary for its solution. But even then the Government seemed to have regarded his austerity planning as an emergency measure, rather than as the first step towards bringing economic power under democratic control. Just as it failed to socialise the management of the nationalised industries, so it left the central control of planning in the hands of an unreformed Civil Service.

Nor was any effort made to encourage popular participation in the new Welfare State. The Labour Movement grew up as a working-class democracy in action. Before 1945, for hundreds of thousands of active trade unionists and Party workers, socialism was a way of life and a vocation. In order to counter the danger of managerialism, it was essential to harness this volunteer energy to the work of social transformation and so to retain for the Party in office the dynamic of Opposition. In the new social climate, there were endless tasks which trade unionists, both locally and nationally, would have been ready to undertake. They were left to infer that collective bargaining, such as they had developed in the capitalist free-for-all, and the humdrum job of Party organisation, were all that was required of them. Municipal socialists—with some of their best enterprises taken over by public corporations—were given no vision of new socialist responsibilities. The Co-operative Movement was not summoned to help in tackling the problems of distribution. Instead, the impression was given that socialism was an affair for the Cabinet, acting through the existing Civil Service. The rest of the nation was to carry on as before, while benefits were bestowed from above upon some, and taken from others. Thus the first stage of socialism was executed primarily by anti-socialist managers and neutral Civil Servants.

We are a nation deeply imbued with a sense of social status and inhibited by an oligarchic tradition, which makes responsibility the privilege of the educated minority and irresponsibility the negative freedom of the half-educated masses. At present the educational system, the parties and the trade union machines, instead of acting as a social solvent, are accentuating the segregation of élites. The leaders—and this applies at least as much in the Labour Movement as outside it—profoundly distrust active democracy.

Yet whether the next stage in our journey is towards socialism or a veiled form of totalitarianism largely depends on how far the state and industry are run by segregated élites, with the rest of the people passive executants of their orders. This applies to public as well as to private industry, to the trade union and Party hierarchies as well as to business concerns. In a world organised in ever larger and more inhuman units, the task of socialism is to prevent managerial responsibility degenerating into privilege. This can only be achieved by increasing, even at the cost of 'efficiency', the citizen's right to participate in the control not only of government and industry, but of the party for which he votes, and of the trade union whose card he carries. After all, it is not the pursuit of happiness but the enlargement of freedom which is socialism's highest aim.

PLANNING FOR FREEDOM

Based on a Fabian lecture, given in November 1955 under the title of 'The New Despotism'. A considerably lengthier text of this lecture was published as a pamphlet in the following February. Though it aroused a certain interest abroad, it fell completely flat in this country. It was not until some seven years later when I covered much the same ground in an introduction to Bagehot's 'The English Constitution' (Fontana, 1963), that it was possible to rouse much interest in the Labour movement for the notion that the prime purpose of socialist planning should be the enlargement of human freedom.

i

IN August 1955 I attended the Congress for Cultural Freedom at Milan. There I had the pleasure of meeting John K. Galbraith, the author of the most arresting study of modern American capitalism. We were discussing the problem which confronts the American Fair Dealer in working out a convincing policy for the Democratic candidate in the forthcoming Presidential election, when Galbraith said to me, 'There's an awkward thought which lurks at the back of our minds. Both the American Liberal and the British Socialist in the 1930s assumed that capitalism was not only immoral but unworkable; it was a system which must destroy itself because of its own inherent weaknesses. And this meant that, in your British philosophy, a Socialist revolution was not only desirable but inevitable. Now suppose that assumption is not true. Would that not mean the snapping of the mainspring of the Labour Party?'

Would it? I propose to pull this ugly thought out of its dark corner and examine it.

Since 1945 the evidence, both from the United States and from this country and Western Europe, seems to suggest that, instead of being the most difficult and fundamental problem of Western society, mass unemployment is something which can be dealt with relatively easily by any Government which understands the economic system and has the right instruments for controlling it and manipulating it. There is still room for argument about these instruments. Are credit contraction and credit expansion—combined with the right budgetary policy—sufficient? Or are physical controls necessary as well? But these are secondary questions—disputes about tactics rather than strategy. What Socialists have to decide is whether John Maynard Keynes was right in asserting that the new capitalism has developed into a workable system—provided that it is worked intelligently.

Let us start by recalling Keynes's picture. The way he proposed to deal with mass unemployment was to dig a very deep shaft, bury millions of bank-notes at the bottom of it and then pay wages to workers for digging the bank-notes out again. There, he said, is the simple method of resolving the inherent contradiction of capitalism. Whether the work is socially useful or socially useless is of secondary importance: what matters is the provision of work. Hitler and Schacht were the first people to demonstrate this, when they used an arms programme, fiscal controls and bilateral trade treaties to produce a full-employment economy in Germany. And we should not forget that the New Dealers did not succeed in abolishing mass unemployment in the United States until the war and the arms programme came along. So, too, when the Germans invaded France, there were still 843,000 unemployed in this country. It was only at this point that the British Government was stimulated to indulge in the arms expenditure which absorbed all the unemployed.

It is high time we pulled this thought from the back of our minds and had the courage to think it through to its final consequences. I believe that Keynes has shown this particular kind of pessimism about the Western economy to be unfounded. It is not an inherently unworkable society, but a workable society which is appallingly wasteful of human and material resources and which contains gross injustices. Only when we have frankly admitted this can we begin to think sensibly about the next stage of Socialism.

Why do so many Socialists hesitate to accept this? After all, we detest the denial of freedom in a Communist State, and it should be a vast relief for a democratic Socialist to realise that there is no need for totalitarian government control in order to abolish mass unemployment.

One reason for our hesitation is a practical one. It was difficult enough to persuade people to become Socialists when we could tell them that capitalism is not only immoral but also unworkable. Will it not be much more difficult, we ask, to persuade the majority of our countrymen that a workable system must be changed, simply because it is immoral and unjust? Don't most people care more about security than they do about social justice and equality? If welfare capitalism can provide the majority with security, how can we ever persuade them to prefer Socialism?

The doubts awakened by these questions have, I think, been accentuated by our experience of the mixed economy established by the Labour Government between 1945 and 1950. If we are honest, we must admit to ourselves that it was the least dogmatically Socialist parts of what the Labour Government did which were most popular and which worked best. What we describe as the Welfare State has been immensely successful and immensely popular, whereas national-isation has not changed the lives of the workers in the industries affected in the way they expected.

It has been a disappointment to the trade union movement. The Socialist planner may envisage a future in which there are added to the Coal Board, the British Electricity Authority and the Transport Commission forty or fifty other Boards of the same type, imposed on other industries. But would this prospect, if presented to the public, win votes for Labour or reawaken the enthusiasm of the trade union movement? I suspect that we all know the answer to this question. It would not. If that is all that socialism means, the people of this country will reject it.

I put some of these problems to a Fabian Summer School at Oxford in 1955, and we had some of the best discussions I have ever heard. Most of the younger Fabians there agreed on one thing. They said to me, 'If you are going to have Socialism and a planned economy, why not make a real job of it? Why be content with this half-baked mixed economy and why imagine that you will rouse the Labour move-ment from its lethargy by proposing that the next Labour Govern-ment should nationalise two or three more industries? For heaven's sake, make up your minds on the National Executive. If you are still Socialists, go for it one hundred per cent.' I had anticipated that this would be the reaction, and I had taken the precaution of asking A. J. P. Taylor to come to the school. He listened to these younger Fabians and then he said, 'Very well, my friends, answer me one

question. If you really believe all that, why don't you join the Communist Party? If you want one hundred per cent Socialism, what's
wrong with the Soviet Union?' They could not give much of an
answer to A. J. P. Taylor's question. They wanted one hundred per
cent Socialism—but they didn't want the Soviet system.

All the week we roamed round the problem, until we began to have
the feeling that maybe the British people is now getting the worst of
both worlds. Under the mixed economy now carried on by the Conservatives what we have is not monopoly (a market dominated by a
single mammoth concern), but oligopoly (a market dominated by a
very few mammoth concerns). In Britain this oligopoly is protected by
a vast, bureaucratic State and so starved of the competition which,
according to Mr. Galbraith, produces the new equilibrium in
American society.

Both the American and the Russian systems are working far better
than anyone expected twenty years ago. Even more important, they
are working far better than the British system either under Labour or
under Tory management. That is why not merely intellectual sceptics
but a good many loyal Labour Party supporters are beginning to
wonder whether there is any third way between these two great
systems. Are the only alternatives left to the Socialist in the 1950s
either to watch Mr. Macmillan bring the British mixed economy into
line with the American system or else to join the Communist
party?

ii

These doubts can only be removed by re-thinking the foundations
of our Socialism.

Surely it is time to recognise that Socialism cannot and should not
be based on any particular economic theory. Judged by the standards
of predication and verification, economics is still very far from being
a science. To rate it at its highest, it is a technique, combined with
historical analysis. Moreover, those who based the case for Socialism
on the 'inherent contradictions' of the capitalist system were depart-
ing from the tradition of British Radicalism and introducing a foreign
element into the philosophy of our Labour Movement. Labour's real
dynamic has always been a moral protest against social injustice, not
an intellectual demonstration that capitalism is bound to collapse; a
challenge to capitalist privilege, not a proof that those privileges must

inevitably be replaced by a classless society. Keynesianism may have
undermined the old-fashioned economic case for Socialism, but it
has left the political and moral case for it completely unaffected.

The case was formulated in its classic form by Professor R. H.
Tawney. He showed that Parliamentary democracy will only become
a fully effective guarantor of individual freedom when it is combined
with social control of economic power. Power, he argued, always
degenerates into privilege when those who hold it are accountable
to no one but themselves. In a democracy, therefore, those who own
or manage the means of production must be made responsible to a
popularly elected Government, and the most effective way to do this
is to substitute public for private ownership of large-scale industries.
Tawney's case for Socialism was not that it is easier to work than
the acquisitive society but that it is morally superior—and politically
essential to the realisation of freedom.

Has Tawney's denunciation of the acquisitive society become less
relevant in the last thirty years? On the contrary. One of the main
post-war features of the Western world has been the steady concentration of economic power in the hands of the managerial class, whose
responsibility to their shareholders is frequently titular. In Tawney's
sense, the men who run our great industries today form an irresponsible oligarchy; and the degree of public control we have achieved
is quite inadequate to ensure that they are in any sense accountable to
the community.

The first task of Socialism, therefore, must be to expose this growth
of irresponsible power; to challenge this new managerial oligarchy;
to show that its monopolistic—or oligopolistic—privileges are a
threat to democracy and to demand that it should become not the
master but the servant of the nation.

At this point, however, we must drag out another of those doubts
which are lurking in the dark corner of our minds. We say that we
must denounce great concentrations of irresponsible power. But are
they all on one side of industry? Is it only the privately owned companies which threaten our freedom?

When I look at the Coal Board (a public corporation), what strikes
me is that it shares certain characteristics with I.C.I. Under its constitution the Coal Board must pay the same kind of attention to its
balance sheet as any private corporation. It cannot pursue an unorthodox price policy, based on the national interest. It is certainly
not fully accountable to Parliament and the degree of workers' partici-

pation in management which it has achieved is not markedly higher than in a progressive company. As for the technician and the scientist, they may actually feel more frustrated under the rule of the accountants, ex-civil servants, ex-generals and ex-trade union officials who compose the Board of a nationalised industry than they did under private enterprise. Nationalisation, in its present stage, has certain solid economic advantages, including Government control of the capital investment and the broad lines of policy of the nationalised industries. Moreover, it is a stabilising factor, since it eliminates those increases in unearned incomes and capital gains which provoke wage demands and stimulate inflation. But it is very far from the kind of Socialism envisaged in Tawney's *Acquisitive Society*.[1] It is only the first step towards our goal.

Moreover, these oligopolists—some in charge of nationalised and some of private industries—do not comprise the whole of the managerial society. There is also the State bureaucracy to contend with; and here too the old distinctions between public and private enterprise are becoming blurred. Of course, the orthodox Tory still instinctively suspects any Government Department of over-staffing and muddle; and instinctively assumes that I.C.I. is a model of individual initiative and business efficiency. Unfortunately the loyal Labour supporter is far too inclined to believe that his Socialist loyalty requires him to say the exact reverse. He believes that, whereas large-scale private enterprise is a threat to freedom, the State must be 'a good thing'.

Actually, the growth of a vast, centralised State bureaucracy constitutes a grave potential threat to social democracy. The idea that we are being disloyal to our Socialist principles if we attack its excesses or defend the individual against its incipient despotism is a fallacy.

Here again, Tawney's principle is relevant. Our aim is to enlarge freedom by making those who control great concentrations of power fully accountable to the people. But that must apply to the Chiefs of Staff or the Milk Marketing Board or the National Assistance Board or the Foreign Office as well as to the Directors of I.C.I. For the Socialist, as much as for the Liberal, the State Leviathan is a necessary evil; and the fact that part of the civil service now administers a Welfare State does not remove the threat to freedom which the twentieth-century concentration of power has produced. It is the

[1] G. Bell & Sons Ltd., London, 1921.

gigantic size of the modern unit of organisation, whether in industry, in the press, in the armed services or in the Welfare State, which presents the citizens of an advanced Western nation today with the choice between accepting the inroads on freedom of an increasingly managerial society or risking the advance towards a fully Socialist society.

Let me try to sum up the conclusions we have so far reached.

(1) The probability suggested by John Maynard Keynes that Western capitalism is no longer bound by its own inherent contradictions to collapse in ruins, may well demand a radical rethinking of classic Communist theory in order to bring it into line with Russian practice. It presents neither a theoretical nor a moral problem to the democratic Socialist.

Our Socialism is based on the traditional Radical demand for a society of free and equal citizens, reinforced by the empirical postulate that great concentrations of power become a menace to freedom and equality unless they are subjected to public control. If the Western economies continue to expand without more than minor recessions, that expansion will bring with it an intensification of the oligopoly which provides the Socialist with the justification for imposing democratic controls on these vast aggregates of economic power. If, on the other hand, the Americans are unintelligent and let themselves drift into a slump, then we shall be faced with a crisis in which the case for Socialism scarcely needs to be argued in rational terms.

(2) Since our Socialism is based on the moral demand for greater equality and an enlargement of freedom, and postulates that irresponsible power corrupts, the Socialist must be courageous enough to admit that the evils of oligopoly are not limited to the private sector of the economy. Public corporations and Departments of State can also exhibit managerialist tendencies, favour inequality and become a threat to freedom. If it is to appeal to the younger generation, Socialism must challenge power which is either irresponsible or only semi-responsible—in whatever hands that power rests.

iii

So far our enquiry has been confined to two points. First we have cleared a number of preliminary obstacles in the way of a reaffirmation of Socialist principles. Then we have defined the enemy we have to fight and the objective for the sake of which we are challenging him. Our next task is to study our own order of battle. Who are our allies? We are used to talking about the 'Trinity of Labour', the Trade Unions, the Labour Party and the Co-operative Movement. We should now briefly consider each of them as an ally in the battle to curb irresponsible concentrations of power.

No organisation with which I have any acquaintance has more genuinely Socialist aims and a more thoroughly democratic constitution than the Co-operative Societies, linked together in the Co-operative Movement. The Co-operatives are a great and living example of the ability of the British working class to organise and manage its own institutions, and I believe that this movement can join us in our Socialist crusade. But we must face certain practical difficulties.

In the first place, democracy, although it is immensely strong in defence, has obvious weaknesses in attack. When a general launches an offensive, he must be sure that the units under him will respond to his commands. What he needs is centralised power, and that is precisely what is lacking in the Co-operative Movement. Here, in response to the principles of democratic Socialism, power has been dispersed from the centre to the individual societies. Moreover, the Co-operative political party, as distinct from the Co-operative Movement, still receives little support from the majority of Co-operators.

In the second place, we cannot overlook the fact that most Co-operative Societies, though they began with the revolutionary aim of transforming society, have integrated themselves into the existing mixed economy and their main aim is not to change its structure but to ensure that their members prosper under it.

I admit that the 1945 Labour Government showed very little imagination in its approach to the Co-operative Movement. Indeed, it fell over backwards in assuring private enterprise that it was showing no favours to a Socialist system of distribution. Nevertheless, we would be unwise to assume that any initiative for a revival of our creed will come from the Co-operatives. If the Labour Party gives a lead, political interest in the Co-operative Movement may revive, on the one condition that the next Socialist programme does not include items which directly violate either the principles or the interests of Co-operators. More than this we should not expect.

What about the trade unions? The first and simple answer is that, without their assistance, a Socialist crusade is a fool's errand. You can have a Labour Party, based on the trade unions, which is not a

Socialist party. But you cannot have a Socialist party divorced from the trade unions. One of the characteristics which distinguishes a democratic Socialist from a Communist is his acceptance of the need to carry the trade unions with him, even though this means slowing the rate of progress.

For Lenin the trade unions were a lever of revolution, an instrument to be used by the trained Bolshevik élite in the achievement of power. But Lenin was justified by his theory in destroying the independence of the trade unions along with the soviets as soon as he had achieved power. For the democratic Socialist, on the other hand, they represent the working-class electorate, who must be persuaded voluntarily to vote for a Socialist programme—and, even more important, to accept it when it is put into action.

Having said this, I must add that the Western trade union move-is not merely a reaction against the harshness of the capitalist system but, to some extent, a product of it. It is not surprising, therefore, that it should exhibit certain capitalist characteristics. Whereas the Labour politician can, if he is determined, make it his chief aim to extend public ownership, the first aim of the trade union leader, who feels a sense of responsibility to his members, must be to improve their wages and conditions within the existing system, even if that means bolstering this system up. Whereas the Labour politician can freely discuss a national wages policy and even reach the conclusion that it would be essential in a Socialist planned economy, the trade union leader will be inclined either to write off such discussions as 'academic' or condemn them as dangerous heresy.

That is why, inside any Labour Party, there will always exist a tension between the representatives of trade unionism and the Socialist politicians—a tension which will be found not only in the Executive at the top but in every Council group and constituency party. That tension can be healthy. It can produce keen and constructive discussion and result in a balanced policy, in which both sides of the Party can have confidence. But this balance can be easily upset. If, for instance, the politicians try to move too fast towards Socialism, there is a danger of a breach between them and their trade union colleagues; and if that breach develops into a Party split, the Socialist politicians are soon isolated from organised Labour and become the leaders of the kind of ineffective Socialist party we can see in several European countries.

The equal and opposite danger is that the trade union leaders should exert too much influence on policy making. If they do so, a Labour Party soon becomes merely the political agent of trade unionism, concerned to get its slice of the economic cake and its status in society for one section of the community. In that case it develops the philosophy of Labourism and degenerates into a class party which can only achieve power by the mistakes of its opponents.

The danger of this degeneration is always there. For it is not only in the management of industry that we find the tendency towards concentration of power. Inevitably the same process has been at work in the trade unions. Our modern Labour movement was rapidly constructed before the first world war as a rough battering ram for the purpose of breaching the walls of privilege. At that time there really were 'two nations' in Britain; the working class was excluded from its rightful share not only of wealth and opportunity but of social and political status as well. Because they grew up when the class war was a grim reality, the British trade unions adopted certain patterns of behaviour which were sharply at variance with the liberal tradition of British Radicalism. Men who are compelled to wage class war cannot worry unduly about minority rights. It is not surprising, therefore, that some Labour leaders, at the head of fighting organisations of the 'other nation', should have made a dogma of majority decisions and developed a habit of obtaining those decisions without too much regard for minority opinion.

In an industrial dispute it is difficult for the trade unionist to be tolerant of the industrial conscientious objector, since such tolerance will leave room for the blackleg. So, too, it is impossible to achieve the solidarity of the closed shop while preserving to the minority in a trade union all the rights which are assured to the Opposition at Westminster. Before 1927, Socialists may have regretted these encroachments on individual freedom. But they realised that the Labour Movement was facing an immensely powerful enemy and, in the heat of battle, they accepted the sacrifices of personal freedom as an inevitable evil, forced upon the Labour Movement by the class war.

A different situation arises however when the battle has been won and the enemy forced to come to terms. Today the British trade union movement is an essential institution of the modern mixed economy. Trade unionists are no longer denied their proper status and their leaders are always welcome at Downing Street, whatever Government is in power. In a fully employed economy, indeed, those who

manage a trade union exert a bargaining power in wage negotiations
at least equal to that of the managerial class who represent an industry. Moreover, the strike weapon is now regarded by many leading trade unionists as a clumsy and antiquated weapon, which be-
longs to the bad old days. Finally, it must be noted that, in modern
large-scale industry, there are certain common interests uniting
organised management and organised labour. For instance, it is
obviously convenient for both sides that power should be concentrated in fewer and fewer hands.

I am not here concerned to criticise this social revolution—for
that is what it is. It was a magnificent achievement to win status
and power within the Establishment and, by winning it, the trade
union leaders conferred immense material benefits on their members.
But anyone who is true to the principles laid down by R.
H. Tawney must raise one question. Rough justice to break-away
minorities and intolerance of opposition to majority decisions—these
were inevitable in the trade union movement of 1910. Are they
still inevitable in the completely changed circumstances of
1956?

The older generation of trade unionists will be impatient that such
a question is even raised. But young people are inclined to ask awkward questions, and it is no good dubbing them Communists because
they do so. Is the control, they ask, exerted by the membership of
a big industrial union over the General Secretary and his appointed
officials a real and effective control? Or is it not in danger of becoming a myth, as fictional as the right of the shareholder to shape the
policy of I.C.I.? When they read about the Tolpuddle Martyrs, they
see that these early trade unionists fought and suffered for the right
of individual workers to organise collective self-defence. Is that right,
they ask, still a reality today, or has it been transformed into a
privilege of well-established trade unions?

How should these questions be answered? It is sometimes argued
that, since concentration of power is inevitable, we should accept
the oligarchic characteristics of modern trade unionism and conceive
of industrial democracy today as an equilibrium of power between
a few very powerful men on both sides of industry. That seems to
me merely the old Manchester theory of economics, restated in terms
of the managerial society. A hundred years ago the Liberal theorists
maintained that, despite the social outrages of early capitalism, there
was a secret harmony of interests in a free-enterprise economy, which

would manifest itself if the economy was left free of political interference. This Liberal theory was exposed by Socialists as an optimistic
illusion, and I see no reason to imagine that it is less illusory in an
age of large-scale industrial organisation.

Surely we are Socialists precisely because we deny that there is
a natural harmony of interests and believe that an equilibrium of
forces which is achieved by power politics will always favour the
strong against the weak, the few against the many and the wielder of
power against the powerless individual. That, indeed, is why we
state as our first principle that those who hold economic power must
be made subject to law and politically responsible to the people's
elected representatives.

Is there then an inherent conflict between the practices of trade
unionism in a highly industrialised nation and the principles of
Socialism? Most American trade unionists would say 'yes'. I do not
accept this view. What saves us is that, in British politics, individuals
count for at least as much as vested interests. At all levels, from
the General Secretary's office to the branch, the active trade unionist,
thank heavens, is frequently an active Socialist as well. He is the
yeast in the non-political dough of the trade union movement, and
he is also the link which binds the T.U.C. and the Labour Party
together.

What we must realise, however, is that the pace at which the
politician at Westminster can move towards Socialism will depend
on the success of Socialist trade unionists in permeating the trade
union movement with their ideas. Neither the Labour Party nor
even a Labour Government can order the trade unions to reform
themselves. The initiative must come from the inside. The success
or failure of the next Labour Government will very largely depend
on the readiness of the trade union leaders to adapt their functions
and procedures to the requirements of a democratically planned
society.

iv

The conclusion we have so far reached is clear. We must not expect the initiative for the next stage of Socialism to come either
from the Co-operative Movement or from the leadership of the trade
unions.

It is, of course, essential for the Labour Party to retain the confidence of its two main allies. But it would be unrealistic to overlook the fact that both have now become established institutions, with deep roots in the existing social order, and display for this reason a quite natural reluctance to accept any radical change which seems inimical to their own interests. The dynamic of change today must be found in the Socialist membership of the Labour Party, or nowhere else.

That dynamic, I believe, will only become really effective if we ground our Socialist case not only on economic arguments about increased productivity and improved living standards but also on the defence of personal freedom and personal responsibility in a managerial society. From this point of view the case for Socialism can be stated very simply. Since the process of power concentration is inevitable in a modern economy, the only alternatives are either to permit the oligopolists to dominate the community or to subject them to public control.

At this point, however, I must insert one reservation. There does exist another possible way of dealing with oligopoly. Instead of socialising the economy, the attempt could be made to break up the concentrations of power, or at least to ensure that they were subject to genuine competition. This, of course, is the tradition of American democracy, with its anti-trust legislation. There the trade union movement is violently but quite rationally opposed to the concepts of Socialism and central planning because it believes that the workers' freedom and living standards can best be safeguarded by independent trade union action in a keenly competitive society. This American philosophy is inapplicable to Britain. In the first place, Britain is too small. And, secondly, British capitalists are as afraid as British trade unions of genuinely competitive free enterprise. The only democratic alternative to Socialism, therefore, is ruled out in Britain by the need for enforced standardisation and by the restrictive practices which have characterised both sides of our industry for a generation. However much Conservatives may talk about their belief in the virtues of free enterprise, the Tory Government has done little to stimulate it since 1951.

So in Britain we are faced with the following dilemma. Since the abuses of oligopoly cannot be checked by free competition, the only way to enlarge freedom and achieve a full democracy is to subject the economy to public control. Yet the State bureaucracy itself is one of those concentrations of power which threaten our freedom. If we increase its authority still further, shall we not be endangering the liberties we are trying to defend?

This dilemma in inherent in the nature of the modern, highly industrialised community. It is not, as is often suggested, exclusively a dilemma for Socialists; it faces every democratic Government, whatever its complexion.

The Conservative solution is to concentrate attention on the threat of State despotism (Crichel Down, for instance) and conveniently to overlook all the other concentrations of power which threaten our liberties. Modern Conservatives wish to weaken the central Government and encourage the Executive to sign a Magna Carta which guarantees the liberties not of the individual but of our new-style feudal barons. In fact, they accept the notion of an equilibrium within the managerial society, which we have already discussed and abandoned as a modern version of the Manchester Liberal illusion.

Where this leads is clear enough. Representative institutions will become less and less effective, and Parliament a ceremonial façade, which conceals the fact that power has been taken from the people and divided between the barons who control industry, Fleet Street and radio, the Departments of State and the party machines. On the pretence of defending the individual against the horrors of State Socialism, modern Conservatism will let democracy drift into a kind of voluntary totalitarianism.

The main task of Socialists today is to convince the nation that its liberties are threatened by this new feudalism and to show the way to overcome it. There are two requirements. (1) If the Executive is not to surrender to the oligopolists, it must be able to control them, and that means that they must be made equally subject to its control. (2) If the Executive is not itself to become a despot, it must be fully and continuously responsive to the popular will.

I shall not spend long on the first of these requirements. It is, of course, the traditional Socialist case for public ownership. That case is even stronger today than it was before the growth of modern large-scale organisation. Although coal, electricity, gas and transport are not yet socialised, the national Boards which run them are partly accountable to the Government and the main lines of their development can be laid down by a strong Cabinet. If the Executive is to curb oligopoly without any loss of productive efficiency, then public ownership must be extended a great deal further.

But neither the workers in industry nor the voters are well acquainted with the serious Socialist case for nationalisation. We would be prudent, therefore, to select industries where even the non-Socialist can be convinced that it is desirable. If the tenant of a rent-restricted house realises that he cannot obtain a bathroom under his private landlord without an exorbitant increase of rent, he may accept the Socialist case for municipalisation. If the road-user sees the chaos caused by pouring new cars on to an antiquated road system while passenger trains are half empty and the railways lose money, then he may accept the case for an integrated and publicly owned transport system. If retirement on half pay only becomes a possibility as a result of nationalising superannuation, then the extension of public ownership into the sphere of insurance will be as popular as the National Health Service.

It is no use, however, believing that we have finished the job when we have nationalised an industry or part of an industry and given it a Consumers' Council. We have plenty of Consumers' Councils already and they are not very effective bodies. There is only one defence for the consumer, and that is through his elected representatives, whether in local or central government. That is why every nationalised industry must be made fully responsible to Parliament, just as municipal trading concerns have always been fully responsible to the Council.

Our Socialist aim has always been two-fold. We seek to make economic power responsive both to the community as a whole (the consumer) and to the worker in any particular industry (the producer). Plans for nationalisation which do not satisfy the aspirations to workers' control are the technocrats' perversion of our Socialist ideal. We must frankly admit that, so far, our nationalised industries have been little better than that.

What is to be done about it? Some Socialists, and most trade union leaders, argue that this is a subject not for legislation but for education. The machinery, they say, for the individual worker to be promoted to management, and for production committees between workers and management, is already there in our nationalised industries, and all that needs to be done is to encourage both sides of the industries to work it.

If this were true, the prospects of a second stage of Socialism would not be bright. It seems to me obvious that any proposal for extending public ownership will not be welcomed by the trade unionists in the industry concerned unless they can foresee an improvement in their own status resulting from it. No one can responsibly promise that, as a result of nationalisation, an industry would be able to offer higher wages or even, in all cases, a more attractive superannuation scheme than a powerful private monopoly or near-monopoly. What publicly-owned industries could offer to their workers is a real share in the control of the industry.

On this problem I believe that the Labour Party would do well to study closely the experiment now launched in Western Germany. Here *Mitbestimmungsrecht* (or workers' participation in management) has been enforced by law on the coal and steel industries. Although they remain privately owned, the boards of directors of all these companies are now composed of an equal proportion of workers, employers' and State representatives, with an independent chairman.

The difference in structure between German and British industry would make quite inappropriate the idea of importing *Mitbestimmungsrecht* into Britain. Moreover, there are many snags in the German plan. Will it denude the trade unions of their best leaders? Will the workers' representatives be cut off from the rank and file and lose its confidence? Have they been promoted to a stratosphere, where they can exert no effective control? These are all questions to which answers are only now emerging. Moreover, *Mitbestimmungsrecht* was regarded by the German trade union movement as an alternative to nationalisation, whereas British Socialists must treat workers' participation in management as an essential part of socialisation. Nevertheless the Labour Party should study the German experiment and ask itself whether the principle could be successfully applied to Britain.

v

Assume, therefore, that the next Labour Government will extend public ownership and simultaneously make our nationalised industries more responsive to democratic control. Assume that it will also encourage municipal enterprise and co-operation. All this will reduce the area of the private sector of the economy and so facilitate the Socialist task of making economic power responsible to the community. But there will still be a great deal of economic enterprise in private hands, some of it in mammoth concerns. How are we to prevent these private oligopolists from achieving irresponsible power? How can we ensure that instead of their telling the Government what to do, the Government tells them?

Here the first thing to realise is that what a British Cabinet lacks is not power and authority but eyes and ears. The last Labour Government was unable to plan largely because it did not know what was going on in the economy. Indeed, the Federal Administration of the United States knows far more about the working of American free enterprise than our Labour Government did about the working of British industry and British financial institutions.

One of the first acts of the next Labour Government should be to remedy this fatal defect. It should expand the miserably small body of economists and statisticians at present available and create not a central planning board (planning is a function of Government, not of experts) but a central fact-finding bureau. And it must make sure that this bureau is not a part of the Civil Service, responsible to the Treasury, but an independent body, responsible directly to the Prime Minister. It is really no good talking about democratic control or democratic planning so long as the Cabinet relies for its information on interested parties. With a central fact-finding bureau, it would acquire its own eyes and ears and be able to reach its conclusions on the basis of unprejudiced facts.

Here we have touched on one of the main difficulties of democratic government in a managerial society. Of course we continue to assert that civil servants only advise Ministers and that Ministers themselves take all the decisions. But we know that, under modern conditions, this statement is becoming a polite fiction. The modern Cabinet Minister has so many little decisions to make that often the big decisions are made for him! He is responsible for so much in his Department that he sometimes ends by being little more than a public relations officer. And if he does master his own Department and impose his will upon it, then he will scarcely have the leisure to read all the other Cabinet papers and contribute to the general discussion of Government policy.

The problem, therefore, is how to enable the Ministers to regain control of the huge State bureaucracy. It is fashionable to say that all British representative institutions are better than all American, and that one of the worst aspects of American political life is the spoils system, the general post which comes when there is a change of Administration. Of course the spoils system is harmful. But it has one advantage. When I was in America recently I was talking to a civil servant working under the National Security Board. 'Of course, your politicians,' he said 'cannot really challenge the Chiefs of Staff or the civil servants in the Service Ministries. Over here the politicians have a good deal more grip because the two top echelons from each Department go out when a new Administration comes in. Below this level the spoils system ceases to function.'

I do not recommend that we should adopt the American system. But I do revive the suggestion that, in the next Labour Government, each Labour Minister should be encouraged to bring with him to his Department, a small brains trust of three or four people to act as his 'eyes and ears'. He should have, in fact, a little departmental 'Cabinet.' Some of them might be drawn from the Civil Service, some from the universities, some from politics; and they would act as a team, reading the papers for him and enabling him to have a well-informed judgment when he faces the permanent officials.

On this issue there are startling differences of opinion among Socialists with much more experience of Government than I have. There are some who have seen the working of Whitehall as temporary civil servants, who strongly incline to the proposal I have made. There are others, particularly a number of outstandingly successful ex-Ministers, who are convinced that no change is required. A really capable Minister, they argue, who selects the right private secretary and who is prepared if necessary to change his Permanent Under-Secretary, can impose his will on his Department. And they would add that, even if a departmental brains trust does have certain advantages, those advantages are outweighed by the resistance it would awaken in the civil service, which (they claim) is loyally prepared to obey Ministerial instructions even from Labour Ministers.

This conflict probably arises from a difference of opinion about what is and what is not practicable for the next Labour Government. Last time we took over a controlled war economy: next time we shall be dealing with a free-enterprise economy, and it would be far more difficult in peace-time to establish brand new controls—especially if there was full employment—than it was in 1945 to maintain the war-time system.

If the next Labour Government, therefore, is prepared to leave the private sector of industry virtually free from controls, it can reasonably be argued that there is no need to disturb the civil service by proposals for Departmental Brains Trusts and for central planning. But in that case we should frankly admit to ourselves that the progress of that Government towards Socialism will be very slow and very limited in extent. The decision on this issue, in fact, is not a minor decision about administrative detail but a major decision of Socialist policy. I myself cannot help believing that, if we are to make realities of Ministerial responsibility and Cabinet planning, something of the kind will have to be adopted. Once it was adopted, it would start a revolution in democratic Government.

The second stage of this revolution would be to tackle the swollen State bureaucracy. Beneath the brilliant jesting of 'Parkinson's Law', there was a substratum of fearful truth. A bureaucracy does swell automatically: swelling staffs do create work for themselves. Most serious of all, the multiplication of advice rendered may blunt the edge of a Minister's decision and so increase the dead weight of Government inertia. It is difficult enough for a Minister to make a bold decision even when he is surrounded by a small circle of sympathetic advisers. Faced with the lowest common denominator of bureaucratic caution, he may well find it impossible to do so.

Any Labour Chancellor of the Exchequer must prevent the automatic increase in the size of Departments if he is to pay for the extended social services and education the nation requires. In the past he has been deterred from such economies by his colleagues' view that the efficiency of their Departments would suffer. I believe this is a delusion. A Conservative Cabinet, with no motive for drastic change, can afford to take the inhibiting advice of a swollen bureaucracy. A Socialist Cabinet does so at its peril. Instead it must deliberately try to unswathe itself from the bureaucratic cocoon which cuts it off and makes it unresponsive to public opinion.

vi

I now come to the second of my two requirements. Suppose we have achieved a position where a Socialist Cabinet was no longer blindfold but had eyes and ears and was really capable both of planning the economy and managing the Civil Service. How are we going to ensure that these Ministers, now that we have given them this gigantic power, do not become dictators? How can we make them responsive (a) to Parliament and (b) to the electorate?

At the beginning of the century Britain lived under Parliamentary

Government. So long as parties were little more than local caucuses, Ministerial responsibility was a real check on bureaucratic incompetence or despotism. If Departments were bad, Ministers could be sacked; if Ministers disagreed with their colleagues, they could resign without losing caste. Now, both resignations on principle and dismissals for incompetence are becoming rarer. An incompetent Minister, with a Departmental muddle to cover up, can be kept in office for years: and the louder the press clamour for his dismissal, the more loyally the Premier will usually support him.

Along with Ministerial responsibility, the responsibility of the individual Member of Parliament has withered away. In the nineteenth century the Member was genuinely responsible to his constituents and it was this that made the House of Commons the most important check on Executive despotism. Now the prime responsibility of the Member is no longer to the elector but to the Party. Without accepting the discipline of the Party, he cannot be elected; and if he defies that discipline, he risks political death. No wonder the modern MP accepts the precept that the test of his loyalty—now the prime political virtue—is his readiness to support the official leadership when he knows it to be wrong. In practice, therefore a Government is no longer fully responsible to Parliament.

If the main task of Socialism is to bring irresponsible concentrations of power under popular control, is it not time to consider whether Parliament should not once again be used for this—its original purpose? Certainly a Socialist will want to be sure that the next Labour Government will have sufficient power to carry through its programme speedily, and that requires a strong political leadership and a disciplined Party at Westminster and in the country to back it up. But the next Labour Government will not only need to nationalise: an almost equally important task will be to democratise the vast institutions already theoretically responsible to it.

I take as an example the National Assistance Board. Before the war Public Assistance was a local responsibility and the officials who administered it were directly and intimately responsible to elected Councillors. Now a great administrative improvement has been achieved by the creation of a central National Assistance Board.

But to whom is that Board responsible? To no one, not even to the Minister of Pensions and National Insurance though he is its link with the Commons. This means that the very poorest people in this country, while they have gained materially, have undoubtedly lost the personal contact with elected representatives which an active Public Assistance Committee in a Labour Borough or County used to give.

Another example, from quite a different field, is colonial administration. Here are some fifty territories for which the British Parliament is theoretically responsible. Yet who is responsible for them? A single Minister. Lastly, I have already mentioned the problem of the nationalised industries, which the Labour Government deliberately cut off from detailed Parliamentary supervision.

I believe the time has come when there should be a standing Parliamentary committee responsible for each nationalised industry, in just the same way as a committee of Councillors is responsible for a municipal trading concern. There should also be standing committees supervising the National Assistance Board and the Agricultural Marketing Boards, another whose task would be to give detailed attention to defence, and another for the colonies. At present Parliament only turns its attention to a colony when a crisis has blown up. Would it not be wiser that they should be visited and inspected before and not after the trouble has started?

Such a reform of Parliament is not only sound in terms of the principles of democratic Socialism: it would have the further advantage of raising the status of the back-bench M.P. At present his jobs are (i) to obey the Party Whips in the division lobby, whatever his conscience may say, (ii) to act as a kind of political welfare officer for his constituents, and (iii) by questions and speeches to ventilate the causes he believes in. There is no doubt that his standing has declined in this century: he can now rarely feel the sense of solid achievement which a Councillor has in an active Council. A House of Commons, a large part of whose time was spent in supervising the work of public corporations and certain Departments of State, would have less time either for ceremonial shadow-boxing or for idle gossip. That surely in itself would be no bad thing. Moreover, this reform would remove from the Cabinet and from individual Ministers some part at least of the detailed administrative chores which prevent them from concentrating on their main task of formulating national policies and preparing plans which require legislation.

vii

To restore Parliamentary control of the Executive, however, is not
sufficient for our Socialist purpose of liberating the community from
the abuse of arbitrary power. The next step will be to reform the
Judiciary, so that it can regain its traditional function of defending
individual rights against encroachment. That function has been
steadily narrowed for the last hundred years, as small-scale capitalism
has been transformed into oligopoly and the flimsy structure of the
Victorian State has developed into the Leviathan which now dominates our lives.

Once again we must observe that Conservatives only have an eye
for one aspect of this problem. They denounce the dangers of State
despotism, exerted through Orders in Council (against which, in
many instances, there is no appeal to the Courts: instead, the Minister's decision is final and sometimes he need not even state his
reasons). Certainly the bureaucracy is one aspect of the new Despotism—but it is only one. The trade association, with its Star
Chamber trials of the cut-price dealer; the professional bodies which
can ruin a doctor or a lawyer whose conduct is condemned as
irregular; the trade union whose rules may prevent a member from
suing it even when he has been unjustly treated: all these are
examples of authority arbitrarily exercised, which it is the task of
Socialism to curb.

In the early days of the Labour Party it was natural to assume that
the Courts and the Police were on the side of property and to suspect
the Judiciary as a defender of established rights, most of which the
worker did not possess. Since then, as we have seen, both the trade
unions and the Co-operative Movement have been recognised as
important parts of the social order, and a majority of what was
once a property-less proletariat now has a stake in the country and
rights to defend. Yet far too many Socialists regard it as reactionary
(or at least as no part of a Socialist's duty) to take up the cudgels
for the individual citizen who feels that his rights have been violated
by a Department of State, a public Board or a semi-public authority.
That kind of political activity, they think, should be left to Tories or
Liberals.

Surely this attitude is a betrayal of the British Radical tradition.
What was wrong with the Conservative agitation about Crichel

Down was that it was so palpably inspired by anti-Socialist prejudices. It singled out one abuse of power by civil servants in order to leave the impression that the central bureaucracy is the only threat to personal freedom in the modern State. I believe that it is a grave mistake to leave this topic to Conservatives and Liberals. On the contrary, the Labour Party should give a very high priority to it in the reformulation of Party policy which is now proceeding.

What is required is nothing less than a new statement of what we mean by personal freedom and how we should safeguard it under Socialism. For this purpose we need to redefine the rights of the citizen in this era, when the unit of political and economic organisation grows ever larger. And, having done so, we should then go on to discuss the reforms of the law and the reorganisation of the Judiciary which will be required to defend the individual against the oligopolists and oligarchs who threaten his freedom. Indeed, it is precisely because a Socialist Government, in its effort to curb irresponsible power, will be compelled to extend the power of the State and enlarge the area of public ownership that this enquiry must be initiated by the Labour Party. For independent voters, particularly of the younger generation, will certainly oppose any Socialist extension of State power unless they can see that it is matched and counterbalanced by new Socialist defences for individual freedom.

viii

But even if we succeed in restoring a degree of Parliamentary control over the State bureaucracy; even if we extend that Parliamentary control to cover some of the great concentrations of power outside; how can we ensure that Parliament itself becomes truly responsive to the electorate?

Some people will tell me that this question is unnecessary, since our electoral system provides a sufficient guarantee. But, here again, we must be careful to distinguish between myth and reality. The elector's right to vote every three or four years for a candidate preselected by a great Party is not in itself sufficient to ensure that Parliament is responsive to his will.

Mr. Robert McKenzie, in British Political Parties, has shown conclusively that the two great parties have developed in accordance with the law of increasing oligarchy which operates in industry, in the trade unions and in Fleet Street. Here too power has been concentrated in fewer and fewer hands. The individual party member, like the individual shareholder and the individual trade unionist, now exerts very little effective control over the Party managers. The two big parties are both in danger of becoming Party oligarchies.

This fact is not solely the concern of the parties themselves. Their constitutions and procedures have become essential parts of the unwritten British constitution; and the way they conduct their business vitally affects the health of our democracy. When we are rethinking our Socialism therefore we should have a look at the Labour Party and say to ourselves, 'How can we reshape it so that its leadership is strong enough to fight the battle against the oligopolists and yet be democratically responsive to the rank and file?'

Many Socialists, when challenged in this way, will talk about the block vote of the trade unions at our Annual Conference. I myself am not against the block vote. In a party with a democratic constitution, you have to find some method of counting heads, and I see no alternative to making the number of votes any delegation wields relate to the number of members in the organisation it represents. Of course, the block vote can be misused by the General Secretary of a big union, but I am much more concerned with the politics of the members that General Secretary represents.

One of the things the Labour Government carried out, almost automatically, when it came to power was the repeal of the Trade Disputes Act. This restored to trade unionists a freedom denied them by a vindictive Tory measure.

Yet one consequence of this change disturbs me. To-day hundreds of thousands of workers are affiliated to the Labour Party through their trade unions, not because they positively believe in Socialism but because they have not taken the trouble to contract out. I have an uneasy feeling that the Labour Party may have been financially poorer but spiritually richer when each trade union member had to assert his adherence to it before his dues were paid.

What, then, about the sponsoring of candidates by trade unions? From the financial aspect there is no essential difference between this practice and the acceptance of a large annual contribution from a middle-class candidate. On the other hand, we have already seen how essential it is that the Labour Party should be firmly rooted in the trade unions. One corollary of this is that trade unionists should form a large segment of the Parliamentary Labour Party and be well represented in the next Labour Government. At present, however, there can be little doubt that, if sponsored candidates were forbidden, the number of trade union M.P.s would drop and the trade union movement would be dangerously under-represented in Parliament.

The long-term solution is easy to state and is in the hands of the trade unions themselves. Each of the big unions must select and train a sufficient number of candidates, able to compete at a selection conference and win the candidature without the extra inducement of a financial grant from their union. If the quality of trade union candidates were raised, sponsorship would be unnecessary and trade union contributions, which now are often poured into safe seats that do not need them, could be paid into the central funds and distributed to the marginal constituencies, where they are really needed.

Lastly, I must add a word about Party discipline. Here again, the Labour Party seems to me to be suffering from the carry-over of an illiberal tradition into a period when intolerance is no longer justified by the exigencies of the class war. No sensible politician denies the need for unity and discipline at Westminster, in Council Groups and, to a lesser extent, in the Party organisation outside. But are unity and loyal support of the leadership best achieved by elaborately drafted Standing Orders, which enforce acceptance of majority decisions on threat of expulsion? When the Labour Party is considering Parliamentary and local democracy, its spirit of toleration and, in particular, the rights it accords to minority opinion, is almost too strictly in line with the Liberal tradition. But when it approaches the problem of discussion and debate inside its own ranks, it adopts a doctrine almost as harsh as Lenin's Democratic Centralism. Specialist minorities (trade unionists, for instance, pacifists or teetotallers) are tolerated. But any sustained criticism of the official policy tends to be treated as an act of disloyalty, which must be dealt with by disciplinary methods.

It is at least arguable that the severe discipline enforced in the Parliamentary Labour Party and Council Groups has actually stimulated rebelliousness; and that the existence of Standing Orders tends to transform debates on great issues into arid arguments about procedure, as well as hardening disagreement into a conflict between loyalists and critics. Any vital Socialist party is bound to have within itself a Right, a Centre and a Left, and no amount of discipline will prevent either the clashes of opinion or the personal rivalries which are the stuff of which politics are made.

It is time we adapted our methods of discipline to the requirements of an epoch in which freedom of debate within the great political parties has become an essential element of Parliamentary democracy itself. Certainly the political leadership must retain the power in the last resort to discipline and to expel. But the test of good leadership is how sparingly that power is used, just as the test of a successful minority is how genuinely it welcomes the adoption of its views as official policy.

In this essay I have confined myself to the single issue of Socialism and freedom. Of course, this would be only one of several themes in a Labour programme; and, in terms of appeal to the mass electorate, it would not be the most important. Responsibility is an acquired taste and the majority will always be far more concerned with material benefits and social security—at least until, in some particular case, their own personal freedom is threatened. Yet I believe that a Labour Party which neglects this theme, either in its appeal to the younger generation of electors or in the conduct of its own domestic affairs, is imperilling its cause and its future too.

For far too long we have assumed that the only changes in society which we have to make are changes in its economic structure and in the distribution of the national wealth. Of course, those changes are a vitally important part of Socialism. But surely we have learnt the lesson of Fascism and Communism. This lesson is that constitutional reform, designed to enlarge freedom and stimulate an active democracy, is at least as important as the extension of public ownership and redistribution of wealth—which are important only as another means to the same end. Indeed, unless the two march in step, we shall merely create a new Leviathan, in which a Socialist managerial oligarchy replaces a capitalist managerial oligarchy or, even worse, shares the power with it.

The modern State, with its huge units of organisation, is inherently totalitarian, and its natural tendency is towards despotism. These tendencies can only be held in check if we are determined to build the constitutional safeguards of freedom—and personal responsibility.

I am convinced that these constitutional safeguards of freedom against the new despotism can only be built by a Labour Government. But if it is to do the job, that Government must return to the first principles of Socialism and decide boldly to make all irresponsible power accountable to the community. And if that is to be our aim, we had better realise that the way we manage our democratic institutions—including the Labour Party and the trade unions—is just as important as the way we manage the economy of the nation.

THE AFFLUENT SOCIETY

Based on a Fabian lecture given a few weeks after the election *debacle* of 1959. I spoke a day or two before the ill-fated post-mortem Blackpool conference at which Hugh Gaitskell first announced his adherence to the Revisionist philosophy which had already been outlined by a number of its most faithful supporters. As the controversy deepened throughout the winter, I found the tape-recording of my impromptu lecture increasingly irrelevant, and finally wrote what was almost a completely new pamphlet. Published in the early summer, it received a surprising amount of attention; but outside the Labour Left was treated with almost universal derision.

1. INTRODUCTION

MY topic is the future of the Labour Party in the British version of the Affluent Society which has emerged under successive Tory Governments since 1951. The fact that the Conservatives won their third successive victory last October has shocked the Labour Party into a bout of introspective self-analysis —inspired by an almost masochistic determination to find the fault in ourselves and not in our stars.

Already one group of Labour Party economists has come forward with a 'Revisionist' diagnosis of what is wrong and a formula for remedying it. Mr. Roy Jenkins, Mr. Douglas Jay and Mr. C. A. R. Crosland predict that Labour will decline into a minority party, representing an ever shrinking working class, unless it scraps its old-fashioned critique of capitalism and modernises its policies, its images and its constitution. Mr. Roy Jenkins, for example, recently listed what he regarded as the five major obstacles in the way of a Labour victory at the next election: (1) fear of a financial crisis if Labour came to power; (2) blame for unofficial strikes; (3) resentment against the anti-libertarian behaviour of Labour groups on certain local councils; (4) a widespread feeling that Labour is a narrow, class party; and (5) the unpopularity of nationalisation. His conclusion was that, if we could only excise these five tumours from the body of the Labour Party, its health would be restored and it would have a good chance of benefiting next time from the swing of the pendulum. Mr. Crosland and Mr. Jay, I fancy, would not dissent from this view. They agree with Mr. Jenkins that, since the Affluent Society has come to stay, the over-riding task of the Labour Party is to persuade the electorate that a Labour Government can take over the modified form of capitalism which has emerged since 1945, without precipitating a crisis, and manage it, at least as well as the Conservatives. Only if we convince the voter of this, it is argued, will he give us the chance to introduce our Socialist improvements, designed to make the Affluent Society more equitable and just. In fact, the *leitmotif* of our next general election campaign must be, 'Vote Labour because you will be as safe with Gaitskell as you were with Macmillan'.

Implicit in this kind of Revisionism is the theory of the 'swing of the pendulum'. British two-party politics, we are told, function healthily only if the two big parties change places regularly and if neither of them is excluded from power for a long period. Thanks to an intuitive appreciation of this requirement, the British electorate tends—all else being equal— to favour a change of Government at each general election. Normally, therefore, the odds are slightly against the party in power and in favour of the Opposition. Applying this theory to the recent general election, the Revisionists conclude that, despite Mr. Macmillan's skill in choosing a particularly favourable moment, Mr. Gaitskell could and should have won, if the confidence of the electorate had not been unnecessarily alienated by the image of the Labour Party as dogmatically wedded to wholesale nationalisation.

An important corollary of this 'swing of the pendulum' theory is the view that it is the main function of the Opposition not to *oppose*—to attack the Government or to crusade for radical causes— but to provide the alternative Government, which can expect under normal circumstances to take office after the next general election, without any violent break in policy. The idea of the Opposition as 'the Alternative Government' is a relatively new growth in the Labour Party. Its development was fortuitously assisted by the practice, adopted by Mr. Attlee and expanded by Mr. Gaitskell, of adding to the twelve elected members of the Parliamentary Committee on the front bench some forty-five nominated Shadow Ministers and Shadow Parliamentary Secretaries. In this way a complete Alternative Government was created to face a real Government across the floor of the Commons. As a result, the phrase 'Shadow Cabinet', which at first was, quite wrongly, used to describe the executive committee of twelve, elected by the Parliamentary Labour Party in order to conduct its business, has begun to approximate to the truth. More and more the leadership of the Parliamentary Party behaves as though it were a Shadow Administration. Instead of concentrating on a strategy of attack, exposing topical grievances while crusading continuously for three or four clearly defined Socialist objectives, the Opposition tends to behave with the cautious responsibility normally associated with a Government.

This shift from the dynamic of opposition to the balanced postures of shadow responsibility is intelligible enough on the assumption that, if nothing is done to upset the normal course of things, the Shadow Cabinet will become the real Cabinet after the next election. If 'the swing of the pendulum' accurately describes the rhythm of British politics, then it is natural that a party out of office should present itself not as an 'irresponsible' Opposition but as a staid Alternative Government. It is also clear that, if it is to play this role, the Labour Party must be prepared to abandon the claim that it is the party of radical change. What it must become, in fact, is not the anti-Establishment party but an alternative team of management inside the Establishment—a party not unlike the Democrats in the United States. And this is precisely the change in the Labour Party image which the Revisionists recommend.

ii

It will be convenient to consider separately the theory of the swing of the pendulum and the concept of the Opposition as the Alternative Government. Taking the 'swing of the pendulum' first, I suggest that, at least since the coming of democracy, it has not operated in British politics. Last October, for example, there was no sign of it. Even if the Tories had fought the last election badly and the Labour Party had not made a single mistake, there is no reason to believe that we should have seen a change of Government. Mr. Macmillan was able to ride back to office on a wave of universal complacency, and nothing the Labour Party said or did had more than a quite secondary importance. The most that a faultless Labour campaign could have achieved was the election of a Labour Government without a mandate for change and based on an inadequate majority. So far from profiting from a desire for a change of Government, the Opposition had to deal with an electorate strongly prejudiced in favour of the *status quo*.

Nor can we find any evidence in history for the swing of the pendulum. Those who believe in it usually quote electoral statistics starting from the Great Reform Bill of 1832. It is true enough that, if we count years of Coalition in the figures for both Left and Right-wing parties, we reach a total of seventy-one years of Labour/Liberal rule and seventy-seven of Conservative rule. When we break these figures down, however, we discover that whereas—after a period of Whig rule—the swing of the pendulum *did* operate in the middle years of the last century, when the middle class were first admitted to power, it was replaced by a very different electoral rhythm as the country moved towards universal suffrage.

If we take the year 1884—the introduction of universal household suffrage—as our starting point, we find that, in the course of the seventy-five years up to 1959, there have been only two Left-wing Governments with outright majorities, the Liberal Government elected after the Boer War and the Labour Government elected after World War II. Moreover, within five years each of these Left-wing Governments had lost most of its popular support: at the succeeding election Mr. Asquith and Mr. Attlee only just scraped back to office—without effective power. Indeed, the most obvious characteristic of these first seventy-five years of British democracy has been the success of the Conservatives in retaining working-class support and either keeping effective power for themselves or rapidly denying it to the Left-wing parties whenever they do attain office. There have been two lengthy periods dominated by the Tories. The first lasted from 1884 until 1905—with the exception of the three years of Gladstone's last Government. The second covered the inter-war years, from 1923 to 1940—from the break-up of the Lloyd George war coalition until the formation of the Churchill war coalition. During these seventeen years there was almost continuous mass unemployment, as well as the disasters of appeasement. Yet the Conservatives retained control—apart from the brief and ill-fated interludes of the

two minority Labour Governments, headed by Ramsay Mac-
Donald.

Those who rely on the historical evidence for the swing of the
pendulum should pay particular attention to the election of 1935.
After the anti-Socialist landslide of 1931, this was an occasion when
the electoral pendulum, if it existed, should have made itself evident.
Yet the Labour Opposition made only modest gains and there is no
evidence to suggest that the next election—bound to take place before
1941 if the war had not intervened—would have ended in a Tory
defeat. Throughout the 'years of the locusts' a large majority of the
British people remained staunchly anti-Socialist.

What lesson can we draw from the history of these seventy-five
years, during which we passed from household suffrage in 1884 to
full adult suffrage in 1928? The first thing a Socialist should observe
is the failure of Mr. Asquith in 1910 and Mr. Attlee in 1950 to
retain the momentum of change. Both had been given a clear mandate for a big leap forward. Both lost that clear mandate in a very
few years. We should learn a lot about the rôle of Left-wing parties
from a detailed study of their failures.

Meanwhile we can point to the danger into which a Left-wing
leadership falls once it surrenders to the temptation to cling to office
—without effective power. That was the situation of the Liberals
after 1910 and it was the situation of the two minority Labour
Governments. The 1931 *debacle*, which nearly destroyed the Labour
Party, was largely due to the eagerness with which not only Ramsay
MacDonald but a majority of the Labour leadership seized the chance
of office, even though they knew that, as a minority Government,
they had neither a mandate for radical change nor the power to carry
it out. It seems to be a rule of British democracy that parties of the
Left can retain their strength and enthusiasm through extended
periods of Opposition, provided the leadership remains committed
to radical change. But that strength and enthusiasm rapidly ebbs
away if ever the leadership becomes obsessed by electoral considerations and succumbs to the temptation to jettison its radical policies
for the sake of office.

The study of history, in fact, refutes the theory of the swing of the
pendulum and suggests that there are two preconditions which must
be fulfilled before a Left-wing Government is elected with an adequate
majority. (1) The country must have been through troubles sufficiently serious to destroy confidence in the Tories. (2) The Opposition

party must have won the confidence of the voters by opposing the Government, even when it was popular, and putting forward its own radical remedies when they were ridiculed by the Establishment.

A Left-wing Government is required only where the change must be radical and involve a repudiation of orthodoxy; and the occasion for it will be a crisis in which the people, shaken out of its complacency, loses confidence in its traditional rulers, berates them on the ground that they have betrayed the nation and quite deliberately insists that what the country needs are new men and a big step forward.

If this, and not the swing of the pendulum, is the true rhythm of British political development, it follows that the prime function of the Labour Party, as of the Liberal Party before it, is to provide an ideology for nonconformist critics of the Establishment and a political instrument for interests and social groups which are denied justice under the *status quo*.[1] So far from trying to show that its leaders can manage capitalism as competently as the Tories and reshaping itself in the image of the American Democratic Party, the Labour Party, if it is ever to return to power with a mandate from the people, must remain a Socialist challenge to the established order.

A Labour Party of this kind is likely to be out of office for much longer periods than the Tories. I have heard it said that such an admission is defeatist and that, if it is publicly made, most of the talent and ambition will be forced off the Opposition front bench, since gifted political leaders cannot be expected to be content to be deprived of office and responsibility for the best years of their lives. I find this is a quite astonishing argument. No doubt it is frustrating for those who have held high office to sit for years on the Opposition front bench as mere members of a Shadow Administration. No doubt

[1] The following anecdote suggests that the rhythm of American political development is much the same. 'Roosevelt told Robert H. Jackson that he had once suggested that Wilson withhold part of his reform programme for his second term. Wilson replied in substance: We do not know that there will be a second term, and, if there is, it will be less progressive and constructive than the first. American history shows that a reform administration comes to office only once in every twenty years, and that its forward impulse does not outlast one term. Even if the same party and persons remain in power, they become complacent in a second term. "What we do not accomplish in the first term is not likely to be accompished at all." (When Roosevelt told this story to his press conference in the first year of his second term, he lengthened the period of possible accomplishment from four to eight years.)' (*The Coming of the New Deal*, by Arthur M. Schlesinger, Jr. Heinemann, 1960.)

it is true that the effectiveness of our democratic checks on the Executive would be endangered if the electorate began to rate the Labour Party as a permanent minority and to feel that there was no prospect of ever getting rid of the Tory Government. To be effective, an Opposition must be a genuine threat to the Government and that means that it must have a genuine will to turn it out. Nevertheless, those who assert that the sole object, or even the main object, of the Labour Party today should be to regain office seem to me to misconceive not merely the nature of British Socialism but the workings of British democracy. For politicians whose sole object, or even whose main object, is to regain office tend to be opportunists, to hedge and to equivocate in order to appease the voter. The Conservative Party, with the clear purpose of retaining power for a traditional ruling class, is fully justified in abandoning established policies, extricating itself from its promises and betraying the pledges to large groups of its supporters, if by so doing it defends the Establishment. Appeasement and equivocation are tactics essential to the great Tory tradition by which the British ruling class has adapted itself to changing circumstances. But a Left-wing party which adopts such tactics destroys itself.

iii

Which role shall the Labour Party play in the three or four years before the next election—a Fighting Opposition or the Alternative Government?

The truth is that there is no principle by recourse to which the eternal conflict between Right-wingers and Left-wingers, between administrators and crusaders, between professional ex-Ministers and professional Oppositionists can be settled in the abstract. The only rational way to settle it is to examine the kind of problems we shall face in the 1960s and to ask ourselves what kind of Labour Party will be capable of dealing with them.

I believe that, in posing the problem in this way, I shall win cordial assent from Mr. Crosland, Mr. Jay and Mr. Jenkins. Their proposals for changing the image of the Labour Party and eradicating many of its radical traits are all based on certain assumptions about the nature of the post-war world and the prospects of the British economy in the next decade. Both in his book, *The Future of Socialism*,[1] and in

[1] Published by Jonathan Cape, 1956.

the occasional writings which have succeeded it, Mr. Crosland has consistently maintained the view that the inherent contradictions in capitalism, which formed the central feature of the old-fashioned Socialist analysis, are now outmoded myths, since we have developed an economy so different from the 19th-century capitalism that it merits a new name. So he looks to the United States as the model of the new, managed capitalism in which it is possible permanently to avoid mass unemployment and to achieve a steady and satisfactory rate of economic expansion without falling into inflation. Of course, each of these post-war Affluent Societies still shows grave imperfections—here too slow a rate of growth; here headlong growth alternating with indiscriminate restriction; here injustice committed to a whole social group; here an imbalance between the private and the public sector. But none of these imperfections, in his view, is inherent in the system and most of them could be evened out by a sensible, moderate Left-wing Government, led by men who both understand the management of modern capitalism and feel an urge to remove its injustices and inequalities. A Labour Government, in fact, once it can persuade the electorate to give it an adequate majority, will, if Mr. Crosland's analysis proves correct, be able to plan and control the economy without any radical changes in its structure and, in particular, without any drastic enlargement of the public sector.

Let me say at once that, if I agreed with this picture of our post-war economies and accepted the Revisionists' optimistic predictions about the way the world will move during the 1960s, I should at once accept their political conclusions as well.

But are they right in assuming the stability of the Affluent Society? Are they correct to anticipate—if it is properly managed—a satisfactory rate of economic expansion? Is their confidence justified when they believe that the contradictions of pre-war capitalism have been removed? Or does our new post-war capitalism contain within it new contradictions, which cannot be resolved so long as the 'commanding heights of the economy' are privately owned and controlled?

I realise, of course, that the optimism of the Revisionist analysis is shared by the vast majority of the opinion-makers throughout the Western world. Most of them, indeed, are reluctant to admit the strength either of their war-time fears that peace would bring a return to mass unemployment or of their post-war sense of relief as, year by year after 1945, the 'inevitable' slump was postponed. At the end of the war, even John Maynard Keynes himself assumed that the American economy would drift into a crisis that would probably engulf Britain as well. In the United States, where fear of unemployment is much less acute, uncritical confidence in free enterprise was rapidly restored. In Britain, on the other hand, this swing of opinion away from Socialism back to free enterprise was postponed during the period of office of the Attlee Government, who were able to convince the electorate that they had averted a return to unemployment by the application of Socialist planning and controls. Actually the Labour Government did very little planning, in the strict sense of that word, *i.e.* the settling of social priorities in terms of a long-term plan. True, they transferred to public ownership a number of basic industries and services and this enabled them to control investment in the newly created public sector. But, so far as over-all planning is concerned, all the Attlee Government did was to retain the cumbersome system of wartime controls and apply it—not unsuccessfully—to the increase of exports, the prevention of a post-war collapse of agriculture, the stimulation of private investment and the maintenance of full employment. Inevitably, as the war receded into the past, these wartime controls became more and more unpopular; even worse, they became more and more irrelevant as wartime shortages disappeared and the terms of trade unexpectedly improved. Already by 1950 the Attlee Government was uncertain whether to liberalise the economy or to substitute a new system of Socialist peace-time planning for the war economy it had taken over in 1945.

The irrelevance of wartime controls, however, was not fully realised until after the Tories just scraped home in 1951 and proceeded to 'set the people free'. In the 1951 election, the Labour Party piled up the biggest popular vote in its history, largely as the result of predicting that the return of the Tories would lead not only to war but also to mass unemployment, and it was the falsification of these predictions that made the British electorate react so violently against nationalisation. And so when the Election came in 1955, British public opinion had swung from a fatuous pessimism about the prospects of Western capitalism into an equally fatuous complacency.

Throughout the 1950s that mood persisted. Less than a decade of expanding prosperity has been sufficient to erase from the voter's mind the doubts and anxieties about Western free enterprise which were still so powerful when the war finished; and to engender a complacent optimism which dismisses nationalisation as an obsolete concept, with no relevance to the second half of the twentieth century. It is worth noticing, however, that these bland assumptions are challenged as soon as one leaves the North Atlantic area. Whatever doctrinal differences there may be between the Communists of Russia and of China, of Poland and of Czechoslovakia, they all agree on the premise that, outside agriculture, old-fashioned nationalisation is the prerequisite for the kind of national planning necessary to achieve a balanced economic development.

Which of these assumptions, the Western or the Eastern, is justified by the facts? The best judges, surely, are the leaders of the uncommitted peoples. Though their preference may be for the Western way of life, they have little doubt who, in the last decade, has been winning the peaceful competition between East and West. They can see that, in a Western democracy today, life is far freer and far more comfortable for far more of the citizens than ever before in the history of the human race. Given a free choice between living in capitalist West Germany or Communist East Germany, for example, a majority of Germans opt for the West. Judged in terms of that individualistic 'pursuit of happiness' which the American founding fathers laid down as the aim of their Republic, Communism is still an inferior way of life compared to that of the Affluent Societies of the West. But this does not alter the fact that, in terms of military power, of industrial development, of technological advance, of mass literacy and, eventually, of mass consumption too, the planned Socialist economy, as exemplified in the Communist States, is proving its capacity to outpace and overtake the wealthy and comfortable Western economies. The lead we held is being narrowed by two factors. The first of these factors is the contrast between the economic use of resources possible under the planned economies of the East and the wastefulness of the artificially induced obsolescence which is the motive force of our Affluent Societies of the West. The second reason why the Communists are overhauling us is the fact that whereas, in their planned economies, inflation can be brought under control by planned income distribution, it is still the scourge of our managed Western capitalism.

At first the technological and economic achievements of the Communists were blandly disregarded. Now that it is impossible to deny their reality, three arguments are employed in order to depreciate

their importance and allay the alarm they have caused. We are told
(1) that, while the 'great leap forward' is natural enough in backward
economies, starting on the early stages of industrialisation, this rate
of increase is bound to slow down as the absolute strength of the
Communist States approaches that of the West; (2) that the Russian
sputnik and other achievements in rocketry are the results of quite
abnormal concentration of effort, such as a totalitarian State can
always make and from which no conclusion can be drawn about the
general efficiency of the system; and, finally, (3) that, as living
standards improve and education spreads, a new public opinion will
be created in the Communist States, with liberalistic demands for
extensions of freedom and a shift of balance from production to consumption industries. Provided, therefore, that nuclear war can be
avoided, we are assured that we can look forward for the next fifty
years to a period of peaceful competition, in which the intrinsic
differences between Communism and Western capitalism will become
less and less marked as the backward Communist nations gradually
find fulfilment in a Western 'pursuit of happiness'.

iv

I am not surprised that, with the change in the balance of power,
the fulminations against the wickedness of Communism and the
aggressive menace of the Kremlin's designs have been replaced, in
Washington as well as in London, by such comforting predictions.
But what does surprise and alarm me is that some Socialist economists
should have joined in peddling these complacent illusions. For one
of the main objectives of a fighting Socialist Opposition must be to
expose the false assumptions of our Affluent Society and so force the
British people to face honestly the challenge that confronts them. Far
more than the revision of its constitution or of its electoral programme, the Labour Party needs today a new Socialist *critique*,
applied both to the Western and to the Eastern economies, which
would enable us to foresee and prepare for the 'creeping crisis' that
will confront the West before the end of this decade.

We can be sure that this crisis will not repeat the pattern of the
1930s and present us once again with the spectres of mass unemployment and under-consumption, spreading from the United States to
engulf the whole world. Indeed, we should be wise to assume that, in
the kind of Affluent Society which is now common to Western

Europe and North America, the masses will from now on be provided with an ever wider choice of consumer goods—but only at the
cost of neglecting each nation's long-term interests, scamping vital
public services and imposing gross injustices on the weaker sections
of the community—particularly upon the sick and the old, who rely
so heavily upon State benefits.

Unfortunately Britain is likely to prove the weakest member of the
Western community, since the inflation and over-consumption inherent in the Affluent Society are aggravated in this country by the
deep conservatism displayed by both sides of industry. The employers'
insistence on quick profits and the demand for annual wage rises
forced upon the unions in a free-for-all economy have combined to
keep capital investment down to a dangerously low level. As a result,
this country, in the race for higher productivity, has not merely
fallen far behind Russia but has been beaten by Western Germany,
France and the United States. Moreover, our foreign trade is now
seriously threatened by the emergence of the Common Market, whose
threat has been consistently underrated by successive Governments.
Squeezed between three giants—the United States, the Common
Market and the Communist bloc—there is a risk that, while the rest
of the world is improving its material conditions, the British people
may suffer an actual cut in their living standards.

How can a people as politically mature as the British be so blind
to these dangers? How can the electorate give a third vote of confidence to the Conservative Party, which has so consistently sacri-
ficed long-term national interests in order to provide short-term
improvements in living standards? No objective observer will deny
that, since 1951, there has been a scandalous neglect of many of the
essentials of a healthy community—capital investment in industry,
pure and applied scientific research, technological training, the expansion of higher education, the extension of hospital services and improved retirement pensions. Public connivance in this neglect has
been obtained by two methods. (1) A mass demand for profitable but
inessential consumer goods and luxuries has been stimulated by
extravagantly expensive mass advertising and satisfied at the cost
of the public services, but at a satisfactory rate of profit to private
industry. (2) The commercialised media of mass communication have
been systematically used to dope the critical faculties which would
normally have been stimulated by the improvement of popular education since 1945. By the continued application of these methods it may

well be possible to keep the British people complacently apathetic, while the social and moral sinews of the national organism are rapidly weakened by fatty degeneration.

What will finally confront us as a result of this decline will not be a return of the mass unemployment of the 1930s but a shrinking of the frontiers of democracy as the world balance of power shifts and the uncommitted peoples of Asia and Africa accept the economic aid and political leadership of the Communists in the modernisation of their communities. If the Kremlin were manned by Cold Warriors determined to overrun the West by a display of aggressive brinkmanship, the decline of Western power which we are now witnessing might well result in a series of international crises. In terms of military strength, it is now within the capacity of the Russian and Chinese Communists to force a showdown on such issues as Berlin, Persia and Formosa and to confront the Western powers with a choice between nuclear suicide and a series of Munich-type surrenders. Committed to the defence of a whole series of positions which have been rendered indefensible now that we have been overtaken in the nuclear arms race, we could do little to protest if the Russians were barbaric enough to call our bluff—by proceeding to mop up three key positions which we now hold only by the tolerance of Mr. Khrushchev in West Berlin, Quemoy and Teheran. By signing a peace treaty with the East Germans, instigating a revolution in Persia or providing the Chinese with nuclear weapons, the Russians could now make each of these positions untenable.

v

No one can exclude the possibility of a series of surrenders of this kind. Nevertheless, I am not convinced that this is the main danger which the West now faces. It seems to me probable that the Communists have taken our measure fairly accurately. Unlike Stalin, Khrushchev probably appreciates that the only thing which can rally the West and force it to mobilise its strength is a repetition of the kind of strong-arm action which we saw in the Berlin blockade and the attack on South Korea. In an actual war, or under direct threat of military aggression, the Affluent Societies of the West can be persuaded to cut back their ostentatious spending and accept a degree at least of national planning and international co-operation. Though Mao Tse-tung may be tempted to follow a Stalinite line, it seems to me unlikely that Khrushchev will commit the mistake of saving the Western powers from the comfortable process of peace-time degeneration on which they have now begun. For the Kremlin is now convinced that the only thing which could prevent the ultimate victory of world Communism is nuclear war. Their determination to practise peaceful co-existence, therefore, is a sign not of weakness but of confidence. When they challenge us to disarm immediately and enter into peaceful competition, they do so because they are sure they will win the contest.

Which system is best equipped for rapidly modernising the under-developed territories, raising their living standards and helping to provide mass education—the Western Affluent Society or Eastern Communism? The Kremlin is sure that, in the course of the next twenty years, the North Atlantic area will become a prosperous back-water, while vast areas of Asia, the Middle East, Africa and, finally, South America—which at present still accept some of our ideals of freedom and still look to us for assistance—are absorbed into the Communist bloc. Recent history supports their confidence. Anyone who suggested ten years ago that the new Aswan dam would be financed by Russia and constructed by Russian engineers would have been dismissed as either a fellow traveller or a defeatist. Even five years ago it would have been difficult to take seriously the prediction that a Cuban Government in 1959 would be entertaining Mr. Miko-yan and considering the possibility of buying Russian arms with which to defend its freedom from mainland interference. The fact that these two 'absurdities' have become sober truth illustrates the shift in the balance of power, and they will be followed in the 1960s by even more humiliating examples, unless we are prepared radically to trans-form the nature of our Affluent Societies and, in particular, their economic relations with Asia and Africa.

It has often been stated that the whole future of Western freedom depends upon the amount of aid which the Western democracies are prepared to give to the Indian nation in its effort to modernise and industrialise itself while retaining the political forms of Western democracy. What is not so often stated is that the chances of the Indian Government succeeding in this attempt depend very largely upon the role which the nationalised industries are permitted to play in the Indian economy. If the price of large-scale Western aid is that the Indian Government should increase the proposed size of the private and decrease that of the public sector of the economy, then the aid we gave may actually decrease the chances of success. Political democracy, in fact, can only be assured in this overpopulated and underdeveloped sub-continent in the kind of Socialist planned economy which would be condemned by Top People in London, Washington, Paris and Bonn as totalitarian.

Nor can we assume that public opinion in these countries will always prefer Western democracy to the Communist way of life. For whereas we can still claim that life in Western Europe is much more comfortable and much freer for the masses than it is in Eastern Europe, the same is not true when we compare Eastern Europe with, for example, the Middle East or South East Asia. Many Poles who visit both London and Moscow are deeply envious of our way of life; but an Iraqi, Egyptian, Burmese or Siamese who makes the same two-way trip could reach a rather different conclusion. Instead of preferring Western freedom to Communist totalitarianism, he may well feel he has more to learn in Moscow, East Berlin and Prague than in Washington, London or Bonn about the task of rapidly modernising a backward country and raising the living standards of the masses. The luxuries, gadgets, entertainments and packaged foodstuffs which so many workers enjoy in our Affluent Societies may strike him as irrelevant and even vulgar and immoral, compared with the solid respectability of the Communist way of life. It is, indeed, a most dangerous assumption that, even if they could be given a truly free choice between the 'Roundhead' standards of Communist collectivism and the 'Cavalier' luxuries of Western individualism, all the peoples of Asia and Africa would be bound to prefer our Restoration. And, anyway, such a free choice will not be given them. In the next twenty years the big decisions will be taken in these countries not by mass electorates but by eager, educated elites, to whom the enthusiastic certainties of Communist dogma make a much stronger appeal than the sophisticated scepticism of our Western democracy.

It is possible, therefore, to predict with a good deal of assurance that, until and unless there is a fundamental change in the structure of our modern managed capitalism, the peaceful competition which has now begun between East and West must result in a series of Communist successes.

True enough, the peoples of the West have recently recognised the evils of colonialism and at long last begun to realize that the principles of democracy—equality as well as liberty and fraternity—must be applied between nations as well as within each nation. In Britain,

for example, there has been national approval for the decision of the
Conservative Government to abandon Empire throughout Africa and
to make it clear that the white settler cannot rely on British support
in maintaining his ascendancy. But good intentions—even mass good
intentions—are not sufficient. What matters in relations with Asia
and Africa is not what ordinary people think and feel but what
economic policies our Government adopt. Our Western way of life
may seem tolerable to the non-political worker in the British or
American motor-car factory. It may at first sight seem heaven on
earth to a visitor from East Germany or Poland. But the colonial
peoples are bound to view it more suspiciously, and they will regard
us as enemies if our Governments decide that our economic relations
with those countries should for the most part be conducted by private
financial and business interests, whose sole concern it must be to buy
cheap and sell dear. It is not sufficient merely to wind up colonialism,
in the sense of ending the direct administration of these territories by
European officials. What is even more important is to end indirect
colonialism, and that can only be done by subordinating all private
enterprise in our trade with these ex-colonial areas to strict public
control. Until that is done, no British Colombo Plan or American
programme of economic aid, however ambitious, can halt the advance
of Communist influence in Asia and Africa. This advance has already
begun and will proceed even more rapidly in the course of this
decade.

It is, I believe, for this creeping crisis of the 1960s and 1970s
that the leadership of the Labour Party should hold itself in
reserve, refusing in any way to come to terms with the Affluent
Society, warning the electorate of the troubles that lie ahead and
explaining why they can only be tackled by ensuring that public
enterprise dominates the whole economy and creates the climate
in which private enterprise works. By starting the job now, when
the public still retains its blind trust in the Tory Government, the
Labour Party may incur a temporary unpopularity, but it will be
creating the conditions for gaining the confidence of the electorate
when its harsh predictions come true.

vi

'When its predictions come true? By what right,' it may be
asked, 'can the future be anticipated with such gloomy confidence?

Is not the Socialist who bases his political strategy on this kind of prediction falling into the mistake of those Marxists who discredited their theory of capitalism by demonstrating that its *inherent* contradictions would *inevitably* lead to its breakdown?' It would be folly indeed if we failed to learn from this sad example. But, as Aneurin Bevan and John Strachey pointed out in two remarkable and sadly underestimated books,[1] the failure of Marx's predictions was largely due to his rigid assumption that capitalism could not modify itself. What he failed to recognise was not only that the entrepreneurs' survival instinct would stimulate them to evolve a modern, managed capitalism, but also that democracy was a dynamic force in its own right. Mr. Strachey's greatest contribution to Socialist thinking has been his subtle and perceptive demonstration of the revolutionary changes in the economy produced by the workings of Western democracy. So far from remaining a mere superstructure, wholly conditioned by economic forces, our democratic institutions have revealed a potent power of social and economic change and in so doing have resolved one of the inherent contradictions that Marx attributed to capitalism. On his theory, the capitalist system *must* break down owing to an ever growing unbalance between an exaggerated production of capital goods and an equally exaggerated dwindling of consumers' demand. But in fact, as a result of democracy, the development has gone in exactly the opposite direction, so that now the prevailing characteristic (which is also the greatest weakness) of the Western economies is that they consume too much of their resources and reserve too little for public services and capital development. Ironically enough, the nations which do show the true Marxist contradiction are those of the Communist bloc, where consumption is nearly always starved for the sake of rapid capital development.

The actual developments of the last hundred years, therefore, have completely falsified Marx's central prediction. But the lesson we should draw from his failure is that which both Mr. Bevan and Mr. Strachey drew. Marx was not wrong to insist that Socialists must base their policy and strategy on the best available analysis and anticipation of how the political economy will develop. The errors he made and which we must seek to avoid were, first his refusal to admit that in social change politics may be as dynamic a force as economics;

[1] *In Place of Fear*, by Aneurin Bevan, Heinemann, 1952. *Contemporary Capitalism*, by John Strachey, Gollancz, 1956.

and, secondly, his failure to foresee the strength of the survival instinct and the powers of adaptability which would be revealed by the Conservative forces that control capitalism. These forces, as we now know, are ready to accept even radical changes, such as those recommended by Keynes, in order to preserve their power. As a result, just a hundred years after the writing of *Das Kapital*, the Western world has resolved the central contradiction of pre-war capitalism. But this has only been achieved at the cost of producing a new and equally dangerous contradiction. This new contradiction *can* be resolved, as its predecessor was resolved. Indeed, the main function of the Socialist in the 1960s is to explain how this can be done, and the main function of the Labour Party is to do it. For once again it is perfectly possible to cure what looks at first sight like an inherent and incurable weakness in our economic system by political action, designed to adapt our democratic institutions to the needs of the times.

There is an urgent need for political economists and sociologists to follow up Professor Galbraith's brilliant initiative by driving his analysis to its real conclusion and also by describing in detail the British variant of the Affluent Society.[1] All I can hope to do here is to list in summary form the main features of the central contradiction that now confronts us; to indicate why that contradiction, unless it is resolved, will inevitably make us the losers in peaceful competition with the East; and finally, to suggest the measures necessary to get Britain out of her special impasse.

Our analysis must start by noting two central features—one a strength, the other a weakness—which all the Western democracies, despite the differences between them, have in common and which separate them from Communist governments. The strength of the democracies is the existence of civil and political liberties as organic parts of the State structure. Their weakness is the complete failure to subject irresponsible economic power to public control. One of the most alarming symptoms of Western decadence is the modern tendency to treat the liberties of the citizen as a 'weakness' of democracy and to explain the successes of the Kremlin by pointing to the 'obvious' advantages any Communist leader has as the unquestioned

---

[1] This work has already been begun by Dr. Thomas Balogh. I should like to acknowledge here the debt I owe not merely to his occasional writings but even more to the stimulus of his conversation. I have also profited greatly by reading, in advance of publication, some chapters of his forthcoming book *The Political Economy of Co-existence* (Weidenfeld and Nicolson, 1960).

head of a totalitarian State. The reverse, of course, is true. All the
weaknesses of Communism derive from the crude brutalities of the
one-party State and the absence of the institutions of civil liberty—an
independent judiciary, an independent civil service, independent
organs of public opinion and truly voluntary organisations, including trade unions. Those who imagine that Russian Communism
would be weakened if Khrushchev succeeds in liberalising the system
and encouraging the growth of these free institutions are under a
grave delusion. If the Russian Communists could really add these
democratic strengths to the strength of a Socialist State which has
already conquered irresponsible economic power and subjected it to
public control, they would make their system irresistible.

What enables the Communist States to achieve their successes—
despite all the inefficiencies and brutalities perpetrated by their totalitarian rulers—is the fact that their governments possess (1) the power
to take vital decisions and the knowledge on which to base them, and
(2) the political and social instruments by means of which those vital
decisions can be put into effect. A Communist government, for
example, can allocate the national resources according to a system of
priorities, allotting so much to producer goods, so much to consumer
goods, so much to health, education, defence, thereby reducing the
hazards of investment and accelerating development. In contrast, the
government of a Western democracy, even under the post-war system
of managed capitalism, cannot even begin to draw up a national
resources budget of this kind, far less put it into effect. Whereas it can
impose its will on the small public sector of the economy, it has only
the crudest instruments for regulating the development of the
dominant private sector. This is the reason why growth is retarded in
comparison with that achieved by the Communists.

But the difference goes even further. The motive forces which
regulate the development of a Communist economy are the five-year
plan and the instruments for putting it into practice. The motive
force which drives a modern capitalist economy is neither the Government nor the Government Departments but the decisions of those
who direct the great combines which now dominate the private sector.
In dealing with the oligopolists, the Government in Britain today
is in a position not unlike that of the luckless King John, when confronted with his feudal barons. Like him, our modern Executive has
been constrained to concede a Magna Carta, which lays down the
rights not of the ordinary citizen but of an oligarchy, deeply divided

against itself but united in its determination to resist domination by the political Executive. More and more decisions which determine our development have been removed from Westminster and Whitehall. Then where are they taken? The truth is that normally they are not taken at all and the determination of some of the greatest issues of our national economy is left to the free interplay of the great concentrations of power. Occasionally, however, a decision *is* forced upon the Government by the pressures of the democratic system. If the absence of national planning threatens serious injury to organised labour, to the farming interests, to the Catholic Church or to any other of the well organised and powerful pressure groups that operate in our society, then the Government may be forced to intervene—even to curb the activities of the oligopolists.

An example of this process is to be found in the Government's reactions to local unemployment. Strictly speaking, a modern managed capitalism is not harmed by local unemployment: indeed, the competition on which it depends may be discouraged by governmental action which seeks to bring jobs to the workers instead of compelling the worker to move to the job. Since, however, the British electorate is still quite unusually sensitive to the threat of unemployment, the Government has found it expedient to induce prosperous industries to move into hard-hit areas—Merseyside and the Glasgow area, for example.

It is worth noticing, however, what happens in such cases. There is no question of the Government *ordering* Fords or Vauxhalls or the Rootes Group to establish their new factories in a particular area. It might, like King John, like to do so, but it lacks not only the will to give a command of this kind but the instruments with which to put it into effect. So what happens is a long drawn out negotiation between the Minister and the oligopolists in question, after which they graciously agree to stretch a point and help the nation—provided the Government gives them a suitable reward.

This explains one odd contradiction in the Affluent Society. The ordinary citizen feels that he is living in a community where the State grows ever more powerful, remote and arbitrary; and, from his point of view, this description is correct. But, in its relations with the oligopolists, the 'all-powerful' State behaves very differently, negotiating agreements instead of issuing edicts. The ordinary citizen *must* pay his taxes or go to prison; the oligopolist *negotiates* an annual tax agreement, in which he can often set his own terms.

A hundred years ago, when the scale of industry was small, it was at least rational to argue that, by reducing the power of the State over the economy and substituting the working of free competition for governmental decision, a society might develop more healthily and achieve more human happiness than under a paternal and interfering government. But in our age, with its tendency for ever greater concentrations of economic power and ever more centralised control of commercial mass communications, the relationship between free enterprise and individual freedom or consumer's choice has, as Galbraith shows, become exceedingly remote. Democratic constitutions, therefore, which were traditionally evolved in order to check the power of the Executive and prevent central despotism, are now employed mainly to preserve the irresponsible power of oligopoly from any kind of popular control.

vii

In *The Irresponsible Society*,[1] Professor Richard Titmuss carried Galbraith's analysis of modern oligopoly one stage further by applying it to a single and apparently relatively harmless segment of the British economy. He showed how, since 1945, an immense new jungle of irresponsible power has been created by the growth of pension schemes, stimulated by lavish tax concessions and financed partly by insurance companies and partly by trustee funds. Professor Titmuss declared that the creation of these huge pension funds constitutes

'a major shift in economic power in our society. It is a power, a potential power, to affect many important aspects of our economic life and our social values in the 1960s. It is power concentrated in relatively few hands, working at the apex of a handful of giant bureaucracies, technically supported by a group of professional experts, and accountable, in practice, to virtually no one.'

He showed how these private pension schemes did something to fill the vacuum created by the failure of the State to provide an adequate subsistence pension. But he also showed how this mushroom development has created gross inequalities as between those inside and those outside the schemes. Even worse, it tempts the Government to renege

[1] Fabian Tract 323 April 1960.

on its responsibility for providing security in old age and leave it to Big Business, at its own discretion, to build up its own 'private-enterprise welfare state'. As the scale of organisation gets larger and as the concentrations of power grow ever greater, there should be a corresponding increase of public service and democratic control. But in fact what we see is a dwindling role for Government. 'This is retreat from Government,' he concludes; 'a retreat into irresponsibility'.

At first sight it is surprising that this retreat from Government has been greeted with enthusiasm by the voter in all the countries of the West. When the war ended, public opinion, in North America as well as in Western Europe, still dreaded the return of mass unemployment and was ready to welcome great extensions of public ownership, of State control and interference in the private sector and of State provision of social services. Now, fifteen years later, public opinion has turned not only against nationalisation but against extensions of the Welfare State; and most of the European Labour movements have either abandoned their Socialism already or begun to consider the possibility of doing so. The reason for this extraordinary reversal is clear. Together with the rapid movement towards irresponsible oligopoly, there has proceeded a rapid, if uneven, improvement in living standards. Since World War II, throughout the West, democratic institutions have been used with even greater success than before the war to create effective consumer demand. The constant trade union pressure for higher wages, the success of farmers' organisations in extracting huge subsidies from their governments, and the favour shown by the woman voter to any politician who promises to increase her spending power—these and other factors, when combined with full employment, have obtained huge concessions for the masses and given them the feeling that they 'have never had it so good'.

The oligopolists, moreover, once they had learnt the Keynesian doctrine, were quick to see that it was in their interest to ensure that the volume of private spending was constantly increased, while the volume of public expenditure was kept as low as possible. During the war and the immediate post-war years, a gigantic volume of pent-up demand for consumer goods, household goods, gadgets and luxuries had been created. Instead of having plenty of money in our pockets and little to spend it on except cheap rationed essentials, we all wanted a world in which rationing was replaced by the widest range of consumer choice. And when our natural desire to make up for wartime

scarcity was further stimulated by enormously expensive and sophisticated advertising campaigns and the temptations of hire purchase, the
consumer demand swelled even further.

At the very moment, however, when each of us wanted to re-stock
our homes, the community had equally urgent needs for repairing the
damages of war, for building not only the houses but roads and railways, the hospitals, schools and universities and—most important of
all—for re-equipping our basic industries. Thus a tremendous conflict
developed between the demands of the community and the individual
consumer, and between those of the public and private sectors of the
economy.

It was a conflict, however, in which victory for one side was pre-
determined. Whether, as was done under the Attlee Government,
the attempt was made to exert direct control on the private sector
or whether control was limited, as under the Tories, to fiscal sanctions made surprisingly little difference. For the dynamo which
keeps our modern Affluent Society moving is the big consumption
industries, particularly the motor-car industry. It is only by permitting a constant increase in the size, profitability and political
importance of these industries that an old-fashioned slump is
avoided. The prosperity of America, it has been ironically observed,
and with it the security of the whole Western world, depends on
whether the American people can be persuaded each year to consume
six million new cars. If, in any year, that figure falls to four million,
there is a sharp recession; if to two million, a (non-Communist)
world slump.

There is one important deduction from Professor Galbraith's
analysis which British Socialists have been extremely reluctant to
make. If the health of the Western economies depends on artificially
creating an ever more extravagant demand for increasingly unnecessary consumer goods, then the maintenance of public services will
take second place to the satisfaction of private consumer needs. For
the money to pay for these public services derives from taxation,
whose level, so long as the private sector dominates the economy,
must depend on the profitability of industry. How many schools we
can have, how many roads we can build, how much of our resources
we can allocate to scientific research—the answer to these questions
depends, under our system of managed capitalism, on the number of
golden eggs that are laid by these oligopolistic geese.

Theoretically, of course, the deficiencies in the public service could be made good over a period by imposing taxation heavy enough to raise all the revenue required. A Socialist Government, it is often argued, would be able to finance the huge extensions of welfare education and other public services to which it is committed by encouraging a much faster rate of development in the private sector of industry and then taxing away a sufficient amount of the profits. This was the policy put forward by the Labour Party at the October election and in the short run any Labour Government would have to attempt it. But experience should have taught us that the run might be very short indeed. In the Affluent Society *no* Government is able to give orders to Big Business. After one Budget a Labour Chancellor who tried to squeeze private industry too hard would soon discover that he was not master in his own house and that there is a relatively low level above which taxation rates, whether on the individual or on the company, are only raised at the cost of provoking tax evasion and avoidance so widespread that revenue is actually reduced. If the motive force of your economy is the profit-making of large-scale modern private enterprise, a Labour Chancellor must be prepared to allow very large profits indeed and to admit that the number of golden eggs he can remove is extremely limited.

In recent months we have seen remarkable evidence of resistance by Big Business to public spending, even where national security is involved. When faced with clear evidence that the Russians are rapidly overtaking it in the nuclear race, many of us assumed that the Eisenhower Administration would feel itself compelled to allocate enough of the national resources to nuclear warfare in order to keep ahead. No doubt the White House would have liked to do so, but it proved impossible. Although he knew that the present levels of American defence spending would permit the Russians to forge ahead, Mr. Eisenhower has preferred to accept defeat in the nuclear race. As a Socialist, I do not myself believe that, by accepting Russian dominance in nuclear weapons, the Americans subject themselves to any very acute military risks. But the American politicians and Big Businessmen who refused to increase the defence budget did so though they were convinced that they were thereby putting their country in the deadliest peril. Nothing could demonstrate more clearly than this the inherent contradiction which ensures that, in our Affluent Society, while the individual grows rapidly more comfortable, the community becomes even more rapidly weaker and weaker. For the inherent inability of the system to allocate suffi-

cient resources for national defence is repeated in relation to education, scientific development, health and welfare services. The price
which the modern, managed capitalism pays for avoiding the old-
fashioned crisis of mass unemployment is the continuous sacrifice of
public service, community welfare and national security to private
profit.

viii

That is why we can predict with mathematical certainty that, as
long as the public sector of industry remains the minority sector
throughout the Western world, we are bound to be defeated in every
kind of peaceful competition which we undertake with the Russians
and the Eastern bloc. It is not that our workers are less skilful and
energetic, that our managers are less competent, or even that our
politicians do their job any worse. The truth is that, whatever our
intentions, wishes or individual capabilities, the nations of the
Western world will be unable to strengthen themselves by developing adequate public services until the public sector becomes the
dominant sector in our economies. Only in this way shall we make
it possible to work out a true national resources budget, which
strikes the proper balance between production and consumption
goods and ensures that community interests are given their proper
priority over individual consumption.

A Socialist programme of this kind will involve transferring
gigantic powers, which are now dispersed among the oligopolists, to
the central Government and the planning authorities which it
would have to establish. Of course there would be dangers to freedom in this process of subjecting irresponsible economic power to
public control. The increased power of the Executive which Socialist
planning must bring will be in danger of degenerating into the
kind of totalitarianism we have seen in Eastern Europe unless it is
counter-balanced by a revival of the challenge which Parliament used
to make to the Executive. Since the war we have watched a dreary
process by which the House of Commons has been progressively
deprived of effective authority until it is in danger of becoming one
of the ceremonial aspects of the Constitution, alongside the Monarchy and the House of Lords. But this draining away of the power
of decision which used to reside in Parliament has not brought an
increase of Cabinet or Ministerial authority. On the contrary, the

power of decision the Cabinet, before the era of oligopoly, used to possess, at least within limited spheres, has been steadily decreased, until today, as Professor Titmuss has shown, we are witnessing *a retreat from Government*. Democratic control of the forces which determine social and political development is steadily declining and with it the ability of the nation to act as a nation and of the people to exert a free democratic will. If the Western world is free, as it certainly is, from the terrible evils of totalitarianism, it is the victim of an even more debilitating disease—the emergence of a modern feudalism, which is strangling our democracy before it has had time to grow up.

Five years ago I pointed to the danger of this 'new despotism' and indicated the dilemma with which the modern Socialist is faced.[1] And I suggested that this dilemma could only be resolved by ensuring that the necessary extensions of public ownership should be counter-balanced by expanding the constitutional and judicial safeguards of personal freedom; by reviving Parliament's traditional function of controlling and checking the Executive; and by curbing the oligarchic tendencies both in the trade unions and in the party machines. It seems to me that, in the five years since this lecture was published, the case has been strengthened by events. The oligopolists have increased their power; the authority of the Executive has been correspondingly weakened; and the vitality of Parliament has even further declined. That is why I still believe that 'constitutional reform, designed to enlarge freedom and stimulate an active democracy, is at least as important as the extension of public ownership and a redistribution of wealth'.

But this is really the subject for a separate study. In this essay I have limited myself to the single issue of Revisionism. What is wrong with the Revisionists is that they misjudge altogether the times in which we are living and, in particular, the stability and strength of the Affluent Societies in which we have lived for under a decade. I am convinced that the kind of Keynesian managed capitalism which has evolved since the war is intrinsically unable to sustain the competition with the Eastern bloc to which we are now committed. Of this inability we shall see some devastating examples before the end of this decade. I believe that the choice with which the nations will soon be confronted will be between a purely authoritarian regime

[1] 'Planning for Freedom', p. 59.

(there is an ominous example in de Gaulle's France today) and a Labour Government which undertakes as radical Socialist reconstruction, while preserving civil liberties and reviving Parliamentary democracy. But we shall not get a Labour Government of this kind unless we start warning the people now of the coming crisis and preparing the party for the tremendous test that lies ahead.

THE CLAUSE FOUR CONTROVERSY

In April 1960 I was invited by the editor of *Encounter* to reply to a characteristically gay and witty attack on the Left by C. A. R. Crosland. This gave me an opportunity to state the objections which many of us felt to Hugh Gaitskell's attempt to revise the Party Constitution.

'A *spectre is haunting Europe—the spectre of Revisionism.* Mr. Gaitskell is not alone.'

How characteristic that Mr. Anthony Crosland should start his pronunciamento in last month's *Encounter* by a facetious comparison with Karl Marx! His bantering allusion to the *Communist Manifesto* expresses pretty faithfully the mixture of Bohemian flippancy and economic punditry with which he has been conducting his campaign for modernising the Labour Party. Mr. Crosland concluded his book, *The Future of Socialism*,[1] with a plea that British Socialists should cease to be drab and should cultivate gaiety and liveliness. It is ironical that the effect of his Revisionist Manifesto has been to plunge us back into a dreary doctrinal argument which is depressing the Labour Party and boring the general public to distraction.

i

The most recent definition of Revisionism was given by Mr. Crosland in last month's *Encounter*.

The Labour Party should have one overriding aim over the next three years: to adapt itself, without in any way surrendering basic principles, to the realities of social change, and to present itself to the electorate in a mid-20th-century guise.

But what form should the adaptation take and what should be

[1] Jonathan Cape, 1956.

the guise—or disguise—in which the Labour Party should represent itself in the 1960s. I have read and re-read *The Future of the Left* and can only discover one concrete proposal, a revision of the Party Constitution in order to remove any suggestion that it is committed either to wholesale nationalisation or to further nation-alisation of whole industries. Mr. Crosland has no difficulty in showing that practically the whole leadership of the Labour Party —including Mr. Bevan, Mrs. Castle, Mr. Mikardo, and myself— has long since avowedly abandoned wholesale nationalisation as an objective. But he believes that the Party militants still blindly adhere to it, largely owing to the influence of 'the Left-wing leaders who intellectually accept a mixed economy but still cling to the dogma of wholesale public ownership.' These Left-wing leaders, according to Mr. Crosland, can rely on the wording of the Party Constitution because 'the extremist phraseology of the Party's formal aims bears no relation to the moderate practical content of its short-term programme.' And so he reaches his conclusion that the Constitution must be re-written and that anyone who opposes this is suffering from 'schizophrenia'.

Alas! The 'fact' on which his whole argument depends is an un-fact. The 'extremist phraseology' of the Party Constitution quite simply does not exist. Here is the actual wording of the relevant clause.

Clause IV—Party Objects

(4) To secure for the workers by hand or by brain the full fruits of their industry and the most equitable distribution thereof that may be possible, upon the basis of the common ownership of the means of production, distribution, and exchange, and the best obtainable system of popular administration and control of each industry or service.

The more I study this formula, the more admiration I feel for Sidney Webb and Arthur Henderson, who drafted it in 1918. At the Blackpool Conference Mr. Gaitskell urged us to distinguish Socialist ends from Socialist means and to recognise nationalisation as a means. This is just what Clause 4 does. First it distinguishes the Socialist end—the end of exploitation and the most equitable distribution of the fruits of our labours—from the organisation of the economy through which this can best be accomplished. Next it defines the two essential features of the Socialist economy which alone can achieve the Socialist end of equitable distribution. The first of these features is not nationalisation but common ownership, and to this is added a second—'the best obtainable system of popular administration and control'—a rather vague phrase, which at least rejects as non-Socialist the kind of nationalised Board, responsible neither to Parliament nor to its workers, which was set up by the Attlee Government. I can see that Mr. Herbert Morrison, whose brain-child these Boards were, could object to Clause 4 as it stands. But Mr. Crosland's case for re-writing it falls, for the conclusive reason that this clause does not commit Labour either to wholesale nationalisation or to further nationalisation of whole industries and contains none of the 'extremist phraseology' which he strangely attributes to it.

Must we be content, therefore, with the Party's present attitude to nationalisation? On the contrary, we should find a new and radical approach to this topic, based on a ruthless critique of the nationalisation undertaken by the Attlee Government. For the public discredit into which public ownership has fallen is very largely due to the disregard of Socialist principle with which whole industries have been subjected to management by remote, centra-lised Boards, which Parliament is expressly forbidden to investigate or control. Unfortunately, before 1945, the Labour Party had done very little advanced planning and there were no blueprints ready, showing how the industries due for nationalisation were to be organised. Since the detailed job of applying Socialism to the coal-mines, the railways, etc., was left to the civil servants in the Ministries, it is hardly surprising that what we got were not socialised industries but centralised, bureaucratic State monopolies. The nationalised Board—neither a public enterprise responsible to Parliament nor yet an efficient profit-making monopoly—is a hybrid, neither fish nor fowl. It can be made to work fairly satisfactorily in certain public services, such as gas, electricity, and atomic energy. But it is a monstrous burden on most productive industries. So the proper way to counter public hostility to nationalisation is not to re-write Clause 4 but to admit frankly the dreadful mistakes made by the Attlee Government and then to work out precise proposals for decentralising their oligarchies and subjecting them to full public control.

ii

It would be silly to imagine, however, that, having disposed of the case for revising Clause 4, one has finished with Revisionism. The influence Mr. Crosland wields—far greater outside than inside the Labour Party—derives less from his particular proposals than from his new philosophy of Socialism—or, if you prefer it, his revised 'Social Democratic' outlook. This has been received enthusiastically by the whole press, including the Top People who write *The Times*, *The Guardian*, and *The Economist*. Among non-Socialists, indeed, there is virtual unanimity that, unless his ideas are accepted by the Labour leadership—not so much as a specific body of concrete proposals but as a general philosophy of life—the outlook for the Labour Party is dim.

What exactly is Mr. Crosland's up-to-date Socialism? The attempt to summarise a view with which one disagrees is always dangerous. I have tried, however, to be scrupulously fair in listing what seem to me the essential features of his Revisionism.

(1) *Economic.* Since full employment can now be maintained by regulating a free-enterprise system, the old-fashioned Socialist analysis of the contradictions of capitalism is no longer valid. Socialists must now admit the Government won the election because they successfully maintained both full employment and stable prices, as well as achieving a rapid increase in living standards, contrasted with the austerity of life under the Labour Government. The only safe assumption is that the next election will be fought under at least as favourable, if not more favourable, economic conditions.

(2) *Social.* Rising living standards are rapidly undermining the class-conscious solidarity which used to cement the Labour Movement. More and more workers dislike business-men less than they dislike trade union leaders, and vote Conservative because they don't want to feel themselves members of the working class.

(3) *Electoral.* One result of increasing prosperity is to reduce the real differences between the two big parties and so to make it even more important to present the right image to the electorate. To regain working-class votes, Labour must remove the image of austerity and the fear that a Labour Government would upset the prosperity people are now enjoying. With these obstacles out of the way, the swing of the pendulum should bring it to office.

(4) *International.* Socialist doubts about revisionism should be removed by the knowledge that most members of the Socialist International, including the Dutch, Swedes, Swiss, Austrians, and Germans—not to mention the Australians, New Zealanders, and the C.C.E. in Canada—have all accepted the new philosophy. It is a sign of insularity that the British Labour Party is 'a bit to the rear of the column.'

iii

Let me admit at once that Revisionism faithfully reflects the political mood of Britain during the last eight years. But is it an adequate Socialist philosophy for the decade which lies ahead? Mr. Crosland is impatient of anyone who even asks the question. He is sure that we must dismiss the idea of the coming crisis, accept the Affluent Society, and try to make it more just and equitable. It is here that we part company. I believe that we must give warning of the crisis ahead and condemn the Affluent Society as incapable of coping with it. I also believe that, by preaching this austere doctrine now, when its apparent irrelevance makes us unpopular, we shall win public confidence as history goes our way.

There are two reasons why I hold this view. One is practical and concerned with electoral tactics. The other is theoretical and concerned with the shape of things to come.

Assume for the moment that the Revisionist predictions are correct—by 1964 people will be even more prosperous and contented than they are today. In these circumstances Mr. Crosland expects Labour to win, if only it will remove from its image those distasteful features—including the commitment to further nationalisation—which prevent the swing of the pendulum. This hope seems to me to be based on a misjudgment of the electorate and a mis-reading of history. What we have seen since the beginning of the century has not been an in-and-out of two big parties, as the pendulum swings to and fro, but long periods of Right-wing rule, with an occasional swing to the Left when something goes badly wrong. As a nation, we normally accept the Tory Establishment and only put the Left into power when it is time for a big change. Mr. Crosland assumes this condemns us to 'impotent opposition'. Oh dear! how can he fail to see that in a period of complacent prosperity, a vigorous Socialist Opposition will have far more

PS   I power for good than a weak Labour Government with a small majority.

There is another factor to be considered. Leaders seek to change the inmost nature of their parties at dire peril. The Labour Party was founded as a movement of moral protest, which denounced the capitalist *status quo* and preached the need for a Socialist transformation of society. To tell our party workers that the need for a Socialist transformation has been eliminated, and that the leadership must now show it can manage a mixed economy as well as the Tories, will destroy the morale of the rank-and-file without regaining the confidence of the electorate. Those who believe that what the country needs is an alternative Government, as distinct from a radical Opposition, should found a new party or revive Liberalism.

One of the curious features of the present controversy is that the leading Revisionists—Mr. Crosland, Mr. Roy Jenkins, and Mr. Douglas Jay—are all professional economists of note. Yet the expert advice they have proffered since last October has been almost exclusively concerned with mass psychology, electoral tactics, and propaganda techniques. This at least disproves the accusation that economists are 'desiccated calculating machines!' As an old-time professional propagandist, however, I am scared stiff by the obsession they reveal with the techniques of 'winning friends and influencing people'. Mr. Crosland, for example, tells us that the 'one overriding aim of the Labour Party over the next three years should be to adapt itself . . . and to present itself in a mid-20th-century guise.' *'The one overriding aim.'* If there is one thing I learnt from five years of psychological warfare, it is that the best propaganda consists in apparently doing no propaganda at all. An Opposition which spent three years in dolling itself up to woo the electorate would condemn itself to certain defeat. The voters would learn to despise it and its members would lose their last shred of self-respect. What makes Revisionism a vote-loser is its obsession with winning votes.

How, then, should the Opposition conduct itself in these next four years? The best way to regain the confidence of the British people is, first of all, to regain our own self-respect. Instead of veering with every gust of popular opinion; instead of watering down policies in order to paper over differences inside the Party or avoid offending an important interest: instead of pulling punches for fear of upsetting the Establishment; instead of behaving as the public contemptuously expects every politician to behave—instead of all this, we should make ourselves thoroughly unpopular by harrying the Establishment, warning the country of the troubles that lie ahead, and showing how they can only be overcome by a further advance towards Socialism. The best way for an Opposition to survive a period of unpopularity is to stand by its principles—in the confidence that history will prove it right.

iv

Having dealt with the practical objections to Revisionism, I must now turn to consider its theoretical inadequacies. If we were to see the world through Mr. Crosland's eyes, would this help us to understand the post-war era and anticipate the shape of things to come?

In order to adapt our Socialism to the mid-20th-century, we need first and foremost a new critique—a sucessor to *Das Kapital*—which expounds the working of the new, regulated capitalist economics and exposes their new inadequacies and contradictions. Naturally, anyone who undertakes this task will be attacked, as Karl Marx was, by every banker and economic pundit. Nevertheless, the job has been started—in this country by J. K. Galbraith, author of *The Affluent Society*.[1] What saddens me about Mr. Crosland is that, instead of joining in the assault on economic orthodoxy, he seems to be advising the Labour Party to come to terms with it. Whereas, for example, *The Affluent Society* mercilessly exposes the vulgarity, the wastefulness, the incompetence, and the inherent contradictions of Western capitalism, Mr. Crosland's *The Future of Socialism* is chiefly concerned to emphasise its stability and strength. He also seems strangely unaware of the threat to freedom presented by the irresponsible concentrations of power which characterise the modern oligopoly.

My second criticism of Mr. Crosland's outlook is that, although he dubs the rest of us 'insular', he himself displays a most curious provincialism. In the whole of *The Future of Socialism* there is no mention of what is happening outside the North Atlantic area, apart from vague references to aid for underdeveloped areas and colonial equality. He talks a great deal about the stability of the post-war economy and the increase in national wealth under the Tories since 1951, but does not mention that this latter has been mainly caused by a fortunate improvement of our terms of trade. As

[1] Hamish Hamilton, 1958.

a result of these gaps in his analysis, he sees only the negative factors which have caused public ownership to become increasingly unpopular since 1945, and completely overlooks the new factors which may completely change that attitude in the next ten years. Mr. Crosland urges the Labour Party to follow the example of the Dutch, Swedish, Swiss, Austrian, and West German Socialists. What he does not mention is that the Swedish Socialist Party—after a long bout of Revisionism—faces the gravest crisis in its history and that the Austrians have for fifteen years shared power quite happily with their anti-Socialist opponents, while the Dutch, the Swedes, the Swiss, and the Germans are minority parties, without any real hope of ever carrying out a Socialist programme.

What strikes me is Mr. Crosland's failure to observe the terrifying contrast between the drive and missionary energy displayed by the Communist bloc and the lethargic, comfortable indolence of the Western democracies. Revisionism assumes that the expansion of our Affluent Society will continue at a comfortable pace, until gradually the whole world, including Soviet Russia, has accepted its values and admitted that a nation's greatness is measured by the number of washing-machines and motor-cars per head of population. I suggest we should make a very different assumption—that the whole Western world will face a grave crisis as the balance of power shifts and the countries which rely on planning and nationalisation catch up on our rich and easy-going economies.

Mr. Crosland rightly sees that this crisis is unlikely to take the old-fashioned form of mass unemployment—and wrongly concludes that there will be no crisis at all. Thus he fails to observe both the new conflicts and the new solutions, such as have already emerged under de Gaulle since the collapse of the Fourth Republic and such as may well recur in India when Nehru dies.

At present the American Administration and the British Government are nearly as complacent and blind to these new factors as Mr. Crosland himself. But history will force them on our attention, as the Communist countries demonstrate with ever increasing force the efficiency of nationalisation. Progressively year by year we shall see that, judged in terms of national security, scientific and technological development, popular education, and, finally, even of mass living standards, free enterprise is losing out in the peaceful competition between East and West. It would be strange indeed for the Labour Party to abandon its belief in the central importance of public ownership at the precise moment when the superiority of socialised economies is being triumphantly vindicated in world affairs.

The Tories have an obvious reply. They say that the Kremlin's brutal power derives not from public ownership but from the one-party State. A dictator can boost defence and welfare services at the cost of personal consumption. But this is an excuse which no Socialist can accept. To concede that dictatorship is intrinsically more efficient than democracy is to admit defeat before the race begins. Indeed, our whole Democratic Socialist case is surely based on the contention that those who combine planning *and* free choice, social discipline *and* civil liberty, a strong Executive *and* independent justice, are not only better but stronger than their totalitarian adversaries. I fully realise that, for some time to come, abandonment of public owner-ship will be urged upon the Labour Party by all the best people; and that those who predict a crisis of Western democracy and warn that it can only be cured by a radical advance towards Socialism will make many enemies in a political climate as complacent and short-sighted as that of the 1930s. But they are the kind of enemies the Labour Party needs to make if it is to become once again a fighting Opposition.

v

A few words, in conclusion, about the background and the prob-able outcome of the Revisionist controversy. When Mr. Hugh Gaitskell took over from Mr. Clement Attlee, the Labour Party had been tearing itself to pieces for several years. So the new Leader decided to staunch its wounds with twelve wads of Socialist re-thinking, each packed into a bulky policy document. We all agreed to stop the abstract Left-Right argument about public ownership and instead to seek agreement on practical measures which a Labour Government could carry out if elected to power. Both Gaitskellites and Bevanites showed a surprising readiness to make concessions of abstract principle and accept practical compromises in order to achieve a workable agreement.

The result of this cessation of doctrinal feuding was highly bene-ficial. We not only evolved a policy for the next Labour Government and a programme for the general election; we also began to heal those personal hatreds and clique rivalries which had been turning the word 'comrade' into a term of abuse. To the surprise of its friends as well as its opponents, the Labour Party last autumn went into the election campaign with a united leadership and a volunteer organization more numerous and more enthusiastic than at any time since 1945. Even the unexpected extent of the Tory victory did not impair either the prestige Mr. Gaitskell had richly earned during the campaign or the renewed fervour of those who had flocked to support him.

It is against this background that we must view the decision of the Revisionists that the morrow of defeat was the right moment to call for a retreat from nationalisation. Did they seriously assume that, by applying shock tactics in a moment of defeat, they could jerk the wheels of the party machine into Revisionist ruts? If they did, they must be sadly disconcerted by what happened. The Labour Party was shocked not into an acceptance of their proposals but into a cold, frustrated anger at the prospect of another long, dreary period of doctrinal feuding. Since then the Revisionists have been hastily retreating towards orthodoxy. In their flight they have jettisoned nearly all their concrete proposals, until, as we have seen, all that remains of their programme is the single proposition that Clause 4 of the Constitution should be revised.

If Mr. Crosland is right and Revisionism is indeed 'a spectre haunting Europe', it looks as though in Britain it is a ghost that will be laid without too much trouble.

THE LESSONS OF 1945

This essay was originally published in April 1963, as a contribution to the Jubilee Issue of the *New Statesman*.

THERE is one function—the task of self-criticism—which can never be adequately carried out inside a democratic socialist party. In a communist state, this task is the perilous responsibility of the voluntary élite constituted by the party members. It is for them to assess successes, to raise the awkward issues and to expose faults of administration. In our British democratic system, however, where two big parties are competing against each other, self-criticism of this kind is too electorally damaging to be permissible. Since the introduction of universal suffrage, party loyalty has come to be the prime virtue expected of the M.P. and of the active party worker; and the test by which his loyalty is measured is whether he supports his leaders when he disapproves of what they are doing, and whether he defends the party line when he feels in his bones that it is wrong. That is why the task of self-criticism is usually left to those socialist journalists and academics who are professionally free to undertake the kind of cool analysis or outraged exposure that are likely to get a career politician into trouble.

George Bernard Shaw was the first and most famous of these socratic gadflies. In his Fabian days, his incursions into practical Labour politics exasperated the leaders almost as much as they stimulated the rank and file. Since then, a long line of intellectuals has carried on the Shavian tradition, forcing the Labour party to face awkward facts and even on occasion to accept new ideas. Some of them, Kingsley Martin and H. N. Brailsford, for example, have been pre-eminently journalists. More often they have been academics who, in addition to their independent writings, have worked for the party behind the scenes, sitting patiently on its working parties and helping on occasion to draft its manifestos.

But in order to fulfil their function—the provision of an intellec-

tual dynamic to a party that instinctively distrusts intellectuals—
they have been forced jealously to guard their independence and so
have laid themselves open to the accusation of irresponsibility.
Whenever he wanted to wither them with his contempt, Earl Attlee
used to call them 'the Newstatesmen'.

The phrase was coined in irony, but it contains a very large grain
of truth. After the collapse of the 1931 Labour government, the
party faced catastrophe with a magnificent display of instinctive
solidarity. But its political self-confidence had been shattered by the
MacDonaldite betrayal, and the job of creating a programme of
action and a structure of doctrine on which their self-confidence could
grow again was quite beyond the trade union leaders and the professional politicians. The Newstatesmen took it over. It was Tawney,
Laski, Cole—and later Durbin—who analysed frankly and candidly
the defects of the 1929 Labour government and worked out the
changes that the party must accept in its doctrine and in its
procedures, if the MacDonaldite betrayal was not to be repeated in
the future.

This new thinking first appeared in books and pamphlets that
only a minority of practical politicians bothered to read. But by
the time the war broke out, the writings of the Newstatesmen had
been vulgarized into a popular version that could be heard in
speeches at Labour conferences and in parliament. That popular
version found its final and most famous expression in the 1945
Labour party election pamphlet *Let us Face the Future*.

Neither Lord Morrison nor Earl Attlee has ever shown much
anxiety to acknowledge the extent to which the achievements of
their administration were made possible by the critique to which
the Newstatesmen had subjected the MacDonald government, and
by the researches which they and their pupils had undertaken in
order to work out a realistic programme of socialization. If in addition
to borrowing their ideas, the politicians had heeded their warnings,
those achievements could have been far greater.

When one compares the Fifties with the Thirties, one is struck
at once by the contrast between the role of the independent intel-
lectual in those two long periods of political defeat and frustration.
This time, the first years in the wilderness were dominated by the
Bevanite split. This time, the post mortem was conducted not by
Newstatesmen outside the party machine but by the professional

politicians. As a result there was much more verbal fisticuffs than serious self-criticism; and, when exhaustion came, the new socialist policy emerged not from a creative public controversy conducted in books and pamphlets but from a long string of working parties established by Labour's National Executive—each of them responsible for a long and sometimes not very inspiring policy document. No wonder that when the 1959 election was fought many Labour voters were quite unable to name any differences between the Conservative and Labour policies.

The third successive electoral defeat caused a renewed bout of questioning. How could the party achieve victory, the right wing asked, unless it could be dissociated from its working-class tradition and given a new public image? Is it possible to have the kind of controversy required to produce new ideas, the left wing wondered, without precipitating another disastrous split? Hugh Gaitskell set himself to grapple with this problem. By a supreme effort of personal leadership he attempted to provide a substitute for the dynamic controversy which had restored the party's morale and stimulated the new thinking in the Thirties. With a series of hammer blows, first left then right, he began to beat out a New Socialism in terms of his own personality. But he had worn himself out; and with Harold Wilson's election as his successor, the Labour party has whipped back into its traditional posture. It has become once again a party where leaders are expected not to give the marching orders to the rank and file but to express the inner momentum of a mass movement. For the first time for many years, the Labour Party now suddenly feels the need for the stimulus of controversy which will help to create the political climate in which a Labour government can maintain its sense of direction and do a real job of work.

Alas! The time is short. After 1951, as contrasted with 1931, no attempt was made to assess the achievements of the Labour government, and to analyse the reasons for its defeat. To publish criticism of the foreign policy of Ernest Bevin, the economics of Dalton, Cripps and Hugh Gaitskell, or the sagacity of Clem Attlee in timing his appeals to the country, was treated as an act of disloyalty. Indeed, it has taken 12 years to purge the Labour party of the disease of 'ex-ministeritis' which first crippled our parliamentary leadership in the early Fifties and then blighted the self-criticism which should have made the political wilderness blossom with socialist ideas. A

few books—by John Strachey and Anthony Crosland, for example—
and a handful of Fabian tracts were devoted to socialist theory. But
the authors were careful to avoid the one essential requirement for
a creative controversy—a determined attempt to hack away the
jungle of complacent myth and self-congratulatory legend which
obscured the real record of the Attlee government from the eyes of
the faithful.

Now this mood of jellied self-deception has been swept away. The
youth and inexperience of the present Shadow Cabinet may well be
used against them in the coming struggle for power. But it brings
with it one enormous advantage—the release of the Labour party
from pious servitude to its own past.

The force on which Conservative electoral strategy depends is
lethargy. The voter who is permitted to feel himself non-political
between elections can be persuaded when the campaign starts that
he has never had it so good. But it is controversy that provides the
dynamic of a Labour opposition fighting for power. It is the voter
whose mind is opened by argument to the need for radical change
who can be persuaded to prefer Harold Wilson to Harold Macmillan
at Downing Street. In creating this atmosphere of controversy, the
Newstatesmen have a vital part to play. While the professional
politicians concentrate on future planning, I hope that some of them
will undertake that analysis of the Attlee government which should
have been completed years ago. This exposure of the harsh truth
behind the comfortable façade of party legend, will, I hope, uncover
definitive answers to some of those awkward questions that first
began to worry me as I sat on the back benches and watched the
Attlee government in operation.

What shook me then and what has perplexed me since was the
rapidity with which the cabinet lost its initial élan. Mr. Attlee had
arrived at Downing Street with the clearest mandate for radical
change ever given to a premier since 1906. Despite the wrecking
activities of the Irish Nationalists and of the House of Lords, the
Liberals were able to achieve re-election in 1910 and to sustain the
momentum of social change until 1914—a period of eight years. Why
was Hugh Dalton able to reveal in the third volume of his memoirs
that by 1947—only two years after the electoral triumph—the
government was manifestly losing both its coherence and its sense
of direction? Why was it that, once the proposals of *Let us Face the
Future* had been rushed through the Commons, the leadership was

so obviously at a loss what to do next—so that in 1950 there was no programme for a second stage of socialism on which the appeal to the country could be made? Finally, what was it that so rapidly deflated the public demand for social change that had swept the party into power in 1945? What transformed the militant activism of the rank and file into a heroic but unhappy loyalty to a remote leadership?

In their memoirs, ex-ministers such as Lord Morrison have taken the view that if the Labour government was at fault, it erred on the side of doing too much rather than doing too little—passing too much social legislation, pushing too many reforms down the throat of the electorate, and sacrificing personal consumption too recklessly to expenditure on public services and capital investment. Herbert Morrison was rightly proud of the skill with which he steered the legislative programme through parliament and maintained both the morale and the discipline of his backbenchers without resort to standing orders. His record as leader of the House of Commons is indeed beyond reproach. But was he as wise and successful outside the Chamber? Was he right to coin the slogan of 'consolidation', and to argue privately that a public reaction exploited by the Tories against controls, rationing and austerity made it impossible to campaign for a second stage of socialism?

With the hindsight of history, we can now see how flimsy the case for consolidation really was. For when the 1951 election came, there was no violent anti-socialist swing of public opinion. On the contrary the party made headway in the country, polling the highest vote in its history and losing its parliamentary majority exclusively owing to an altruistic re-drawing of constituency boundaries. Although the Labour party had no programme of action, and although its public image had been damaged by the Bevanite split, it still enjoyed more public confidence than the Tories. If only Mr. Attlee had held on, instead of appealing to the country in the trough of the crisis, he would have reaped the benefit of the 1951 recovery, and Labour might have stayed in power for a decade.

If this analysis is substantiated by an independent investigation, it would have an immense importance for the present Labour leadership. For it can hardly be denied that the orthodox socialist legend makes gloomy reading for a future Labour prime minister. After all, the political conditions under which Mr. Attlee took office in 1945 were considerably more favourable than any that are likely to confront Mr. Wilson in 1963 or 1964. As members of the wartime coalition, Attlee and his colleagues had during the war achieved entrenched positions in Westminster and Whitehall. Moreover, they took over an elaborate system of wartime planning and controls which enabled them to tackle any incipient financial crisis and suppress any economic sabotage—provided only they had equipped themselves with a staff capable of assessing the situation well in advance, so enabling the cabinet to base its decisions on a correct appreciation.

In 1945 both the conditions in Westminster and Whitehall and the whole political climate of the country outside were extremely well suited for a big and sustained advance towards a socialist planned economy. If the fate of the Attlee government was really inevitable, if it was beyond its powers to avoid losing most of its majority in the 1950 election, or to control the economic crisis that swept it from power a year later, then we had better admit straight away that our next Labour government will be faced with the choice of either spinning out its term of office by 'doing nothing and doing it very well', or, alternatively, of cramming all its socialist measures into its first months of office—before the inevitable public reaction sets in. To put it mildly, both prospects are depressing.

Fortunately, however, these are not the conclusions likely to be drawn from a candid study of the record of the Attlee government. An independent critic is much more likely to find that the electoral losses in 1950 were quite unnecessary, and that the precipitate decision to resign a year later was not an inevitable result of the crisis, but a consequence of physical exhaustion and loss of nerve. In all the circumstances, Mr. Attlee's decision to go to the country, with more than three years of his term of office to run, was understandable; and his motives for doing so, as explained in a recent book, were unimpeachable. Nevertheless, the results of his mistaken calculation were almost as disastrous to the cause of socialism as the events of 1931. But whereas the MacDonaldite collapse was frankly admitted by the Labour movement and the correct lessons were drawn from it, the failure of 1951 has been treated as a wicked Tory invention.

Once the mistakes of 1951 are freely admitted, it becomes possible to look back objectively on the record of the 1945 government, and in particular to submit its loss of direction and its rapid decline in momentum to frank investigation. Every Labour M.P. who won his seat in the 1945 election will have his personal impression of the causes of that decline. It is my opinion that the Attlee government revealed three grave defects, of which the first and most culpable was its failure to do its homework in the years before it achieved power. Of course the cabinet had its socialist successes—nationalised electricity and civil aviation among them—and one socialist triumph. Despite more than a decade of Tory erosion, the National Health Service still stands out as the only example of a radical, socialist solution, imposed by a minister who knew how to split the powers that be and call the bluff of the professional pressure groups. But there were ministers charged with huge plans for nationalisation who took office without any adequate blue print for the job.

Labour's plans for the Welfare State were equally vague, and the Minister of National Insurance found himself almost automatically committed to the Beveridge system of flat-rate contributions and benefits, which was obsolescent years before it was introduced. Even more serious was the little advance thinking that had been done about the way of achieving the transition from a wartime siege economy to peacetime socialist planning. This intellectual vacuum was only too easily filled by a continuance of wartime controls and rationing. Socialism as a result became disastrously identified in the consumer's mind with shortages and austerity; and industrially with bureaucratic interference from Whitehall.

When the fuel crisis hit us in 1947, it blew this gaff. So far from imposing a full-scale national plan on the economy, the Attlee government had not furnished itself with the information on which any plan must be based—far less with the instruments for carrying it into effect. In the convertibility crisis a few months later, the socialist Chancellor of the Exchequer at the Treasury was far less well informed about the flight from the pound than his opposite number in Washington.

The final exposure of this failure to forestall trouble, by advanced planning based on the best available information, and so designed to meet predictable difficulties, came with the outbreak of the Korean War. The government's attempt to spatchcock a huge rearmament programme into a fully-employed economy, without either import controls or an incomes policy, only aggravated the inevitable inflation and indicated clearly enough the inadequacy of the planning staff on which ministers were relying. It was because he had lost control of the situation that Mr. Attlee decided to resign.

My second main criticism of the Attlee administration relates to personnel. As members of the wartime coalition, its senior ministers had already been accepted into the Whitehall Establishment; and it did not occur to Mr. Attlee that the election of a Labour government pledged to radical social reform required any radical changes in the civil service. The claim that top people in Whitehall could serve a post-war Labour government pledged to socialisation just as faithfully as they had served a pre-war National government pledged to prevent socialism, was accepted with complete sincerity. In a nervous attempt to avoid the charge of 'jobs for the boys', ministers fell over backwards in appointing administrators who could show an unblemished record of anti-socialism to run the new nationalised boards, in collaboration with a few retired generals and ageing trade union leaders. Railway nationalisation was the extreme example of this uncritical reliance on Whitehall. A huge price was paid for a private enterprise on the verge of bankruptcy, which was then allowed to run down under an ineffectual minister at the beck and call of his civil servants.

How much more humane and imaginative our post-war reconstruction would have proved if government departments had been invigorated by an influx of experts with special knowledge. But once again, as after 1918, the best of the temporary civil servants returned to their peace time occupations, and the old Establishment ruled unchallenged over a bureaucratic empire which had been both enormously enlarged and dangerously centralised during the war.

At the Foreign Office, Ernest Bevin soon got rid of Philip Noel Baker, his only minister with any knowledge of foreign affairs. As a result, while the Prime Minister and Sir Stafford Cripps—confident in their personal knowledge of India—were pushing independence through in defiance of the civil servants, Mr. Bevin was building his reputation as a great Foreign Secretary by giving a trade union gloss to Sir Winston Churchill's Fulton speech. The economic ministries—above all the Treasury—were nearly as successful in excluding unorthodox outsiders. If in 1931 the MacDonald government was killed by the aristocratic embrace, in 1951 the Attlee government quietly expired in the arms of the Whitehall Establishment.

In describing these first two defects of the Attlee government, I write without inside knowledge and must base my judgment on the impressions of a backbencher who had only one opportunity to observe for himself how Mr. Attlee and Mr. Bevin put their socialist principles into practice. In 1945, I was appointed to the Anglo-American Commission on Palestine, and from then until the loss of Abadan I saw at close quarters each stage of Mr. Bevin's disastrous Middle East policy—in particular his self-inflicted defeat by the Palestine Jews. Seldom can a socialist Foreign Secretary have accepted more conscientiously the advice of the Foreign Office and the Chiefs of Staff, or spurned more roughly all those who suggested that he would best serve the cause of expediency, as well as of honour, by keeping his promises and sticking to his principles. The record of the Attlee government in the Middle East is a classic example of what happens to a powerful trade union leader who takes over the Foreign Office, full of good intentions and bursting with self-confidence, but without either prepared plans or selected personnel to carry them out.

So we come to the third defect—the breakdown of the government's relations with the rank and file of the Labour movement. When the story of the Bevanite revolt comes to be written, it will be seen that the cabinet quarrel about teeth and spectacles was not the cause of the trouble. It was merely the occasion of an explosion of rank-and-file disillusionment which blew Morrison and Dalton off the Executive and created the rift between 'loyalist' M.P.s and the party outside that is still not completely healed today. For years before the three ministers resigned, a crisis of confidence had been brewing between the Labour Establishment—politicians and trade union leaders alike—and their active supporters throughout the country. In this oligarchic country of ours, the people traditionally think in terms of 'We' and 'They'. 'They', of course, are the rulers and 'We' the ruled. When Mr. Attlee was summoned to Buckingham Palace in 1945, he was felt to be forming a government on behalf of 'Us' as distinct from 'Them'. And Lord Shawcross sensed the mood in his notorious remark 'We are the rulers now'.

But that dawn was soon over. Long before the election of 1950 had made us a party in office but without power, and therefore at the mercy of the enemies of socialism, it was clear that the Attlee government dismissed the vision of a government that would make 'Them' responsible to 'Us' as silly syndicalism. In the history of the British Left, there can seldom have been an administration so conservative in its solicitude for the stuffier constitutional conventions, so instinctively suspicious of all suggestions for popular participation in decision-taking and workers control, and so determined to damp down the fiery demands for a new social order that had won them the election.

Already in 1913 Robert Michels had written the classic description of how a democratic Labour movement, dedicated to the cause of social revolution, becomes enslaved to its own leadership. I read *Political Parties*[1] in the Twenties as a deadly account of what was wrong with Weimar socialism and I gaily assumed that it had no relevance to Britain. Reading it again in 1947, I began to have doubts. Today I recommend it unhesitatingly as a text-book analysis of how the Labour movement's complex structure of internal democracy was being almost unnoticeably changed into a system for maintaining in power a self-perpetuating industrial and political oligarchy—until the Bevanite revolt upset the process.

If Michels' picture is regarded as a perverse caricature and I am asked for a realistic study composed by a fairminded academic, I need only turn to Robert Mackenzie's *British Political Parties*.[2] The facts described by both observers are exactly the same. Michels, however, believed that the job of a Labour party was not to manage parliamentary democracy as well as the Tories, but to transform it into a social democracy, in which the ordinary people for the first time lost their sense of helplessness and shared in the task of taking decisions. And in this transformation, he saw that a Labour party's internal democracy had an essential role to play. Hence his horror at its destruction. Mr. Mackenzie sees things differently. His book is inspired by the warmest admiration for the way in which the Labour party under Mr. Attlee's leadership was becoming an oligarchy almost indistinguishable from the Tory oligarchy. His analysis completely confirms Michels' famous 'Law of Increasing Oligarchy'. But unlike Michels he seems to regard this process as praiseworthy.

Was Michels or Mackenzie right in his conclusions? I myself have no doubt of the answer. Surely when it was faced with a tacitly hostile Establishment in Whitehall and an actively hostile press in Fleet Street, the Labour government should have felt the need for a politically conscious and politically educated rank and file, such as

[1] Constable, 1959.
[2] Heinemann, 1955.

was beginning to emerge in the Thirties with the help of the W.E.A. and the N.C.L.C. Surely after 1945 the party machine should have been instructed to organise a nation-wide crusade of workers' education so as to give the rank and file the feeling that they were needed by the leadership, not merely to man the electoral machine, but to create that pressure of active left-wing opinion required to combat Tory propaganda. If a Labour government is to survive the attacks of its enemies and to make some advance towards socialism, it cannot do so by treating the party that puts it into power merely as a useful vote-getting machine. It was because the Attlee government trusted the Whitehall Establishment and distrusted its own movement that its dynamic was halted within two years of its election victory. After that, disintegration was inevitable. The Bevanite split finished off a dying administration. But as a result the Labour movement was saved as it had been saved in 1931.

Of course there is another side of this picture which the historian of the Labour party will have to take into account. Within its limits, the Attlee government was competent and successful. It not merely prevented a relapse into pre-war conditions, but consolidated the social revolution that the war itself had brought about, and so prepared the way for the development of the new managed capitalism and the Affluent Society of the Fifties. In this respect, its historical role is of the greatest importance. But in this essay my concern has been not so much with the past as with the future. It is only by forcing ourselves to see the errors of the Forties that we shall prevent a repetition of them in the Sixties.

SCIENTISTS IN WHITEHALL

Based on a Fabian lecture delivered in the autumn of 1963, this essay was first prepared for publication as a Fabian pamphlet. When this proved impossible, this version appeared in the July issue of *Encounter*.

I N November 1959, the Labour Party began to conduct a collective post-mortem on its third successive electoral defeat. Re-reading recently some of the lectures, articles, and pamphlets,[1] I found it extraordinarily difficult to recall how we were thinking and feeling in that antediluvian epoch—less than five years ago. But the effort is worth making if only to remind oneself how unpredictable British politics are. In the winter of 1959, the Macmillan Comet was at its zenith, and the Labour Party seemed down and out.

Looking back now at this ancient history, the first thing that strikes me is the degree of agreement the party had achieved under Hugh Gaitskell's leadership. As a result of all the work that had been done during the years before the 1959 election, there was virtually no disagreement about the programme that a Labour Government, if elected, would carry out. The disagreement concerned what we heretics on the left called 'our socialist philosophy', and what the pundits on the right preferred to describe as 'the Party image'.

Our heresy consisted in a stubborn determination, despite the three successive electoral defeats, to stick to our 'irrelevant' socialist principles until another crisis made them relevant—even if this meant a long sojourn in the wilderness. Their orthodoxy consisted in a fervent

---

[1] E.g., C. A. R. Crosland, 'The Future of the Left (included in his book *The Conservative Enemy*, Cape, 1963), and my reply, 'The Spectre of Revisionism,' in *Encounter*, March and April 1960. Also Crosland's Fabian pamphlet, 'Can Labour Win?' and my own 'Labour and the Affluent Society,' which was based on a Fabian lecture delivered in November, 1959. Last November I was once again invited by the Fabian Society to give a lecture on 'Scientists in Whitehall,' from which this article is adapted.

determination to regain electoral popularity, even at the cost of jet-
tisoning a whole cargo of socialist goods, ranging from nationalisation to Clause 4. We, in fact, were Traditionalists, convinced that
we had history on our side. They were Revisionists, convinced that
the only hope of revitalising the Labour Party was to break with
tradition, and turn it into a British version of the American Democratic Party or the German Social Democrats. Although we had
achieved by long and painful discussion agreement on policy, we were
still divided—by mistrust. We doubted their sincerity: they doubted
our capacity. What we needed to dissolve this distrust was first a
new, creative socialist idea, and secondly a situation to which it was
demonstrably relevant. Both these requirements have been met today. But they seemed depressingly absent in that winter of 1959.

The second thing that strikes me, looking back on those far off
days of defeat and recrimination, is the exaggerated importance politicians attribute to their ideas, and the scant attention they pay to
the objective factors which so largely determine elections. Each fac-
tion believed that the ideas and attitudes of the other had damaged
the Labour Party's chances, and denied it the victory that would
otherwise have been its due. Yet everyone can now see that our
defeat was due neither to the Revisionism of the Right nor the
Traditionalism of the Left. We lost quite simply because the British
people, in the golden autumn of 1959, were content with their
Government. They felt they 'never had it so good' as under the Tories
and they were very much afraid that a Labour victory would
threaten their new found prosperity. And to clinch our discomfiture,
the complaisant materialism of the ordinary voter was not in those
days condemned as immoral. The man in the street would vote against
change with a good conscience when Top People were unanimously
assuring him that Harold Macmillan's Britain was as sound as a
bell.

Four years ago it was not only leading Socialist Revisionists who
were telling us that 'economic stagnation was something of which
a Tory Government could never again be accused by a sensible Labour
Opposition'. Private affluence and public squalor is now a cliché. But
four years ago it was dismissed by responsible people as a clever-
clever paradox. We were still in the pre-Galbraith era. The economy
of the United States was still the faultless paradigm, and the watch-
word of orthodoxy ran. 'We must make our British economy expand
as steadily and as fast as that of the U.S.A.'

All my life I have watched the gyrations of the British Establishment. They move like a flight of starlings. One turns, all turn ! One month, they are all optimists—confident we can rely on the stability of the American economy. Next month, they are all pessimists—convinced that we must take refuge inside the Common Market. The U.S.A. and the Commonwealth are suddenly out of favour, and you can hardly enter the Athenaeum if you mention our obligations to New Zealand. Then, one fine day, General de Gaulle stops the negotiations and the Common Market phase ends as suddenly as it began. The starlings swoop over to another perch, and sit there twittering in unison. Let no one tell me that academic education inspires independence of thought, and discourages tame conformity. The behaviour of the British Establishment since 1959 demonstrates that this proposition is untrue, and if some of our Labour Revisionists flew with the starlings, at least they were wrong at the right time and in the right company.

Of course I am describing ancient history—history before the flood that swept Macmillan out and Home in. The last two years have seen an ideological upheaval so violent that the Conservative Party has espoused an incomes policy, planning and controls. Affluence is a dirty word, and *The Times* thunders in terms of Galbraithian economics. Once again the Establishment starlings have taken off with brilliant simultaneity, and are poised to land on a new orthodoxy.

But if history made the Revisionists look pretty silly, we heretics also got a number of things quite wrong. I confess, for example, that I failed to foresee either the economic consequences of Mr. Selwyn Lloyd, or the political consequences of Miss Christine Keeler. Instead I convinced myself that faith in the Conservatives would be undermined by a Munich-style crisis in Quemoy or in Berlin, where our bluff would be called and we would have to surrender to the Russians because we had nothing with which to defend ourselves except nuclear weapons. In fact, I was possessed by the atmosphere of the Eisenhower-Dulles era, and completely failed to foresee a Kennedy era or a Cuba crisis, in which it was the Russian bluff that was called, and the Americans who showed statesmanship by forgoing the fruits of victory.

Another thing we got wrong was the pace of change, the rapidity with which the voters' complacency would be undermined by events. We had assumed that it might well be a long time before the electorate began to realise that 'you've never had it so good' was a fraudulent slogan. If only I had written 'two years' instead of 'a few years', for in March 1961 came the Orpington by-election; the trend was reversed and disillusionment took the place of complacency.

What caused the astonishing switch since those far-off days? Mr. Gerald Kaufman has recently analysed all the by-elections and showed —to my mind pretty conclusively—that it is difficult to correlate it with anything any socialist leader, orthodox or heretic, said or did. Indeed, it was while the Labour Party was still divided and weak that the public began to feel it was time for a change. And as soon as the political climate changed, suddenly the affluent society was out of fashion; *The Times* began to thunder against its immorality, and economic pundits started arguing that stagnancy could only be ended by economic planning and an incomes policy. Even the poor derided nationalised industries began to creep back into favour. As so often before in British history, heresy had become orthodoxy almost overnight.

This upheaval was largely unforeseen by Government and Opposition alike. What first set it going? And what, once it had started, kept it moving at a constantly accelerating speed? The answer is now glaringly obvious; yet four years ago only a handful of individuals—among them Harold Wilson and Morgan Phillips—saw the two most important factors in the situation. In this respect, socialist heresy and orthodoxy were equally blind.

The first of these factors was the constantly accelerating rate of technological change, particularly since the end of World War II. Since Harold Wilson's speech at Scarborough, this has been impressed so deeply on public opinion that this new and powerful argument for socialism is in danger of becoming a cliché. Of course, it is not new to say that changes in the techniques of production, distribution, and exchange largely determined social change. But in 1867 when *Das Kapital* was first published, the actual rate of change was much slower than Marx realised, and it was this fact that caused his predictions of world revolution to be falsified by history: Technology was developing so slowly during the 19th century that Governments were able to adapt themselves in time to avert catastrophe. But a hundred years after Marx, the pace of technological change has been so speeded up that the social revolutions he anticipated are now physically possible. In fact they are taking place

throughout Asia and Africa wherever industrialisation and modernisation impact on primitive economies.

In itself, this accelerating rate of scientific and technological
growth is formidable enough. But there is a second factor which
aggravates it still further—the social explosion which is caused by
the injection of these new technologists into an unplanned society.
I was very struck the other day when I read in a text by Barbara
Ward of the effect of the 'urban explosion'. We all know, she pointed
out, the destructive power of the nuclear bomb; but we don't realize
that the city has as destructive a power as the H-bomb. At a recent
conference of town planners and architects, held in Athens under
the chairmanship of Mr. Doxiades, it was stated that every day the
city grows larger by seventy houses and thirty foot of road. Here
was a great dragon, eating up everything, destroying the old social
organism, creating an asphalt desert, in which human beings have
yet to learn how a civilised life can be lived. As Miss Ward pointed
out, the cancer of the modern conurbation is the result of the impact of rapid technological advance on a society used to a slow rate
of change.

The second example I want to take in order to illustrate the explo-
sive impact of new technology is in the field of education, for the
techniques of communication are being transformed as fast as the
techniques of destruction or the techniques of urban development. I
do not only refer to changes caused by television or the computer.
In linguistics, mathematics, and physics, revolutionary new teaching
methods are being developed by a minority of progressive teachers.
Where are they most fiercely resisted? In the teaching profession,
of course. But in this they are not peculiar. All of us resist any
change which affects our own skill and our own status in society.
Ask the political leaders what kind of change they think would be
desirable in the House of Commons, and you will find a strange
coalition of conservatism between the two front benches; it would
probably even include the leader of the Communist Party, if there
were communists in the House of Commons. Like the teachers, the
politicians do not want to have a scientific study made of their own
institutions, or to ask themselves whether those institutions are
capable of being adapted to the incredible modern rate of change.

But in the last four years, we have at least become aware of it.
We are now beginning to see that the impact of new and peaceful
techniques of production on unplanned societies, unwilling and un-

prepared to receive them, is a fact at least as important—and possibly as perilous—as the nuclear bomb. In nuclear warfare, statesmen can purchase a stalemate and so push the bomb out of the way, preventing it from detonating. But urban expansion is detonating every day, owing to the absence of adequate town planning; and the population growth caused by improved health services is causing havoc because of a lack of family planning. All these forces are exploding in a society which drags along behind science and technology, unable to adapt itself to them. The question forced upon us is how we can become the masters, not the slaves, of technological change.

Directly this question was asked at Scarborough recently, we realized that here was the new, creative Socialist idea needed to reconcile the Revisionists of the Right with the Traditionalists of the Left. Harold Wilson succeeded where Hugh Gaitskell failed because he did not propose a substitute for the old Socialism. Instead he offered a reaffirmation of its traditional moral and political arguments in ultra-modern terms. The basic moral case, for example, has always been the outrageous fact of the two nations—one poor, one affluent—living alongside each other. Socialists have always maintained that a society of this kind is intolerable because it is unjust : it will only be made just when the privileges of the minority are transformed into the rights of every citizen.

This traditional moral argument becomes not less but more powerful in a period when technology can double the standard of living in a dozen years. True, mass poverty has been abolished in the U.S.A., where only thirty per cent are now living in agrarian squalor, and in the blighted areas of the towns. But an affluent majority which permits a third of its fellow citizens to exist on the poverty line is not morally superior to the old affluent oligarchy which used to permit seventy per cent of its citizens to die in squalor. On the contrary ! The fact that poverty can now be abolished altogether makes the fact that it is tolerated in the U.S.A. even more scandalous. This country, too, is rapidly moving towards a situation where a majority of the population is living well and improving its living standards year by year. But the affluence achieved during the Tory decade only strengthens the case for Labour's New Deal plan to abolish poverty in the midst of plenty by means of modern social security.

The traditional political case for socialism can also be restated in new scientific terms. Democracy, R. H. Tawney told us just after World War I, is 'about power'—how to make power responsible, how to tame it by public controls. Parliamentary institutions can be democratised by universal suffrage; but that leaves the problem of economic power unsolved.

Exactly how economic power must be tamed (how much public ownership, for example, will be involved) is a secondary question. The basic principle is that power must be made accountable, and that principle has been strengthened—not weakened—by the increasing rate of technological change, and the consequent concentration of economic power.

But now, to the traditional moral and the traditional political, has been added a new scientific case for socialist planning. Nothing will halt the scientific and technological revolution under which we live. And in this case, a community which does not take control of these forces is doomed to suicide, either by the nuclear weapon or by one of the other disastrous explosions which occur when these new technologies are injected into an unplanned society, unattuned to change. Even the Government has been forced to face up to it: the creation of N.E.D.C. and the publication of the Buchanan Report are evidence of that.

History now requires of each industrialised nation a continuous and purposive adaptation to its environment. And this means that our British Establishment must become 'science-based.' Throughout this century, it has been not only unscientific in its outlook and in its education, but actively hostile to science and technology. Out of our 625 M.P.s in this Parliament, I reckon we have under twenty with any scientific qualification (and among them are listed neither the Minister for Science nor his Shadow[1] !). This is not the first time this kind of educational inadequacy has characterised the ruling class in British history. At the beginning of the modern age (say, in the 15th century) literacy was just about as rare in Parliament as numeracy is to-day. In those days, the sound, sensible men of affairs who ran the country regarded the clerks on whose reading and writing they relied, with a mixture of envy and suspicion and were determined to maintain them as a small élite circle so as to keep them well under their thumbs. In due course that changed; and the modern state came into being when it was found necessary to require literacy of the ruling class. We shall only be able to talk of a modernised Britain when numeracy as well as literacy becomes a requirement of the ruling class.

[1]   Quintin Hogg and the Author.

What is enormously exciting is the realisation that we are now living in the precise epoch in British history when this requirement will have to be met. The Labour Government which we are determined shall be in power within a matter of months may well be the first science-based government this country has ever known.

Over the last year, it has been my job to organise the working parties that have been studying how science and technology can be applied under a Labour Government. It has been an immensely exhilarating experience, because of the astonishing stream of talent that has come pouring in as soon as we made it clear that we are not preaching to scientists and technologists but asking them for active help.

Already, however, I see two dangers in the success we have achieved. First, that we should be tempted to 'sell science' to the electorate as a 'gimmick' which the Labour Government would be able to employ in order to solve all its problems; that sort of talk would of course be pure political claptrap. Suppose, for a moment, that we have won the election; carried out our plans for making our existing ministries science-based; established a new ministry with the function of injecting government-financed Research & Development into the economy on the massive scale at present reserved for military R. & D.; suppose, finally, that the new Premier has organised scientific intelligence sufficiently thoroughly to select the three or four points where a first attack would be launched. Even so, even when all this has been accomplished, it would be five years at least before any concrete results could be expected. There are no short-term economic advantages which accrue from bringing the scientists into Whitehall, and the sooner this is made clear to the general public, the less danger there will be of science being perverted into one of those political fads which become the mode and then are equally rapidly discarded.

The second danger we have to avoid is a very simple piece of self-deception which is often offered to us by the scientists themselves. The main thing wrong with Whitehall, they say, is its 'anti-scientific bias'. Scientists and technologists are deliberately kept out of all the key positions which are reserved overwhelmingly for professional administrators with a non-scientific (or an anti-scientific) bias; and even in Ministries where scientists are employed, they are segregated and treated as technical experts with no direct access to the Minister.

There is of course some truth in this complaint, as indicated by the following from *Hansard*:

> MR. BOYDEN: to ask the Chancellor of the Exchequer how many assistant principals in the Civil Service have degrees in scientific subjects, and what proportion these form of that grade.
>
> MR. BOYD-CARPENTER: 14, which is 7 per cent of the grade.

Obviously there are some areas of government administration where the scientists are in a relatively good position. They have no complaint, for example, against the standing accorded to them in the Ministry of Defence; nor has anybody suggested that they cannot get the ear of the Minister. The same seems true of the D.S.I.R., of the Ministry of Aviation, and of the Ministry of Works (as it has been recently reconstructed under Mr. Rippon).

But when all is said and done, the sections of Whitehall where the scientist is given a hearing are extremely limited. There are many Ministries which need scientific advisers on their Establishment that have not got them, and there are many more where the anti-scientific attitude of the higher civil servants prevents the Minister from really understanding the nature of a problem before he comes to his decision. The Labour Government will have to remedy both these defects; (1) immediately, it must see that professional scientific advice is available in every Ministry wherever it is required throughout Whitehall; and (2) it must ensure, as a matter of long-term policy, that a steadily increasing proportion of the posts at Assistant Secretary and Permanent Secretary level are held by civil servants with a scientific (and not with an exclusively arts) background.

Nevertheless, to talk as though all we needed in order to put Whitehall right is to inject a lot of natural scientists into key positions in the Ministries is to disregard what is really wrong. The more rapid the rate of technological change to which Government is subjected, the more urgent will be the need to maintain a permanent cadre of professional administrators who can combine very high intellectual calibre with absolute incorruptibility. I would hope that when we get the balance between Arts and Sciences in our schools and universities right, we shall be able to achieve not only a fair balance between scientists and humanists at the top of the civil service, but also a new kind of civil servant whose general education is both scientific and humane. Meanwhile, we must make do with the cadres we have. The one thing which would certainly undermine the morale and the efficiency of our civil service would be the fear that a Labour Government intended to replace a large number of our senior permanent administrators with scientific experts of its own choosing. By doing this, we should destroy the morale of the civil service without any assurance of improving its efficiency. For what is wrong to-day is not merely the lack of natural scientists in Whitehall but the fact that specialist knowledge of all kinds— whether of natural science or of social science or even of human psychology—fails to get through to the politicians in time to influence the decisions that are being made.

If we are to make Whitehall responsive to technological and social change, the problem we have to solve is how to marry a permanent civil service with outside expertise. And this problem of getting the expert analysis through to the top civil servant and to the Minister has been greatly complicated by the change in the organization of Whitehall that has taken place since 1918. Before World War I, the various departments were more or less specialised. A young man recruited to the Board of Education expected to stay there all his life, and his best chance of becoming a head of a department was to work his way up to the Permanent Secretaryship of the Board. The situation began to be transformed on September 14th, 1919, when Lloyd George decided to unify the service and to recognise the Permanent Secretary of the Treasury as Head of the Civil Service. Since then, the consent of the Prime Minister and the Head of the Civil Service has been required to vital appointments in all Whitehall departments, and the departmental Minister has retained not the rights of selection but merely of proposal and veto.

The effect of this change was two-fold. In the first place, the appointment of outside experts to important jobs in the departments became increasingly rare. The key positions were all manned by men who had been promoted within the civil service and for whom it had been a life career. Secondly, the heads of departments were no longer normally recruited from inside the department. 'Specialism' had become the characteristic of the second-class administrator, and the topmost positions had been reserved for the 'trained mind', the professional administrator who can run any department equally well.

And so we have seen the emergence of the Whitehall Mandarin— the pure professional administrator without specialist knowledge or specialist interest.

I was brought up on Plato. But the part of Platonic philosophy I always doubted was the doctrine of philosopher-kings. I doubted it before the scientific revolution really got under way, and I must say my doubts are even stronger to-day. Was it really wise to permit Whitehall to be dominated by a single-type, trained to suit the requirements of a highly centralised bureaucracy, and each of them confident that, if the word is given, he can move from, say, the Ministry of Transport to become head of the Ministry of Education, knowing his capacity to do the job? I cannot help wondering whether the combination of the anti-scientific bias which he has so often acquired at school or university with the anti-specialist bias which was a factor, at least, in the obtaining of his promotion in Whitehall, provides the ideal conditions under which he would be inclined to welcome new ideas coming from outside.

Nevertheless, the centralising revolution in Whitehall has been completed; and it is unlikely that it will ever be reversed. What we have to evolve are ways of getting new ideas and new techniques from the outside world to the professional administrator, and it would be foolish to pretend that we can achieve this by a stroke of the pen or a verbal declaration. Certainly the problem will not be solved simply by saying that more of the permanent civil service shall be science-trained.

Is the problem then insoluble? Of course not. It was solved in part during World War I; it was solved completely during World War II. In every war, we maintain our cadres of professional civil servants, and then introduce temporary civil servants from outside to achieve the victory which would be impossible by running the country along the old peace-time lines. New ideas stream in to Whitehall, new procedures are adopted. University dons who had previously shown only a capacity for Latin verse or philosophical speculation suddenly reveal extraordinary powers of administration. Business executives show that they can put country before self-interest. From all over Britain, the best people are found to win the war.

Between 1940 and 1945, Britain was probably the best-governed country in the world. Our centrally planned economy achieved far more with far fewer resources than the modified *laissez-faire* of the U.S.A. and was infinitely more efficient as well as more humane than the totalitarian planning of either Germany or the Soviet Union. The reason for our success was, first, that we were able to

construct our war economy around the firm scaffolding of a professional civil service; and second, that we were able to make it flexible
and open to innovation by introducing into Whitehall an army of
outsiders, uninhibited by civil service procedures, or by any desire
to remain in government after the war was over.

Of course, appalling mistakes were made. But our wartime administration was, in the truest sense of the word, science-based—and also
social-science-based.

The conclusion is inescapable. In the technological revolution to
which we are now committed, we shall be in a state of permanent
emergency in which we shall permanently need the marriage of
established civil service and outside expertise that we developed as
a temporary expedient in World War I and perfected in World
War II.

The kind of planning we require now, however, is very different
from the siege economy which was developed after 1940, with its
single narrow objective and its negative controls designed to stop
production of anything except weapons and the necessities for survival. Because we shall not rely on rationing either of raw materials
or of consumer goods; because we shall not employ direction of
labour; because we shall take account of changes in consumer taste,
both at home and overseas, our peace-time planners must evolve a
flexibility and a sensitivity to consumer demand both at home and
abroad which set them completely apart from the planners of the
wartime and post-war epochs.

But there *are* two ways in which peace-time planning resembles
wartime planning. (1) It requires definition of clearly-defined targets
to which the community's efforts can be directed; and (2) it can only
be successfully achieved by the systematic use of scientific methods
both in the investigation which precedes selection of the aims, and
in the plans worked out in order to achieve them. Fifty years ago,
when the rate of technological change was still relatively slow, scientific planning of this kind was unnecessary; now, it has become a
necessity of survival. This is why we now need, in peace as well as
in war, the constant reinvigoration of our professional administrators
in Whitehall from outside.

Partly this can be done by greatly strengthening the professional
scientists already in government service (ensuring, for example, that
the Chief Scientific Adviser in each Ministry has direct access to the
Minister). But if our aim is to ensure that all government policy

is science-based, and that Ministers make their decisions upon the very best information available, it is not sufficient merely to increase the number of whole-time scientists working in government departments. We must also stimulate a steady movement between government and the universities, the universities and industry, and industry and government, so as to ensure that the rigid procedures of the professional administrator are rendered flexible by constant contact with outside realities. (Although on much too small a scale, a circulation of this kind has already been achieved in the Ministry of Defence: we must extend it to every area of government activity; and we can be sure that everybody will be a gainer.) The vitality of our academic research will undoubtedly be increased if leading university scientists, social scientists, economists and administrators, as a matter of regular routine, spend two or three years on contract to the Government in Whitehall and perhaps another period of two or three years working in industry as well. The same is true of industry. Here, too, new links must be created with government on the one side and the universities on the other, and the best way to do this is by ensuring a regular interchange of personnel.[1]

A sharp increase in the size and in the status of our scientific civil service; a full recognition of the vital role of the outside specialist on temporary assignment to Whitehall—these two measures should provide us with the manpower required to ensure that the Government adapts its thought and its procedures to technological change, that 'planning is science-based', and that Cabinet decisions are arrived at on the basis of a scientifically-assessed intelligence.

But what exactly do I mean by 'scientifically-assessed intelligence'? Fortunately, an answer to this question has been given us recently in the Robbins Report. It seems to me that this Report is epoch-making, far less for its recommendations—the more I look at them, the more dubious I find many of them—than for the appendices in

[1] But if we want to enable our temporary Civil Servant to play a role in peacetime planning as creative as he played in wartime Whitehall, we must make his transfer as easy as possible. Obviously it is impossible ever to achieve equality of salaries. But I suspect that the kind of man we want will be prepared for the two or three years of his contract to sacrifice considerable economic advantages for the sake of the experience of government that he gains. But one thing he cannot be expected to sacrifice is his pension rights; and that is why the Labour Party has included in its new Social Security plan a demand that pension rights should be made fully transferable. So long as it is only the employees' contributions which are returned if he decides to move to a new job, superannuation will remain a major obstacle to that mobility—especially among professional men and women—which it is essential to maintain if we are to adapt Whitehall to the modern pace of change.

which the evidence on which those recommendations are based is presented to us. Of course, there have been plenty of previous Committees which published the facts and calculations on which they based their findings. But the Robbins Committee is surely the first which made the bold attempt to look twenty years ahead to assess the rate of growth in terms of population, requirements, and resources, and so to work out a scientifically phased and costed plan of expansion.

What Robbins showed was that a Government which is prepared to rely on modern techniques of social investigation and statistical analysis can plan well into the future without relying on mere guesswork. Of course this kind of planning is still in its infancy; and so are the techniques for amassing the collection of the intelligence on which it is based. But there seems to me no inherent difficulty to prevent the next Labour Government rapidly creating an organisation which will ensure that its decisions in other fields will be as demonstrably 'science-based' as the decisions this Government has been able to base on the work of the Robbins Committee.

In this context, however, it is important to realise that first-rate scientific intelligence is not only produced by scientists or even by social scientists. What is needed is a team, a mixture of talents, derived from the ranks of the professional administrators, the social scientists, statisticians, economists, natural scientists, and technologists. One of the most important qualities of a Minister in future will be an ability to pick teams of this sort, capable of carrying out the social investigation which will enable him to undertake really sensitive and accurate planning. It seems to me that this organisation of scientifically prepared intelligence in industry, in the departments of Whitehall, and finally—and most important of all—in the central Ministry of Production, will be the most important application of science in Government which a Labour Cabinet will have to undertake.

Part III

PROBLEMS OF THE COLD WAR
1950–1963

NATIONALISM

First published in May 1950 in the New York monthly *Commentary*, this essay was composed as a contribution to the discussions preceding the writing of the New Fabian Essays. I have thought it worth preserving because what was then regarded as its perverse description of the intimate connection between nationalism and democracy seems to me to have stood the test of time.

O NE of the queerest phenomena of the 20th century has been the cult in America and Britain of 'internationalism'. Despite the teaching of Woodrow Wilson, who rightly saw that national self-determination is a precondition of political and economic liberty, we have come to associate progress with the formation of supra-national unions and to treat nationalism as a sentiment unworthy of the progressive mind, or even as an enemy of democracy. The young men of the Oxford Union who, on a famous occasion in 1932, refused to fight 'for King and Country', would have been ready to die for the League of Nations, and some of them did die fighting in Spain with the International Brigade. But at that time they felt that a war fought to defend the nationhood of Great Britain would be a futile—possibly even an unjust—war.

Such sentiments are not nearly so strong today—at least in Britain. Now that our own independence is gravely endangered by economic and strategic weakness, we are beginning to realise that national self-determination is the most priceless possession of a free people. Our associations with other nations—whether in Western Europe, in the Commonwealth, or across the Atlantic—are undertaken not with the object of transcending nationalism, but of creating conditions in which the British nation can survive. When experts tell us that we must federate with Western Europe or take the consequences, our instinctive reply runs as follows: 'We are not prepared to sacrifice our basic freedom for the sake of an economic theory, or even as the price of dollar aid. We would rather starve on our island than be forced into the prison of an artificial super-state. Alliance? Yes. Military integration? Yes. Internationalisation of public utilities, such as transport and power? Yes. But each step must be designed not to abolish nationhood but to defend it. Nations are not industrial concerns, which can be amalgamated at will in order to increase their efficiency and profitability. They are living organisms out of which individual freedom grows. Destroy the nation, and you destroy freedom itself.'

I do not wish to suggest that nationalism is not frequently a reactionary force, and an obstacle in the way of human progress. Certainly it can take obnoxious forms, as, for instance, in the persons of Hitler or Stalin, Sir Oswald Mosley or Senator McCarthy. Often enough, it may well become a drag upon progress, and hysterically achieve a curtailment of human freedom.

But it is wrong to conclude from the excesses of nationalism that it is always and everywhere reactionary. In fact, nationalism is a necessary and creative concomitant of real popular liberty. A state ruled by a small capitalist or communist oligarchy, or by an aristo-cratic élite, can always be more internationalist, more one-world minded, than a state where the masses really have their say. The more the common people take over the decisions which affect their lives from traditional ruling élites, the more divided and varied will the pattern of human life in the world become. Nationalism, in fact, is an essential stage in the self-assertion and emancipation of man. In its modern form it really began when the Protestant countries, including Britain, revolted against the world order of the Middle Ages. Henry VIII was the ancestor of Marshal Tito. Its second wave came when the American revolutionaries revolted against Britain, and the ideas of the French Revolution overthrew the divine right of monarchs. In its third wave, nationalism came as the Russian revolution against Western capitalist domination and in its fourth wave, the wave which is now undermining the foundations of both the Eastern and the Western blocs, it is the self-assertion of the millions in Asia and Africa against white ascendancy, whether that white man be a Russian commissar, a British proconsul, or an American oil magnate.

Nationalism, when it is healthy and democratic, is never purely nationalist. Every national, democratic revolution is also a social revolution, a struggle of the under-privileged inside each nation against exploitation by the élite. Seeking security and status, the under-privileged reorganise the economy of the state in a struggle to achieve full employment, fair shares, and equality of opportunity. But in so doing they tend to transform their nationalism into isolationism. The Left is internationalist and fired with the ideal of the brotherhood of man so long as it is in opposition. The testing time comes when it achieves power. Then, far too often, it uses that power not merely to destroy privilege within the nation, but to maintain or establish a privileged position for the nation over against the community of nations. And just because the Left is democratic and expresses the fears of the masses, who know little of other countries, it finds it especially hard to sacrifice national interests for the sake of an international society. The American wants to use the taxes he pays for improving the conditions of the Americans, and not for loans to other nations; the British worker, determined to maintain full employment, suspects any plans for European union which would give the foreigner free right of entry to his country; and the Russian Communist, who long ago, when he was in illegal opposition, planned for an international order, has become more suspicious of the foreigner, more fearful of contact with him, than the most reactionary landowner of capitalism. The danger of the national democratic revolution, which always begins as an emancipating, liberating force, is that it will end in the dead end of chauvinist self-sufficiency.

When we look at the present world conflict against this background, we realise that nationalism is the ally and the enemy of both contestants. The more the Kremlin seeks to integrate Russia's allies into a larger Russian-controlled economic and political unit, the greater the tension inside the Communist world. The more, under the pressure of the cold war, it tightens its grip on the satellite Communist parties, the more the nationalist dynamic, on which Communism relied in its revolutionary phase, is turned against Russia itself. That is the lesson of Titoism. Tito is the national Communist who wants his Communism to be for Yugoslavia, and though his military power may be small, he is relying on an elemental force which in the long run is more powerful than the Red Army. Hence the paradoxical position that Communism is no longer an integrating force inside the Eastern bloc. Where the Red Army has never been in occupation—in the Far East, for instance, and in Africa—it still has the power to disintegrate an empire or an effete order. But it is fast losing its power to unify a new Communist world—except by brute force.

This failure is all the more remarkable because Russian Communism originally had an enormous opportunity. It appealed not only to the proletarian class within each state but to the proletarian nations; and it could offer them a revolutionary short-cut to emancipation and modernisation which was not available to the Western democracies. If the Kremlin could have given Tito 'dominion status,' if it could have treated Poland and Bulgaria as Britain treated Canada and South Africa, conceding to their demands of sovereignty and retaining leadership by sacrificing power, the Russians might have created a world Communist society. They will fail to do so, and they will end in disintegrating their own empire, because their Marxist philosophy prevents them from realising the historic fact that, when matched against each other, nationalism nearly always defeats class war.

The great strength of the Western democracies is that they are not blind to this fact. Indeed, they all accept national self-determination as the foundation of their freedom. This is why America is still fundamentally isolationist, undertaking reluctantly, and without ideological conviction, her vast overseas responsibilities. It is because Americans really do not want to dominate other nations or impose a philosophy on them that the Atlantic pact is a less unstable unit than the Eastern bloc. It is because Britain understood the force of nationalism and voluntarily abdicated from the empire that India, Pakistan, and Ceylon—the only bulwarks of Western civilisation in the Far East—have remained within the Commonwealth.

Does this argument imply that we shall have to exploit the spirit of nationalism in order to make Germany and France tough allies in the cold war? Are General de Gaulle and some neo-Nazi German leader to become the twin defenders of Western European culture against Communism? These are legitimate questions. Nationalism—particularly when it is combined with anti-Communist hysteria—degenerates only too easily into Fascism, particularly in a country like Germany, which has no stable democratic tradition. But this obvious danger should not make us dismiss any and every revival of German national feeling as a revival of Hitlerism. To desire a unified Germany is not a sign of original sin, but a healthy symptom of German recovery, provided that the Germans who desire it renounce war and and totalitarianism as the instruments for achieving their ends. The

Weimar democracy collapsed partly because the German democratic parties allowed themselves to be the passive executants of the Versailles Treaty. As a result, the Nazis and nationalists were able to identify democracy with treason and patriotism with totalitarianism. If he is to fight the revival of Fascism, the German democrat today must uphold the principles of the Atlantic Charter as they apply to Germans, and must claim that in any Western union the Germans must be treated as equal partners.

It is, I believe, the abject failure of our appeal to nationalism which explains our defeats in the Far East. Here Communism not only caters for empty bellies, but is a popular movement against Western imperialism. Among the coloured peoples, racial inequality is at least as effective a breeding ground for Communism as poverty and disease, since it provides the intelligentsia and the more idealistic section of the ruling class with a motive for siding with social revolution. Indeed, it is only where the educated classes are ready to lead the workers and peasants that Communism becomes really dangerous. What differentiates the position in Western Europe from that in Asia is the fact that, in the former case, for national reasons, the educated classes are mainly anti-Communist, whereas in Asia nationalism drives them to school with Marx and Lenin. A young professor of economics in Peking may possibly calculate that American dollars would do more to solve the social problem than a Chinese Communist regime. But this rational calculation is pushed aside by his patriotic hatred of Western imperialism. American aid is received as an insult by any nation which has not already fought and won its own war of national independence against its own George III. And even those nations whose nationhood has been secure for centuries will resent assistance if it is accompanied by demands for any form of union which seems to threaten their sovereignty. As democrats, we are all isolationists at heart.

But this does not mean that we can afford to wallow in our isolationism. A stable world cannot consist of selfish nations, each planning its economy in reckless disregard of the others, and extorting all it can in every economic negotiation. Just as Russia may well destroy its empire by the imposition of a ruthless discipline in defiance of nationalism, so the Western democracies may well destroy their freedom by permitting it to degenerate into anarchy. When Wendell Willkie wrote *One World*, he was right in one respect: in order to maintain our national self-determination, we must accept a unified economic order in which the richer nations systematically assist the poorer and backward peoples. If the American worker is to make the Fair Deal for which he strives a stable Fair Deal, he must help to organize a world Fair Deal. If the British worker wants his British socialism to be permanent, he must help to organise a world of full employment and fair shares, in which the coloured peoples take a full and equal part.

Let me sum up my conclusions.

1. The only idea strong enough to compete with Russian Communism is that of a strong, popular nationalism. We can see it working for us in Yugoslavia. We can see it working against us in the Far East.

2. Any suggestion that the United States intends to use the big stick in order to wind up the untidy mess of European nation-states and to replace it by a neat, efficient, federal super-state plays into the hands of the Kremlin. Sandwiched between two hostile non-European powers, most European nations today would like to be neutral if they could. Since this is impossible, they look westward, and not eastward, because they believe that assistance from America does not involve accepting a foreign way of life, or submitting to political and economic integration ordained from outside.

3. Primarily Europeans detest Communism not because it is communistic, but because it has become a weapon of Russian imperialism. We resent Communist parties less for the doctrines they preach than because they take their orders from a foreign power. American foreign policy has tacitly recognised this in its handling of Yugoslavia. Instead of 'containing' Communism here, it is seeking to split Communism by helping Tito's national Communism to defend itself against Russian Communism.

4. Our declared aim should be not to contain Communism, but to contain Russian imperialism. We are opposed to Communism in our own countries; but we accept the right of other nations, with quite different social problems, to establish Communist regimes, provided those regimes are genuinely independent and respect the rights of other nations to their own forms of government.

5. Outside Europe—immediately in the Far East and, later on, in the Middle East and Africa—it is probable that revolutionary dictatorships will be established as a transitional stage to modern national democracy. Our aim must not be to stop this social and national revolution, but to prevent it from falling under Russian

domination. We must remember our own infancy as nations and the excesses of our own revolutions. We cannot, without violating the whole idea of democracy, seek to impose free enterprise on collectivist countries, or parliamentary institutions on peoples who lack the centuries of development which our specialised form of Western democracy requires. The colonial and coloured peoples must be given the freedom to make all their own mistakes, and they must be convinced by the Western world that we respect their demand for national self-determination, even if it takes social revolutionary forms.

The mental readjustment required for such a re-definition of our foreign policy is, of course, enormous. Anti-Communism is an ideology almost as vulgar and easy to swallow as Communism itself. Moreover, just like Communism, it provides a rationale for the aggressiveness and contempt for human rights which is instinctive in both dominant nations and dominant power groups. It is always tempting, when you have the power to do so, to force others to be free according to your own definition of freedom, instead of tolerating the growth of freedom through its adolescent phase of social and nationalistic violence. Yet, as British history teaches us, a great power which yields to this temptation is guilty of imperialism, however much it may persuade itself that its intentions are purely defensive.

I am convinced that the world-wide spread of the idea of nationalism is already sufficiently strong to prevent world empire by a single power, or even by an agreement between great powers. The strength of a great power today resides in its industrial potential, in the number of divisions at its disposal, and in its stockpile of atom bombs. But in the long run this mere physical strength avails nothing against the obstinate resistance of national democracy, the protest of the peoples against an imposed uniformity, whether Communist or anti-Communist. Our supreme job in the Cold War is to insure that this democratic demand for nationhood and social justice can be fully satisfied inside the Western World.

'THE COLD WAR'

From the first days of the Attlee Government, the official attitude of the Labour Party towards Russian Communism began to harden. Until the summer of 1947, however, the Left of the Labour Party refused to abandon hope of East-West collaboration. We pinned our faith in a European Third Force led by Britain and mediating between Russia and America. The Marshall Aid offer and the Russian rejection of it destroyed these hopes. As the Berlin blockade succeeded the rape of Czechoslovakia, we recognised that the kind of democratic socialism that we had envisaged in 1945 was being rapidly ground to pieces between the blocs. Those of us, however, who had never been pacifists and rejected neutralism supported N.A.T.O. and began to try to work out a new socialist philosophy in terms of the Cold War. The task was not rendered easier by the United Nations action in Korea, which converted a large section of the Labour Party into passionate anti-communist crusaders.

I wrote this essay in the crisis atmosphere of December 1950, when General MacArthur had just been routed by the Chinese, and it was generally held that the Korean War was merely a prelude to an attack by the Red Army on Western Europe. This belief was of course the main motive for the Attlee Government's second armament programme which, in its turn, produced the 1951 Gaitskell budget and the Bevanite split.

When I agreed to publication in the January-March issue of the *Political Quarterly*, I knew there were Ministers on the point of resignation, and thought it was important to try to work out a realistic position from which a rebel Left could criticise the Labour Government.

i

W HAT exactly do we mean by the Cold War? To ask the
question is not merely a piece of academic pedantry. Since
1946 this concept has increasingly dominated the policies
of the western democracies and moulded the lives of their inhabitants. We have gradually come to take the Cold War for granted,
without any precise understanding of what we mean by it or—even
more important—what difference it makes to our other political
preconceptions.

Superficially, the definition of Cold War seems obvious enough.
It describes the fact that we are neither at war nor at peace with the
Soviet Union, but in a state of undeclared hostility. So far the
statesmen have failed to find not merely an agreed solution of a host
of particular problems, like Germany and Japan, but any basis on
which communist and non-communist states can agree to exist alongside each other.

A moment's reflection, however, will reveal that this is not a
complete account of what we mean by Cold War. After all, ever since
1917 communist and non communist states have been existing side
by side, and the Kremlin has been framing its policies, and the
policies of communist parties all over the world, on the Leninists'
assumption of inherent conflict between capitalism and communism.
On this definition, Russia has been waging Cold War or Hot War
ever since the Bolsheviks seized power, and nothing has happened
inside the Soviet Union since 1945 to change the situation. If Cold
War is used to define the objective relations between communist
and non-communist states, then we must admit that it has been
going on for thirty-three years and not, as most of us tend to assume,
only since the Foreign Ministers' Conference broke down in the
winter of 1947. There may have been tactical reasons why the Bolsheviks allied themselves now with the Weimar Republic against
France and Britain, now with the League of Nations against Nazi
Germany, now with Nazi Germany against the western powers, and
now with the western powers against Nazi Germany. But these
were merely actions of expediency, manoeuvres, which did not
change the basic struggle between communists and non-communists.

But to say this is to make nonsense of plain English. What we
mean by the Cold War is something which began since the end of

the war, a new phenomenon which distinguishes the decade we live in from the war years and from the 1930s. This new element can have nothing to do with the Soviet Union, since it has not modified the principles of its policy one iota. It must be something which has happened outside Russia, in the western world.

Directly we state this, we can see what was wrong with our first definition. Though only one is needed to make a Hot War, it takes two to make a cold one. What is new since 1947 is the acceptance by the western powers of the Russian challenge, and their determination to reciprocate in kind. The Russians have not changed their attitude to us; it is our attitude to them which creates the new condition of Cold War. Instead of pushing Marxism aside as irrelevant, and treating Russia as though she were merely another nation state or empire, we are now inclined to accept the Russian account of the relationship between communism and capitalism at its face value. Reacting against Russian methods of power politics, we are beginning to base our own policy on the Leninist assumption that peace is only war prosecuted by other means; that the aim of negotiation is not to reach a genuine agreement (in our democratic sense of the words 'genuine' and 'agreement'), but to achieve a tactical advantage over the enemy, or to make a tactical detente for short-term purposes. Up to 1914, the Russians waged ideological war against us, while we continued to treat them as though we were not doing so. Now both sides are active, and it is this fact which we describe as the Cold War.

ii

It is not surprising that the philosophy of Cold War has been most fully worked out by ex-communists, such as Arthur Koestler and Burnham. Trained for many years in the Marxist school, they have no difficulty in elaborating a doctrine of anti-Marxism as coherent and as total as that of the Stalinites. Mr. Burnham's recent book, *The Coming Defeat of Communism*,[1] is a very fair sample of this approach, and has the unusual advantage of a brilliant lucidity of style. Just as the Stalinites portray the capitalist enemy, in bold, over-simplified lines, as a vast conspiracy, relentless in its constant offensive for world domination, so Mr. Burnham permits no fine distinc-

---

[1] Jonathan Cape, London, 1950.

tions in his description of Stalinite aggression. In scores of pages he describes the complex power, the ruthless cunning, the implacable hostility of the communist enemy, and prophesies the inevitable world clash between this monstrous demon and an almost defence-less free world. Constantly he warns us that only a picture painted in these blacks and whites can rouse the democracies; and those who prefer the sober greys, daring, for instance, to suggest that the Chinese communists may possibly be different from the Russian communists, are written off as fellow-travellers. Mr. Burnham states bluntly that, in order to win, we must believe that the third world war has already begun and that the issue whether we should start the actual shooting or not must be treated, not as a matter of morality, but in terms of strict expediency. There is no basis for a settlement between democracy and communism other than a sur-render whose terms, as he outlines them, are so severe that it would in fact be unconditional.

The value of Mr. Burnham's book is that it is a logical extrapola-tion of a good deal of our present policy. Many of its practical sug-gestions for a gigantic political warfare offensive by an American-organised anti-Cominform are plainly absurd, but this fact should not make us overlook the importance of what he has done. If we reject his practical conclusions for the obvious reason that to adopt them would transform the western world into a totalitarian state, we must at least be willing to ask ourselves whether, in accepting Cold War and waging it, we are in fact accepting a denial of democracy. Once we admit that there is a real incompatibility between the communist and non-communist world, are we not guilty of cowardice if we flinch from the practical consequences? Once we borrow the Russian dogma of permanent war, must we not scrap our belief in international law and the sanctity of treaties, and our opposition to preventive war, as antiquated and positively subversive notions? Must we not agree with the ex-communists that the com-munist parties, to which we grant political freedom, are really a fifth column organised by an enemy power, and deserving only of liquidation? Wars and conflicts between old-fashioned nation states could end in peace treaties and even in enduring alliances between the belligerents. But a Cold War, arising out of an inherent contra-diction, can never be ended by a peace treaty. It must be total, in the sense not merely that any and every means to victory will be employed, but also that it can only have two possible ends: either the total destruction of one system or the total exhaustion of both. There is no third possibility in Cold War, when it is defined in these anti-Marxist terms.

iii

The Burnhamite view suffers from two defects, the first theoretical and the second practical. Mr. Burnham talks freely of inherent contradictions and inevitable conflicts. But if the history of the last hundred years has shown anything, it is the futility of this Hegelian logic when applied to human history. Most of Marx's prophecies have failed to come true because he tried to force facts into a system of dialectic. We can now see that, although the abstract capitalism which Marx described was inherently contradictory, the contradictions did not produce the results he expected, because reality diverged further and further from the abstract system. Instead of behaving as puppets on Marx's stage, the capitalists often saw the contradictions and took steps to smooth them out, under pressure from the labour movements. Instead of ruthlessly following their class interests, they were stirred sometimes by morality, sometimes by patriotism, sometimes by a shrewd self-preservation instinct, and their economic ideas and motives in the western world were deeply influenced by a public opinion which soon came to feel that *laissez-faire* was wicked. British socialism and the American Fair Deal are now emerging out of the capitalism which Marx dogmatically described as a closed, self-contradictory system. There is no scientific validity in the phrases 'inherent contradiction' and 'inevitable conflict'. In so far as they are not just untrue, they merely express a pessimistic conviction that human beings will always fail to find a sensible method of resolving a dangerous situation.

If this is a fair criticism of the Marxist justification for Cold War, it can also be applied to the anti-Marxism which the ex-communists are now trying to foist on the Western democracies. To borrow from the communists precisely that apocalyptic philosophy of history which falsified the brilliant social analysis of Marx is surely a very queer way of combating totalitarianism. In order to frame a sensible defence against communism, it is essential to realise that Russian policy is based on this gross distortion of history; that Stalin will always see the western world through Marxist glasses, which prevent him from ever understanding it; and that we are facing men in Russia whose choice of political instruments is inhibited by no moral scruples. We must accept the brutal fact that Stalinites believe in Cold War and that their whole policy stems from this belief. But there is no reason whatsoever to conclude from this correct analysis of Stalinism that we must adopt every communist intellectual error and moral vice in order to combat them. But this is just what Burnham and Koestler seem to want us to do.

In the second place, the anti-Marxist theory of Cold War is impossible to apply in any western democracy. Because the ex-communists, in changing sides, have brought with them the materialism and determinism which are the chief heresies of communist theory, they completely fail to understand the working of democracy. True to their instinctive totalitarianism, they think of it as something which can be engineered and manipulated from above by an élite imbued with the philosophy of Dostoievsky's Grand Inquisitor; and they are eager to organise the anti-Cominform on the same principles of democratic centralism which brought the Bolsheviks to power. At one point in his argument, Mr. Burnham observes that in the U.S.A. it is the military mind which really understands the communist menace. Of course it is true that the soldier, who thinks in terms of war, and sees diplomacy as nothing but power politics, to that extent resembles the communist. But surely it is the communist transformation of diplomacy into warfare and of planning into a militaristic managerial society to which we, as democrats, are opposed. If President Truman permitted the American Chiefs of Staff to usurp the functions of the State Department in order to organise an anti-Cominform in Europe, or to smash communism in China, the case for European neutrality would become unanswerable. By waging the Cold War according to Mr. Burnham's strategy, America would soon transform the Atlantic Pact from an alliance of free nations into an instrument of American imperialism, and Europe would have every reason to renounce it. Moreover, any American bid for world domination, under cover of waging the Cold War, would fail much more speedily than the communist crusade, because it would not have even the dynamic of a social gospel. An anti-communist world state, dominated by a United States which had accepted anti-Marxism as its philosophy, would be as repellent and probably less efficient than a communist world state.

iv

If we reject the Burnhamite theory of Cold War, what are we left with? Is it possible to fight totalitarianism without becoming ourselves totalitarian? One approach to an answer is to study the lessons of the second world war. Whatever the effects of unconditional surrender upon the Germans themselves, it is certain that this policy was wholly harmful to the interests of Western democracy. By exacting total defeat, Roosevelt and Churchill prolonged the war and permitted the Russians to advance deep into Europe. Even worse, they postponed any consideration of peace-making until it could only be made on Russian terms. By 1944 war had become an end in itself, and not an instrument of policy, with the result that we found ourselves committed to such monstrous proposals as the Morgenthau Plan and to the totalitarian idea that one can impose democracy from above on a defeated, partitioned and occupied nation. All this suited Russia admirably. A People's Democracy must always be imposed from above by a trained élite, but for us to copy the Russians involved a violation of every human instinct and every democratic principle. Instead of teaching the Germans democracy, we merely taught them that Englishmen and Americans—for a few months until the policy began to change—could behave like German *Herrenvolk* or Russian Commissars. During and after the war a few voices were raised in protest against the adoption of Nazi methods in order to defeat Nazism. Those who spoke up against strategic bombing, the Yalta decision to expel millions of Germans from their homes, the Morgenthau Plan, and non-fraternisation were denounced as appeasers who favoured a 'soft' policy. But history is proving the 'appeasers' right. It would have paid us to fight the German war and to organise the occupation according to our own moral code and not that of the totalitarians.

The lesson of Germany has a direct bearing on our conduct of the Cold War against Stalinite Russia. I accept the view that it will probably last as long as the Stalin régime, if not longer. There may be partial agreements and periodic détentes, but peace is not likely in our time. I also believe that it was essential to rid ourselves of the illusion that European socialists can ever co-operate safely with Stalinite communists in Popular Front governments. We have all got to accept the enduring reality of the Cold War. Even if, for tactical reasons, the Russians become reasonable about Austria or Japan, or any other particular problem, we shall have to remain on our guard, we shall have to remain armed, and we shall have to realise that Stalinism, the cruellest form of the managerial society, will remain a menace to world peace as long as it dominates Russia. But this does not mean either that war is inevitable or that we are justified in using any and every means to defeat communism. Today the only inherent reason for war is the statesmen's belief that war is inherent; the only inevitability is the dogma of inevitability, whether promulgated by Marxists or anti-Marxists. I can see no reason why, over a long period of time, the Russian menace should not be over-come peacefully—on one condition. That condition is that, by our own approximation to Russian methods, we do not justify the apoca-lyptic belief in Armageddon. If the world were to be divided, as the anti-Marxists would like it to be, into two blocs, both believing in an inherent Cold War, then the conflict would indeed be inevitable.

v

Fortunately, this is not the case. Despite every provocation, the western world has not adopted *vis-à-vis* Russia the policy of uncondi-tional surrender which it imposed on Germany. On the contrary, the Cold War is in fact providing a new dynamic for Western democ-racy. Despite the confident anticipations of the chronic anti-Americans, the response to Russian aggression has not been atom bombardment, but Marshall Aid in Europe and United Nations action in Korea. Both of these are enormously encouraging experi-ments in collective democratic action, and neither would have been possible without the Cold War. Of course, there are powerful forces in the U.S.A. which regard Marshall Aid and the refusal to use the atom bomb as appeasement, and call for a tough policy and a pre-ventive war. But so far we can say that since 1947 the Cold War, by and large, has been a creative force, forcing the western world to put its house in order and to attend to evils which otherwise would have been left to fester. It is only thanks to Russian pressure that we are organising collective security on a world basis, and it might well be that the main instrument for building the foundations of a World Fair Deal will not be Truman's Fourth Point, but the common defence plans of the west. Those plans will have to include not merely integrated commands and a common strategy, but joint boards to allocate food, raw materials, and labour, and to control both production and prices. During the second world war, such combined boards went a very long way towards the development of a planned economy over a large part of the world. The Cold War, if we use the opportunity aright, may enable us to reconstitute those boards today, just as it may enable the Fair Dealers to switch the U.S.A. back from free enterprise to a controlled economy. If we can move in this direction, we could, in the process of building our military and social defences against communism, evolve a balanced economy in the non-communist world and at long last begin to tackle the problem of the backward peoples.

This concept of Cold War strategy is consistent with the tradition of British socialism. In our own country, our aim has been to subject power to a free public conscience and to civilise the conflicts of capitalism through the development of public ownership and democratic planning. At home we are on the way to completing the task of civilising class conflict, so that it ceases to be conflict. Now we are faced with the grander and infinitely more dangerous job of civilising a world struggle for power so that it does not end in total war. If we accept this challenge in the spirit in which the pioneers of socialism accepted the capitalist challenge a hundred years ago, I can see no reason why we should fail. We have already disproved the Marxist thesis that violence was inherent in the capitalist system and that it could only be transformed by the imposition of a ruthless dictatorship. We must now disprove the thesis of the communists—and the ex-communists—that violence is inherent in the Cold War and unconditional surrender its only logical climax.

To achieve this, however, demands a considerable revision in our thinking. Far too many socialists still believe that the choice is between accepting Fultonism or seeking an accommodation with the Soviet Union: we should either be as tough as Mr. Churchill or as soft as Mr. Nehru. So long as controversy continues in this sterile rut, it will be barren, and the practical result will be annihilating defeats of the Left and a steady drift towards reaction throughout the western world. If the Left is to revive and to fulfil its radical and civilising function inside the labour movement, it must rid itself of its 'Russia' and 'America' complexes. British socialism is neither a mediator nor a halfway house between American capitalism and Russian communism; and socialist righteousness will not be achieved by a disdainful attitude of equidistant neutrality. In 1950 the main enemy of freedom, and in particular of free Labour movements, is the Stalinite managerial society, and the strongest potential ally which British socialism possesses is the American labour movement and the Fair Dealers in Washington.

It is true enough that reactionary forces are still immensely more powerful in the U.S.A.—and indeed in Western Europe—than they are in Britain. But to treat General MacArthur or Senator McCarthy as the main enemy, or even to think of them as a threat to peace as dangerous as Soviet policy, is to neglect everything which has happened both in the U.S.A. and in the U.S.S.R. since 1930. In the U.S.S.R. we have seen the elimination of the last trace of revolutionary communism, and the development of a managerial state run by a privileged and despotic élite: in the U.S.A. we have seen the steady growth of the labour movement under New Deal and Fair Deal governments, defeated only once at the polls in twenty years.

To achieve a genuine socialist policy, therefore, we must accept two hard facts: (1) that Anglo-Russian collaboration (in any sense of those words which have meaning for a British socialist) is impossible; and (2) that the best hope of world peace lies in a constructive alliance between American welfare capitalism and British welfare socialism. The Anglo-American alliance can only too easily be used for reactionary purposes which endanger world peace—for instance, to compel the French to accept the rearmament of Germany or to prop up Chiang Kai-shek. But because there are powerful popular forces in the U.S.A. which share our ideals there is no reason to believe that we cannot defeat such reactionary tendencies. The Russian alliance, on the other hand, is a mere form of words, because Stalinism is far more fundamentally opposed to our democratic socialism than it is to monopoly capitalism, with whose managerial structure it has a good deal in common. If we treat the Cold War as an unnecessary quarrel between potential allies, and the Anglo-American alliance as an unnatural marriage of convenience, we can achieve nothing. Accept the Cold War as the challenge of this century and the Fair Deal as a potential ally, and you have the beginnings of a socialist foreign policy which can achieve the 'agreement to disagree' between East and West which is the only alternative to war.

LOYALTY

As a result of working during the war, first in a secret department of the Foreign Office, and then in A.H.Q. Algiers and S.H.A.E.F., I got to know a good deal at first hand of the problems of security. So it naturally became one of my special subjects when I entered the House of Commons, and I took part regularly in the debates on security leaks which started with Burgess and Maclean, and reached their climax with Vassall and Profumo.

The line I took in these debates was summarised in a comparison of British and American security which I contributed to the Harvard quarterly *Confluence* in 1954.

i

EVERY Englishman who visits the United States, and every American who visits England, must be struck by the difference in political atmosphere of the two countries. In the very first conversation the Englishman discovers that, while his American liberal friends condemn the excesses of Senator McCarthy, they accept the necessity for 'an unequivocal fight' against Communism at home and abroad. The dismissal, for instance, of a school teacher or a civil servant, simply and solely because he was once a member of the Communist party, is now accepted by men and women who, even four years ago, would have been deeply shocked by the suggestion that they would ever condone such measures.

The American in England is in for equal and opposite surprises. I asked one young couple recently what had most impressed them during their stay in Oxford. Immediately the wife replied, 'We found it most interesting to go to St. Giles' in the evening, because a Communist holds a meeting in that street.' And the husband added, 'He always has a good crowd and we were able to ask him questions. That is something we could not do in our country.' I do not know whether these young Americans approved or disapproved, but they were obviously thrilled at being able to do something with perfect propriety in England which, as Americans, they regarded as rather *risqué*.

The fact is that, in our respective attitudes to the Communist in our midst, British and American public opinion are poles apart. In a recent article, *Civil Liberties, 1952—A Study in Confusion*, Irving Kristol, a noteworthy Americal liberal, remarked, 'It is impossible to tell the citizens of Oshkosh, some of whom have suffered personal loss as the result of the war in Korea, that there is no harm in having their children taught the three R's by a Communist.' I am sure that he was not exaggerating. Yet in Wigan (the British equivalent of Oshkosh) avowed Communists are permitted to remain masters and even headmasters, and the Conservative government is still strictly applying the pre-war principle, also enforced by the Socialists since 1945, that there must be no political discrimination in the teaching profession. A Communist cannot be dismissed unless he is proved to have abused his position and systematically introduced propaganda into his lessons; and the whole weight of public opinion, both in the National Union of Teachers and in the general population, is in favour of maintaining this principle of civil liberty.

Broadly speaking, the same is true of the trade unions. One of the biggest unions, it is true, the Transport and General Workers, has made it a union rule that avowed Communists shall not be appointed as paid officials, and a few others enforce a rule that Communists shall declare themselves before standing for election. But the Labour movement as a whole obstinately refuses to discriminate against Communists. The vast majority of unions still stand by their tradition that no one shall be banned from union membership for his political views and that, in the election of branch and district officials, the political affiliation of the candidates shall be treated as irrelevant. The other day, for instance, in my constituency at Coventry, which is dominated by the Amalgamated Engineering Union, I was discussing with some of my Labour supporters how we could defeat a fellow traveller who had been nominated for an important post. 'Couldn't we put up Blank,' I said, 'and let it be known that he is a sound Labour man?' The suggestion was received with stony disapproval. 'We've got to choose the best man for the job,' was the general view. 'And if we can't get a man who will beat the Communist on his merits as a trade unionist, then the Communist deserves to win.'

An even more surprising example of this adherence to political nondiscrimination was last year's conference of the British Legion. Though it is not as reactionary as the American veterans, the Legion is hardly a hotbed of revolutionary ideas. Yet, by more than three to one, it turned down a resolution that avowed Communists should not be accepted as members.

Lastly, the civil service. Fifty years before the United States had introduced any effective counterintelligence, our MI5 had worked out its techniques for dealing with espionage. MI5 has always been a pure intelligence organisation, with no executive powers whatsoever, and responsible solely to the Prime Minister. All it can do is to advise the government that it considers a certain civil servant a suspicious character, and it is up to the minister responsible for the department what then happens. When the Fuchs story broke, Mr. Attlee, as Prime Minister, announced that all civil servants with access to secret information were being carefully screened and that, wherever possible, avowed Communists or suspects would not be dismissed, but transferred to a nonsecurity job. Since, however, these decisions to dismiss or transfer would be taken not on grounds of proven guilt but of suspicion, a small internal committee of appeal would be established. This policy still holds. The remarkable— and, from an American point of view, disconcerting—fact about the British reaction to what must be admitted to be a series of desperately serious lapses[1] in the Government's security arrangements is (1) that public opinion has obstinately refused to be roused, and (2) that neither the Labour nor the Conservative government has tried to stir it out of its apathy. In government circles the argument against rousing public opinion is always the same. 'We remember the spy scare in the First World War when we were inundated with denunciations. Public excitement makes the task of scotching espionage much more difficult.' And sometimes an official will add, 'It may well be that the best thing to do with a spy when you have discovered him is to leave him where he is, and feed him with the information you wish to send to the enemy. Counterespionage is a professional job, and we don't want an excited public butting in and messing things up.' I have no idea whether this defence of British security methods is sound or not. What is relevant to my argument is the attitude of mind which inspires the politicians and the officials

---

[1] There have been many more since this was written but without any marked effect on the attitude here described.

who give it. Whether they are party or non-party men, they are almost unanimous in their determination to preserve the spirit of toleration.

ii

I think I have said enough to show that the British people adopt an attitude toward Communists which would be condemned in the United States as either blind fellow-travelling or frankly treasonable, whereas the American people adopt an attitude which in England would be dismissed as hysterical. What is the explanation? Is it, as Mr. Kristol suggests, because of the American losses in Korea that the citizens of Oshkosh will not permit a Communist to teach their children the three R's? I find this explanation unconvincing. If it were true, it would lead to the conclusion that the British tolerance of Communists is entirely due to the lowness of our casualty rate in that campaign. This is obviously absurd. After all, long before American soldiers were killed in Korea, we had two divisions in Malaya. The contrast between American intolerance and British tolerance cannot be explained by mere arithmetic.

What, then, is the reason for it? Partly, of course, it stems from differences in our national habits. Civil liberty to us means leaving the citizen alone to live as he likes, do what he likes and say what he likes, provided that his eccentricities do not upset his neighbours. Because we are a rooted people with an established pattern of life, we tolerate the nonconformist, the eccentric and the unpopular minority. In the United States, as it seems to me, both the demand and the desire for conformity are far stronger than in Britain, precisely because it is a new country without rooted traditions. Because he is a natural anarchist, the American must enforce social discipline, even at the cost of infringing the liberties of the minority. Because he is a natural conformist, the Englishman can afford to make civil liberties an absolute principle.

Let me at once admit, however, that this easy-going toleration, which is such a striking feature of British life today, does not go very far back in our history. Anyone who has studied the seventeenth century will recognise that Senator McCarthy had his prototype in Titus Oates. Until well into the nineteenth century, British loyalty tests for Catholics were a supreme example of intolerance and discrimination. Even as late as 1914, moreover, it was possible for a few newspapers to smear Lord Haldane, the creator of the British

Expeditionary Force, as pro-German, so effectively that the Prime Minister had to ask him to leave the Government; and to create a spy scare which roused the mob against thousands of innocent citizens with German names. Red-hunting too had a tremendous vogue in the 1920s, when the publication by the *Daily Mail* of the so-called 'Zinoviev Letter' helped to defeat the Labour party in a general election. Political toleration, as we know it in our country today, is in fact a quite recent phenomenon, a habit we have only just acquired.

This very important difference in national habit, however, does not in itself provide a sufficient answer to the question why Britain still assures to the Communist full civil liberties, while Americans feel that they cannot do so. Though we can afford wide differences of application, it is a very unhealthy state of affairs that the principles on which British and American policy are based should stand, as they do, in flagrant contradiction. If we really want the Anglo-American partnership to prosper, we must not be afraid to argue the matter out, and to discover who is right and who is wrong.

iii

It is impossible to discuss the problem of loyalty in isolation from foreign policy. On this point, if on no other, I agree with Senator McCarthy! What tests of loyalty we enforce depend very largely on our analysis of the dangers which face us in the world outside and our definition of the objectives we set ourselves in the cold war. I am not concerned here with the policies of the State Department and the Foreign Office, but with the conceptions which the British and American peoples have of their respective governments' foreign policies. For it is these popularised simplifications of national policy which create the atmosphere in which civil liberties must be discussed. The area of general American agreement, it seems to me, covers the following three concepts: (1) that the enemy we face is a world-wide, highly organised conspiracy, led by Moscow; (2) that the Communist parties inside the Western democracies are fifth columns, organised by the Russians, and that their members are either conscious traitors, deliberately serving the interests of the Kremlin, or dupes whose muddleheadedness is no excuse for the fact that they are indulging in treasonable activities; and (3) that any equivocation by an American citizen about the nature of Communism and any inclination to tolerate Communist activities is to be regarded as evidence of his disloyalty.

These three concepts would, I think, be accepted by most Americans, including liberals. Yet in Britain they would be regarded as hysterical and unsound not only by Liberals and Socialists but also by many Conservatives. Many Englishmen, for instance, outside the Labour party ask themselves whether it is not a dangerous over-simplification to assume that the major premise of our foreign policy must be the containment of Communism. Certainly we must oppose the extension of the Stalinite empire. But are all Communists Stalinites? Yugoslavia, for instance, is still most certainly a one-party Communist state. Then why, if our aim is the containment of Communism, does the United States give Tito substantial military aid? Or, to take an even more controversial case, is it correct to assume that Mao Tse-tung and Chou En-lai are mere agents of the Kremlin? Surely it is at least arguable that the analysis made by the 'old China hands' in the State Department and the Foreign Office just after the war was not based on any fellow-traveller's delusions but on a shrewd appreciation of the facts. Here in Britain (where a Conservative government, despite American pressure, still refuses to de-recognise the Peking government), it is not only fellow-travellers who remember the futile and fatal results of armed intervention against the Soviet Union after World War I. As a people, we are unwilling to repeat in China the precedent we then set with such disastrous results. We can understand why the American people, who were far more deeply and tragically engaged in Korea than we, demand of their leaders an unequivocal attitude, which identifies Chinese and Russian Communism as one single totalitarian conspiracy directed from the Kremlin. But here in Britain only a small minority, neither vociferous nor respectable, shares this view. Partly, no doubt, because of our vital economic interests in Hong Kong and Malaya, we are inclined to treat the 'tough' line advocated by so many Americans as a dangerous oversimplification. We fear that, if it is followed to its logical end, it can only produce the expulsion of Western influence from South-east Asia and possibly from the Indian sub-continent too. Is it not possible, we ask ourselves, that the relations of Peking and Moscow are analogous, on the other side of the Iron Curtain, to those of Britain and the United States? Those Englishmen, of all parties, who believe that this is possible claim no certainty for their view. What we do claim, for Americans as well as for ourselves, is the right to ask such questions without being charged with disloyalty.

The second reason why even Conservative Englishmen cannot accept unquestioningly the American concept of how to wage the cold war is the growth since 1900 of the British Labour party. Because there exists in Britain a powerful party, avowedly bent on social revolution yet undeniably democratic and patriotic, British public opinion is more ready than American to admit that in other countries too there may be Socialist and even Communist movements which are not simply parts of a Russian conspiracy. The world picture of the average American is painted in black and white. Ours is bound to include other colours as well. Hence our differing ideas of loyalty.

But this does not mean, as so many Americans suppose, that British Socialism stands half-way between Washington and Moscow and that its foreign policy can be fairly accused of trying to achieve an equidistant neutrality. The Labour party has always been un-equivocally opposed to Communism. Even during the Spanish civil war, when most American liberals favoured accepting Communists in an anti-Fascist front, the Labour party defeated all such proposals by huge majorities, and prevented anything approaching the systematic infiltration of the trade unions which took place in the United States under the New Deal. What I think is puzzling to an American is the fact that, whereas the Labour party has always opposed discrimination against Communists in the trade unions, this has not prevented it from treating the Communist party as an enemy. British Socialists see no inconsistency in fighting Communism at home and abroad, while simultaneously accepting Communists as fellow trade-unionists, as teachers, or as civil servants. Of course, there has always been a minority in both extremes of the Labour movement who denounce this as a weak compromise. The extremists of the Right, including some big trade union leaders, would accept the American concept of how to wage the cold war, while the extremists of the Left for many years have based their policy implicitly on Anglo-Russian collaboration. But both kinds of extremists have always remained small minorities in the Labour movement and, since the cold war began, both have dwindled almost as rapidly as the Communist party itself, which, despite the freedom it is given, now scarcely numbers fifty thousand.

My third explanation of the difference between the British and

American concepts of loyalty relates to changes which have taken place in the United States since 1945. The traditional neutrality of the United States was based on a firm and sometimes blind sense of security. Because Americans felt themselves safe, they believed they could afford to disregard power politics outside their hemisphere. Now they have swung from an extreme sense of security to an extreme sense of insecurity, from the assumption that America is threatened by no one to the assumption that everyone is her enemy who is not unequivocally on her side. We, on the other hand, have never in this century felt so insecure as the United States under neutrality, and we cannot therefore share the violent revulsion of feeling which Americans are experiencing today. Habituated to power-politics and insecurity, we do not assume that everyone is against us who is not for us. We tend to be sceptical of black-and-white definitions which divide the world into good allies and bad enemies; and we think twice before accepting an invitation to join any ideological crusade!

This scepticism of ideologies provides yet another reason for our tolerance of home-grown Communists and intolerance of any suggestion that their civil liberties should be curtailed. So long as we are not actually at war, we do not believe that it is sensible to treat *all* Communists as traitors, even though *some* of them are engaged in a conspiracy against us. When we measure the possible risk to Britain arising from a Communist party enjoying the freedom which it still enjoys against the actual harm brought about by strong counter-measures, we believe that the cure would be more dangerous than the disease.

Of course, if we were faced by a strong Communist party, with a real hold on the trade unions and the intelligentsia, we should think differently. I am certainly not prepared, for instance, to recommend our good-natured tolerance of the Communists to any Frenchman or Italian who asks for my advice. But in Britain and America the existence of a Communist party, along with its panoply of front organisations and fellow-travellers, presents no such imminent threat to liberty. Espionage is a matter for specialists to be dealt with by the security authorities, and there are good grounds for believing that their task is made more difficult when the Communist party is suppressed or driven underground. But, apart from espionage, the Communist conspiracy in both our countries has only a minor nuisance value. Why, then, should we take measures against it which set the most dangerous precedents in the violation of civil liberty? Why endanger our own freedoms to smash a conspiracy which only possesses the remotest chances of success?

The reply, no doubt, is that we must do so because the Communist party is admittedly not a part of democracy, but a conspiracy against it. It is true that inside each Communist party is a secret Russian apparatus, and that this is a conspiracy in the fullest sense of the word. But the vast majority of the members of a Western Communist party and of their fellow-travellers are not conspirators but misguided idealists. They have no idea how their idealism is being expoited and genuinely believe the myth that they constitute a Left-wing group. In my experience (I have had to fight Communists in Coventry since I first went there as a Labour candidate in 1937), most of them are young people who do not stay long in the party. Indeed, I calculate that the lapsed membership totals something like 25 per cent annually, and most of it comes back to the Labour party. So long, therefore, as the Communist party is tolerated, we are re-absorbing about a quarter of it annually into the free community as disgruntled ex-Communists, democrats who are none the worse for knowing something about the totalitarian enemy from personal disillusionment with his leadership. Indeed, in a strong and virile democracy the Communist party (though, of course, it constitutes a certain danger) also provides an inoculation against serious conspiratorial activity. Like any other inoculation it is worth taking—if your system can stand the shock. On the other hand, if you treat every Communist as a treasonable conspirator and start dismissing people for having once been Communists, you will merely persuade the disillusioned convert to stay in the party. Our method of treating Communists is not merely more humane than the American: it may also be more successful!

THE CONTROL OF PROPAGANDA

Whereas no official history of Psychological Warfare in World War II has been written, there is quite a library of semi-official American publications. This essay (after the normal Foreign Office vetting) first appeared in a volume by Daniel Lerner, entitled *Sykewar* (sic), in 1959.

1. PROPAGANDA AND DEMOCRACY

IN America and Britain, propaganda in peacetime has been an affair for political parties, pressure groups, and economic interests; and the democrat's demand of the State has been that it should safeguard his right to persuade other people, by a self-denying ordinance that it itself should not seek to persuade him. Only in wartime do we relax this principle, and permit the central authority to interfere in our controversies by censorship (negative psychological warfare), and by campaigns to raise the morale of our friends and to destroy that of our enemies (positive psychological warfare). Then, but only then, may the techniques employed previously in a democracy for selling goods and winning votes be used as an instrument of national self-assertion.

This liberal theory of propaganda survived to a remarkable degree in the period between the first and second world wars. Despite the rise, first of Communist Russia—with its ideology of world revolution and its apparatus of psychological warfare against external capitalism and internal sabotage—and, later, of Nazi Germany, which took over and vastly refined the Bolshevik techniques of mass persuasion, the democracies remained psychologically disarmed. The first German broadcast from London, for instance, took place a few days before Munich. It occurred to someone that it might be a good idea to let Germans hear the text of Mr. Chamberlain's broadcast to his fellow countrymen. A friend of mine, interrupted at dinner, was hastily summoned to Broadcasting House to translate Mr. Chamberlain's message and read it over the air. This was the beginning of the European Service of the BBC, which by 1945 had grown to be the most important psychological warfare instrument of the Anglo-American war effort. But in the autumn of 1938, neither Britain nor America felt any need to counter the Nazi and Communist psychological warfare by a government-controlled propaganda. 'Truth will prevail' was our motto, though most of us knew from our experience in commerce, journalism, or politics that truth rarely prevails when it cannot be heard.

It would be easy, now, amid the turmoil of ideological warfare, to dismiss the liberalism of earlier days as idealistic nonsense, and to repudiate the democratic opposition to state-controlled propaganda, along with President Wilson's dream of 'open covenants, openly arrived at.' But that would be throwing the baby out with the bath water. During the war, we discovered that truth is the best propaganda. Those who lose their integrity destroy themselves, if for no other reason than because they come to believe their own inventions; and that, as the Nazis found out too late, is the beginning of the end.

I write this as one who served as a propagandist for five long years, first as director of political warfare against the enemy in the Political Intelligence Department of the Foreign Office, and then as a member of the joint Anglo-American Psychological Warfare Section of General Eisenhower's Staff. Many of us were journalists or academics by profession, and at first we found the unrestricted use of the techniques of persuasion against an unseen enemy a fascinating and absorbing task. Freed from the limitations imposed by democracy, we were able to experiment with any and every black magic in the use of words which might help to 'save lives'; and we were provided—at least, toward the end of the war—with funds, staff, and material far beyond the means of any newspaper, advertising agency or political party. Here was a unique chance for what seemed to be a supremely interesting scientific experiment. We were equipped, so far as technical facilities went, to out-Goebbels Goebbels. As the campaign of 1944 progressed, and the Nazi Reich grew smaller and smaller, our radio transmitters, which in 1940 could scarcely whisper among the roar of the Nazi-controlled ether, shouted the ailing *Reichsrundfunk* down; and our specialized leaflet-carrying Fortresses, with their specialized leaflet-bombs, could pinpoint their propaganda targets virtually without hindrance. We were masters of the enemy mind—to do with it as Roosevelt and

Churchill willed. Why should we pull our punches, or be squeamish about our methods? This was total war. Our job was to demoralise the enemy, so that the Allied statesmen could pastoralise him at leisure.

Yet, remarkably enough, we did pull our punches and we remained squeamish. Indeed, the longer we stayed on the job, and the more professional we became, the greater our squeamishness. It was the occasional V.I.P. from Whitehall or the Pentagon, blowing in to give us a bright idea for winning the war by a single propaganda stunt, who succumbed to Satan.

I will only give two examples, which stick obstinately in my memory. The first occurred during the stalemate winter of 1944. We had been preparing the German mind for the Allied advance into Germany. Since high policy forbade any modification of 'unconditional surrender', we had decided to build up the personality of the Supreme Commander, and step by step to persuade both the German civilian and the German soldier to accept his orders instead of those of Himmler and Hitler. Day in, day out, by radio and leaflet, German soldiers had been informed that 'the way back home lies through the prisoner-of-war camp', and had been shown in photographic detail the comfort and security which really was being given to prisoners of war. Simultaneously, the civilian was being instructed in the Military Government regulations under which he should live when our armies reached the area of his home. If the soldier surrendered precisely according to the instructions which we gave him, and if the civilian obeyed the orders of Military Government, General Eisenhower would see to it that no evil would come to them. Better, therefore, when the great advance began, to 'stay put' than to do as the Nazi radio advised and withdraw into the centre of Germany, where the final Armageddon would take place.

It was a good campaign for several reasons. In the first place, we were telling, as is very rarely possible in wartime, the truth, the whole truth, and nothing but the truth. Our instructions on how to surrender with the minimum of personal risk were accurate; our description of Military Government regulations precise; our build-up of the Supreme Commander not exaggerated. Equally important, this campaign served a very important military purpose—to keep the civilians off the roads, where they would block the advancing armies, and to preserve German manpower to work in the coal mines, the factories, and the fields, and so reduce the problems of occupation.

During one of the smaller initial offensives on the west of the Rhine, a very important person visited S.H.A.E.F., and read in the *Stars and Stripes* of the instructions being issued by radio to the German civilians that they should keep off the roads. 'What nonsense!' he said to the Supreme Commander. 'Why be soft to the Germans? Your job is to stimulate disorder and to block the retreat of the German armies by the methods they used against the French in 1940.'

That night we received orders to reverse our whole propaganda campaign. I shall never forget the blackness of our despair. We realised that, if we carried out the very important person's 'stunt', we should be breaking what had become a solemn pledge by the Supreme Commander to the German people, and so undermining his authority with them. We also realised, I think, that militarily such a step would be of doubtful value, since our soldiers, unlike the Germans in France, would not shoot down helpless civilians, and the crowding of the roads would therefore obstruct our armies more than those of the enemy. Finally, we could not help remembering the indignations expressed in the name of democracy when the Nazis used these techniques four years previously.

The Chief of Staff, General Bedell Smith, was called in, as he always was in real crisis. 'Do something—one single thing—to satisfy the Old Man,' he said, 'and use your brains to ensure that it doesn't contradict or undermine our main campaign.'

How we got out of the difficulty is not relevant here. What is important to observe is that the professional propagandists had discovered by the spring of 1945 that stunts do not pay. This particular one was proposed by a politician, who treated psychological warfare as a 'war game', and not as what it really was—the imposition of the Allied will on the German mind.

My second example comes not from the campaign of which Dr. Lerner writes, but from the Mediterranean. I give it here because it illustrates so aptly the moral which I wish to draw. For six weeks, during the summer of 1943, the Italian armistice negotiations had been dragging on while the Sicilian campaign was wound up. As each day passed, the German strength in Italy increased. When Mussolini fell, at the end of July, there were only two or

three divisions in the northern plains; we could have landed anywhere without resistance if we had had the landing barges. But by
the end of August, when operation 'Avalanche' was only a few
days off, fourteen divisions had streamed in, and Kesselring, by
a simple calculation of the range of our fighters, could guess that
our landing would have to be near Salerno. When Field Marshal
Alexander talked to the propagandists in his Headquarters in Sicily,
he said tersely, 'I have never faced a worse situation, militarily:
I have to rely on you.'

Unless the Germans could be prevented from throwing all their
available divisions in to defeat the landing, its failure seemed certain.
Only one thing could stop them—a situation throughout Italy so
serious that some of their troops would have to be used during
the crucial days after September 6th for guarding the lines of
communication. This is why the armistice became a matter of first-
rate strategic importance. Its announcement was timed for 6.30
p.m. on the evening before the Salerno landing. This was to be
the signal for an American paratroop division to take off from
Sicily for airfields near Rome, where they would be met by Italian
transport and employed, with four Italian divisions, to split the
German Army in half. At 6 o'clock on the next morning, the dis-
embarkations on the beaches would begin.

Our special problem was how to 'authenticate' the armistice
announcement. If it were simply put out over the Algiers Radio
and picked up by London and Washington, it might be considered
a fake, in which case the Italian Army would immediately be available to throw us off the beaches at Salerno. What was required,
to convince both the Italians and the Germans that Italy had really
changed sides, was a speech delivered by Badoglio over the Rome
Radio. Such a speech might, for a few days at least, produce the
confusion necessary to secure a firm lodgment.

It was on this basis that the final arrangements were made with
the Italian General Castellano in a secret conference in a Sicilian
olive grove. We took the precaution of requesting that the text of
Badoglio's speech should be sent to us in good time; but otherwise
we relied completely on the Italians to carry out their side of the
bargain.

The morning of the 6th in Algiers was, as usual, clammy with a
cloudy heat. Owing to the need for secrecy, no advance texts of
the armistice announcements could be sent to London and Washing-

ton. They would have to take their cue from Algiers, where our Anglo-American propaganda team would have its first real test. Apart from General McClure, only two of us, C. D. Jackson and I, with our two secretaries, were in on the secret. The rest of the staff were to be briefed at 5.15 p.m. At midday, the General sent for Jackson and me and informed us that a message had been received from Rome. Everything was off; the airborne division could not land; Badoglio could not broadcast. The Chief of Staff wanted to know immediately our recommendations for action.

We had only a few minutes to prepare our minds for the conference. General Eisenhower was at Tunis; communications with London and Washington took so long that it was impossible to obtain advice from there. The decision had to be made in Algiers by those who happened to be there.

One of the soldiers began by asking whether Badoglio's voice could be simulated. The reply was, 'Probably yes. It would be most unlikely, since reception was so bad, that anyone would notice, except, of course, Badoglio himself.' Then the advice of the psychological warfare staff was asked. One of us said, 'What we have to do is to put ourselves in Badoglio's skin and forget that he's a "yellow Iti". If we fake his broadcast, he will have precisely the justification for cowardice which he wants. We must treat him as a gentleman and shame him into changing his mind.' 'What do you mean?' asked the General. 'We must go on the air at 6.30 and give just sufficient details about the negotiations to implicate him and his staff. Then we must say that it had been foreseen that the Germans might prevent him from putting out an announcement from Rome, and that it had therefore been agreed between the Italians and ourselves that, if this occurred, Badoglio's message should be read aloud over the Algiers Radio. That is our only chance of persuading him to broadcast it.' One of the soldiers observed that there would be no harm in letting the propagandists have a try, and the conference broke up.

For the next three hours we frantically redrafted the announcements. We knew that we were bluffing, since the Italians had actually called the whole armistice off. At 6.30 we went on the air, first with Eisenhower's message, then with our lengthy explanation of the circumstances of the negotiations, and then with Badoglio's message, read by an announcer. An hour later, while we were sitting at dinner, a monitor came in and stated that Badoglio was on the air, reading his message over the Rome Radio. So we had shamed him into it, after all.

These two stories, in their different ways, illustrate the basic principles of psychological warfare, as it was practised by the Anglo-American armies throughout the Normandy campaign: (a) honesty is overwhelmingly the best policy; and (b) if you want to achieve results, you must get inside the other fellow's skin, feel his feelings and think his thoughts. In so far as our psychological warfare was successful, this was because it successfully combined these two basic principles. When it failed, it was because we disregarded them and tried short-cuts.

2. DID 'UNCONDITIONAL SURRENDER' PREVENT AN EFFECTIVE PSYCHOLOGICAL WARFARE?

A people subjected exclusively to one totalitarian propaganda machine is mentally numb, whereas, when two propaganda machines are fighting it out, the controversy between them automatically releases at least a minority from the enslavement of the mind. Just as controversy is the lifeblood of democracy, so it is the poison of dictatorship, and it was the controversy between the Goebbels and the Anglo-American propaganda machines which kept occupied Europe intellectually alive from 1940 to 1944. We had won half our propaganda battle long before D-Day in Normandy, by the simple fact that we had compelled Goebbels to conduct a day-and-night battle with us in the hearing of his slaves. Having broken his monopoly, the next task was to win the confidence of Europe.

Between 1940 and 1942, we had tried every device of Nazi and Communist propaganda and a good many others which the totalitarians had never thought of; but we returned, in the end, to the conclusion that, even by the strictest standards of military expediency, the most effective weapons for demoralising a totalitarian enemy are truthfulness and integrity. If, in a leaflet or a broadcast, the propagandist deliberately deceives a soldier, it will be discovered sooner or later, and then that soldier will not trust the armies enough to surrender when the moment comes. If a civilian in enemy country catches the B.B.C. suppressing the truth over the air, he will have that much less confidence in the Military Government officials when they arrive. Terror propaganda may have its short-term uses in achieving tactical success against half-demoralised peoples, like the French in 1940 or the Italians in 1942, but the long-term problems which tactical terror propaganda presents to the occupying forces easily outweigh its short-term advantages; and, in the case at least of British and Germans, even the short-term terror propaganda—and for that matter terror bombing—did not produce collapse, but actually stiffened resistance. Whether by intent or no, the propagandist builds up a picture of the nation or group of nations for whom he speaks. He creates behind the enemy lines either good will or bad will for the fighting soldiers who will ultimately decide the issue.

The austere objectivity of our psychological warfare not only was due to considerations of military expediency—it was also a direct consequence of Allied policy to Germany. In the first world war, propaganda had been constructive; its purpose had been the overthrow of the Kaiser's regime by a democratic revolution. In the second world war, psychological warfare had no such positive programme. There were no Fourteen Points, and no promises, explicit or implicit, of any benefits which the Germans would enjoy if they transformed their country into a democracy. The policy of 'unconditional surrender' ruled out any attempt to divide the enemy and to rally 'good Germans' against the regime. No overt encouragement could be given to opposition groups. The German Officers' Corps, for instance, from which was drawn the nucleus of the conspiracy of July 20th, was explicitly named as jointly responsible for Hitlerism and, despite constant and urgent requests from the conspirators, this identification of Nazism and militarism was never modified.

On two occasions—the first in April, and the second in August, 1944—General Eisenhower, on the advice both of his psychological warfare and political staffs, sought to persuade the President and the Prime Minister to modify the harshness of 'unconditional surrender'. On the first occasion, a few weeks before D-Day, the case was set out at length in a staff study. This argued that German resistance in Normandy could be considerably weakened if, at an early date, the Supreme Commander were permitted, speaking as soldier to soldier, to inform the German armies of the steps which commanding officers could and should take to avoid a continuance of the useless slaughter. It was assumed that, on the high political level, 'unconditional surrender' would remain the Allied policy; but it was urged that, since no surrender could actually take place unconditionally, common sense demanded the military definition of the terms of surrender. The Secretary of State, Mr. Stettinius, was in London at the time, and agreed to put the S.H.A.E.F. point of view to the President. On April 17th, the reply was received that the President wished that the subject should be given no further consideration without his approval. A second attempt was made towards the end of August, but once again it was vetoed by the President.

How strictly the policy of 'unconditional surrender' was enforced in Psychological Warfare is illustrated by an incident which occurred in October 1944. At that time an offensive against the Saar was being planned, and S.H.A.E.F. regarded it as vitally necessary to persuade the miners to remain at work after the withdrawal of the German armies. P.W.D. was called in to assist and, after discussion with those responsible for Military Government, we drafted an official announcement that all those miners who 'stayed put' would continue to receive existing rates of pay and be permitted to organise Trade Unions. This announcement contained nothing more than the Military Government regulations which would be enforced immediately after the area was occupied. State Department and Foreign Office representatives, however, were so nervous about violating 'unconditional surrender' that they raised the objection that this draft announcement contained a promise to a section of the German people and so transgressed the bounds of high policy. When the issue could not be settled inside S.H.A.E.F., it was referred to Washington. The objection was sustained by Washington and the matter dropped.

Whether 'unconditional surrender' was or was not a wise policy is a question which falls outside my theme. The job of psychological warfare is not to make policy, but to work within its limitations. Surprisingly enough, we found more room for manoeuvre than might have been expected. The Germans had been deeply impregnated with scepticism about Anglo-Saxon promises, and Goebbels almost daily reminded them of the turpitude of the failure to fulfil the pledges implicit in President Wilson's Fourteen Points. Long before the Normandy campaign, we had discovered, while trying to 'sell' the Atlantic Charter, how effective this German counter-propaganda had been. It is by no means certain, therefore, that our appeal to the German people would have been greatly strengthened if we had been able to make use of precise promises about the treatment to be accorded to Germany if Nazism were overthrown. On the other hand, the refusal to permit the Supreme Commander to state the terms and methods of military surrender certainly decreased the readiness of German commanders in the field to surrender, and so quite needlessly prolonged the war.

Because Psychological Warfare could promise nothing, it was compelled to rely exclusively on two themes: (a) the inevitability of Allied victory, and (b) the integrity and decency of the democratic world, in contrast with the corruption and untrustworthiness of the Nazi leaders. The Germans were presented with the alternatives of unconditional surrender to Anglo-Saxon mercy and justice, or continued resistance. Partly because no promises were made, this contrast gained in persuasiveness, once it became clear that a German victory was impossible. A Germany impregnated with Nazism, paradoxically enough, was more inclined to trust an enemy who promised nothing, and told the stark truth with a soldierly objectivity, than 'a Greek bearing gifts'. To this extent, the limitations imposed by high policy became a positive advantage.

But when we entered Germany, we found that, though Psychological Warfare had scrupulously fulfilled its policy directive, it had nevertheless committed the Allies in one important respect. By telling the objective truth, and building an impression in the German mind of Anglo-Saxon honesty and integrity, it had brought the enemy to expect a standard of behaviour on the part of troops and officials which in practice it was very difficult to maintain. Millions of Germans had learnt to know intimately the personalities who had spoken to them day by day over the radio, and the isolation of black listening had made the contact between the remote radio voice and the German audience extremely intimate. The promise of fair treatment and democratic decency had been implicit in all our propaganda output, though on no occasion had any explicit promise been made; and the contrast between the unseen personalities of the B.B.C. and the real behaviour of the occupying forces made many friendly Germans believe that a pledge had been actually broken. This belief would have been far *more* widespread and justifiable if 'unconditional surrender' had been modified.

3. DEMOCRATIC AND NAZI PROPAGANDA TECHNIQUES

It is often naively assumed that, whereas Goebbels lied, we spoke the truth, and that this constituted a real difference in technique. Such an assumption is an oversimplification. It is, of course, of vital importance to a propagandist that he expose the enemy as a liar, so as to reduce confidence in his word. By selecting and repeating *ad nauseam* German boasts which had not come true, and German promises which had not been fulfilled, we succeeded in achieving this object. Throughout the campaign, a very large part of our radio and leaflet output was devoted to discrediting the Nazi leadership by making it clear that the leaders were propagandists, whereas we were just telling the truth as we saw it. We were greatly assisted in this by Goebbels' assumption of the title of Minister of Propaganda as far back as 1933, and by his ingenuous taste for displaying his talents in public. The propagandist who asserts that he 'can play on the public mind as on a piano' is a conceited amateur. If he *can* do so, it is his prime object to conceal his skill from the public and to appear always as a simple man, telling the simple truth.

It is not my impression that German propaganda was guilty of many deliberate lies. In wartime, mistakes about matters of fact are inevitable in any news service, and the enemy always exposes them as lies. During 1940 and 1941, R.A.F. communiques about bomb damage in Germany were often fantastically inaccurate, claiming, for instance, that a town had been heavily damaged, when the bombs had fallen many miles away. I have no doubt that the German propagandists were sincere enough in accusing us of lying when we published those communiques. But, in reality, we just didn't know the truth. In the same way, most of the German lies, which we successfully 'nailed', were probably sheer mistakes, just as most of the German promises which, as we daily reminded the listeners, had failed to come true, were due to the ineptness of politicians. Goering was not knavish but foolish when he once stated in a speech that not a bomb would fall on the Ruhr, and so was Hitler, in October, 1941, when he announced the final collapse of the Bolshevists. But they provided us with the material we required for proving that the Nazis lied; and we used these broken promises, year in, year out, till every German knew them by heart. There is every likelihood that Goebbels, the arch propagandist, was furious when such statements were made. He was far too able a man to make silly propaganda 'commitments' or to perpetuate small lies deliberately. He understood that, if you want to put over a big lie, the way to do it is to be as scrupulously accurate as possible about the small facts.

Where the Germans differed from us was not in their means, but in their ends. The Nazis really believed that the Germans were a *Herrenvolk*, with the right to dominate the world; that democracy was an expression of decaying capitalism, and civil liberty a relic of a decadent bourgeois civilization; that the Soviet Union was simply a Mongolian despotism, and Communism a disease; that the Slavs were natural slaves and the Jews vermin, fit only for extirpation. The real lie of which Goebbels was guilty was the attempt to conceal from the rest of Europe the implications of the *Herrenvolk* idea. This led him into a maze of contradictions in his psychological warfare. Though he believed, for instance, that the French were decadent, he had to pretend, for a time, that France was a centre of civilisation. To a lesser extent, we suffered a similar embarrassment. The directive that we should treat Communists as fellow democrats laid us open to a line of attack which Goebbels was able to exploit to the full, particularly in relation to such countries as Yugoslavia and Poland.

Indeed, one of the most remarkable features of wartime propaganda was the inability displayed, both on our side and on the enemy's, to cover up deeply felt convictions for reasons of tactical expediency. Truth will out. The Nazi who desired to appear respectable, merely disclosed a hypocritical shiftiness. The democrat, by the very vociferousness of his pro-Russian sentiments, revealed the inner conflict between East and West. In so far as propaganda was used in an attempt to conceal real intentions, it usually exposed them. Cleverness defeated itself. We were fortunate because we began our psychological warfare in 1940, when we had nothing to lose by telling the truth and revealing our innermost convictions. Goebbels became a first-rate propagandist only in the last twelve months of the war. When Germany was faced with destruction, he advocated 'blood, tears, and sweat', underlining the bad news in red ink and rallying his supporters with a fanatical self-revelation. But by then it was too late.

Once the distinction between means and ends is clear, the fact that the techniques of psychological warfare did not vary from country to country appears almost self-evident. In this respect, psychological warfare does not differ from other forms of warfare. The use of verbal missiles, just as much as artillery or aircraft, is governed by general rules which apply to all participants in total war, irrespective of the ultimate political object for which they are employed.

4. TRUTH AND CREDIBILITY

Psychological warfare is only one part of propaganda. It is not concerned with home morale, or with public relations with friendly countries, but exclusively with enemy and enemy-occupied countries. It is therefore intrinsically aggressive in character, and can be fully effective only when combined with a military offensive. From 1940 until the landings in Sicily, we had tried to use it defensively. During this period it had a negligible effect in Germany, and was valuable only in keeping alive resistance groups in occupied Europe. But even here it would have been quite ineffective without an assurance that sooner or later the Army of Liberation was coming; and premature 'successes' like the 'Colonel Britain' campaign were highly embarrassing to the Chiefs of Staff, because they raised hopes of an early landing in France, which could not possibly be fulfilled.

The real justification for psychological warfare in this period was that the staffs engaged were learning both the techniques and the nature of the organisation required. By the time of the Normandy landings, we had made most of the mistakes it was possible to make; and, largely as the result of our experiences in North Africa, we had constructed a machine expressly designed to make mistakes unlikely. In the second place, we had, during this period, established a reputation for objectivity and integrity by a calculated policy of admitting defeats—if possible before the Germans announced them —and we had learned to tone down or even suppress news, even if we believed it to be true, which would sound incredible to people living under Nazi rule.

This latter point is of considerable importance. Propaganda, to be effective, must be not only factually true, but credible. In enemy-occupied territory we had two audiences, motivated by precisely opposite emotions—our friends, whose hopes made them intensely credulous of good news; and our enemies, ready to dismiss as

'*Feindpropaganda*' even the most sober statement of an Allied success. Whether on the radio or in leaflet form, the same news had to be selected and presented so as to appear objective to both these audiences, the credulous friend and the sceptical enemy. This demanded a tremendous effort of *empathy*, not merely feeling *with* the listener, but feeling *into* his emotions, so as to avoid statements and forms of presentations which would create hostility and suspicion.

There is no doubt that in this respect Anglo-American propaganda outclassed all its rivals. The totalitarian State, by its very nature, is unable to understand its opponents. It believes them to be the caricature which they appear in its propaganda. In a democracy, so long as objectivity is not regarded as subversive, the enemy can be understood as he really is. A very large section of our Psychological Warfare staff was devoted to 'consumer research', a scrupulously scientific attempt to 'get inside the enemy's skin' or, alternatively, to get inside the skin of a friend living under conditions remote from our own. Our propaganda staffs, by their training, became far more objective in their estimate of enemy morale than the politicians and civil servants who laid down policy; and one important by-product of Psychological Warfare, both in the State Department and in the Foreign Office, was the supply of 'psychological warfare intelligence', which attempted to correct the 'propaganda picture' of the enemy current in London and Washington.

This stress on *empathy* meant that output became more and more specialised in the various language sections. A Churchill speech or a Roosevelt fireside chat would be cut and arranged quite differently for a German, French, or Norwegian audience, because it was felt that the truth would not seem truthful to different audiences unless it were presented to each in the way best calculated to make its message intelligible.

It very soon became apparent that this specialising of appeal had its dangers. It is a short step from *empathy* to appeasement, from persuasive presentation to unconscious misrepresentation. This could be avoided only by a constant and most fruitful conflict between the various sections of the psychological warfare machine, stretching all the way from Washington and London to the combat loudspeakers in the front line. The executants, who were charged with actually putting the propaganda out, were concerned with achieving results within their narrow field, to produce, for instance, in this particular

German division in the Ardennes, a state of mind conducive to surrender. The policymakers, far away in the rear, were struggling to preserve at all costs conformity with high policy and a minimum uniformity of outlook. It was one of the accidental advantages of our complex and unwieldy psychological warfare machine that in this controversy no one had the final word. The B.B.C., for instance, always remained independent of the P.I.D. of the Foreign Office. O.S.S. was at loggerheads with O.W.I. The S.H.A.E.F. staff, who ran Radio Luxembourg in almost open rivalry with the B.B.C., exploited to the full the delicate balance of power between 12th Army Group, in whose area they operated, S.H.A.E.F. in Paris, and the far away policymakers of Washington and London. The leaflet teams, forward with the combat troops, were each responsible to an Army H.Q., itself responsible to an Army Group, which in turn was bound by a S.H.A.E.F. directive derived from an O.W.I.-P.I.D. overall directive, ground out at the highest policy level and in the most generalised terms. At each level, a considerable degree of independence was retained, which permitted friction, harassing at the time, but fruitful in its effect on the output. Our propaganda was constantly in danger of disintegrating into a chaos of conflicting specialised appeals for special purposes—sometimes, indeed, it did so—but this danger was far preferable to the dreary uniformity and lifelessness which the Russians so successfully imposed on their propaganda machine. Theoretically, this lack of system and individualism was utterly intolerable; apart from its other defects, it caused a most wasteful overstaffing at all levels. But the product, in the peculiar conditions of Anglo-American teamwork, was remarkably successful. Our psychological warfare was credible because it was *not* uniform. If the State Department and the Foreign Office had had their way, they would have caused us to be dismissed, by friend and foe alike, as blatant propagandists, and so destroyed our reputation for truthfulness and objectivity.

5. PROPAGANDA 'DIRECTIVES' AND 'TIMING'

The problem was how to combine extreme diversity in the methods of expression with adherence to an overall line which faithfully expressed Allied policy. We soon found that this could not be achieved by the mere issuing of directives. A propaganda directive is either so general as to be valueless, or so detailed that it is invalidated by events before it has been distributed. Directives were, of course, issued regularly. But, from the point of view of the active executant, their chief function was to provide a cover from interference by the policymakers. The higher the official, the more he likes a directive, and the less he peers below it to study the actual output. But every now and then there is a complaint. The high official demands to see the full text—in an English translation !—of the offending leaflet or broadcast. It is then that the directive becomes invaluable. If skilfully drafted, it provides a justification for the man on the job, which prevents interference by the policymakers, whose excessive caution on some occasions and wild stunting on others are inevitably a menace to serious and continuous work.

The speeches of Roosevelt and Churchill were by far the best directives we got. To a very great extent our work consisted of the selection and repetition of passages from their speeches, and of weaving variations on the themes which these two voices introduced from time to time. A speech, however important, is soon forgotten unless its central theme and its key sentences are endlessly repeated in every medium of propaganda.

But obviously we could not rely on the Prime Minister or the President to make a statement on each of the multitude of secondary problems which arose in the course of the campaign in the West. To deal with them, we invented 'The Voice of S.H.A.E.F.' The 'Colonel Britain' campaign in 1941 had been an early experiment in this medium of propaganda. But Colonel Britain's messages to the resistance movement in Europe had been 'pure propaganda'. They were not geared to any strategic plan. 'The Voice of S.H.A.E.F.', on the other hand, was a deliberate and most carefully prepared projection of General Eisenhower's strategy. Before D-Day, a whole series of 'Instructions to Resistance Movements' was issued by radio and leaflet. Despite their name and appearance, they were not designed as orders to the active leaders of resistance—such orders were, of course, transmitted by other means. The purpose of these 'instructions' was to indoctrinate the populations of enemy-occupied countries, who were *not* under the discipline of the resistance movements, and in particular to restrain them from unorganised sabotage, which might disastrously obstruct military operations. 'The Voice of S.H.A.E.F' was sometimes misleadingly described as 'operational propaganda'. As a matter of fact, operational instructions were never given over the radio or in leaflets, except in code. The purpose of

'The Voice of S.H.A.E.F.' was entirely psychological—to create the state of mind among civilians in occupied countries required for the various stages of the campaign.

When the invasion of Germany began, 'The Voice of S.H.A.E.F.' was directed more and more to the Germans. A series of instructions was issued to German civilians, to German soldiers, and to displaced persons. The aim was twofold: (1) if possible, to ensure that the instructions were carried out, at least by a minority of those who received them; (2) to create among the less friendly elements of the population the impression that such instructions were being carried out by others, and so to demoralise them.

In developing this strategic propaganda, we discovered the importance of accurate timing. A propaganda stunt, however brilliant, can have a disastrous effect if it is launched prematurely. In this work, the 'psychological moment' was not a trite phrase but a precise description of what we had to aim at. One ineffective or badly timed piece of propaganda cancels out the effect of months of patient, successful work. It was soon discovered that correct timing demands advance knowledge by the psychological warfare staff of the full details of military operations, and the closest liaison with all the various Staff sections involved. This is one reason why, during the campaign in the West, the day-to-day direction of Psychological Warfare gradually shifted from London and Washington to S.H.A.E.F., which became the central point from which military requirements were transmitted upward to London and Washington, and policy requirements were transmitted downward to the Army Groups and Armies.

Two examples of successful timing will illustrate the methods developed in the campaign in the West. A few hours after the German offensive in the Ardennes began, the first conferences took place to prepare the leaflets which would accompany the Allied counteroffensive. A series of four leaflets was composed and twenty million copies printed while the Germans were still advancing, each leaflet to be dropped at a set phase of our counteroffensive. This work was done by the S.H.A.E.F. staff, working in the closest collaboration with both 12th and 21st Army Groups. To prepare such a series of leaflets was possible only owing to the very precise advance knowledge provided to the S.H.A.E.F. staff. This could not possibly have been disclosed to those directing policy in London or Washington.

Another interesting example of advanced planning was the S.H.A.E.F. instruction 'To German Units out of Contact with a Higher Command'. This 'Voice of S.H.A.E.F.', ultimately used in radio and leaflet form, bluntly ordered German units, which could no longer obtain orders from their own side, to maintain their cohesion, and told them how to make an organised unit surrender. It was drafted, along with other instructions, during the stalemate winter of 1944, and millions of copies were printed and distributed to all our Psychological Warfare units. Then we waited for the psychological moment. Used too early—that is, before the demoralisation of the German Army had reached a point where such an instruction would no longer seem to be a bluff—the effect would have been disastrous. On the other hand, if we had waited until the demoralisation was complete, the propaganda would have been nugatory. By keeping a curve of the morale of freshly taken prisoners on various sections of the front, it was possible to avoid these two mistakes of 'too soon' and 'too late'. The instruction was used with success some weeks before the German surrender.

The one propaganda weapon which needed no timing was the *Passierschein* a surrender pass leaflet promising safety to any German who showed it to an Allied soldier. Very early in the war, crude 'safe-conduct passes' were used by both sides. By 1944, the *Passierschein* had become almost a work of art. A great deal of detailed market research was done to perfect it. It was found that a particular shade of green was the most persuasive colour (possibly because a green *Passierschein* had the authenticity of a 'greenback'); that the text should not be printed only in German, but in parallel German, English, and French columns; and, most important of all, that it must have the signature of the Supreme Commander. The test of its efficiency was not how many Germans actually waved a *Passierschein* when they surrendered, but how many kept a *Passierschein* because it might come in useful. The mere fact that a German soldier hid a *Passierschein* in his pocket was a tiny but important psychological concession to Allied victory.

6. MEDIA

Radio is infinitely the most effective form of strategic propaganda, if we use 'strategic' in the same sense as in the phrase 'strategic bombing'. Its peculiar power is its intimacy. By making 'black listening' a crime, the Germans had already given to us an enormous advantage. Any German, Nazi or anti-Nazi, with a natural curiosity to hear both sides, was branded as a criminal, and so forced into a form of private conspiracy with the enemy. Soon a sense of dependence on the Anglo-American radio was created, not only in the occupied countries but in Germany itself; and this often grew into a devotion to the B.B.C. and the personalities who spoke on it, all the stronger for its forbidden intimacy. Through this medium, once securely established, it was possible to impose the Allied will on the enemy mind. Even though only a small minority might have listened regularly, that minority, feeling itself 'in the know', spread the news to all the rest.

The leaflet had a far more restricted use. Even after the invention of the leaflet bomb and the formation of special leaflet squadrons, it remained a relatively ineffective instrument of strategic propaganda. Its proper use was for soldiers with no access to radio and often starved of reading matter, in the front line. We found that the 'Leaflet Fortresses' based on Britain could efficiently reinforce the forward teams in precision work on small sectors of the front. Printing facilities back in Britain were far better, and greater quantities could be dropped by the Fortress squadrons. The earlier division between strategic and tactical leaflet-bombing therefore tended to disappear. Once we had developed an organization through which the requirements of an Army could be passed via S.H.A.E.F. to P.I.D.-O.W.I. units in London, efficient staff work made it possible to lay on a tactical leaflet raid at forty-eight hours' notice on a single German division by the British-based Fortresses. So too, the daily leaflet newspaper for the German troops could be specially slanted to suit the requirements of one sector of the front and dropped exclusively upon it. Such refinements of tactical propaganda are obviously impossible on the radio, which is heard by everyone.

Whether in a leaflet or on the radio, we found that *news should always take priority over views*. The more hostile the audience, the more rigorously must this Golden Rule of psychological warfare be enforced. A very friendly listener in an enemy-occupied country may tolerate a certain amount of the direct exhortation which most politicians assume to be the natural form of propaganda. But 'uplift' soon palls, especially under the nervous conditions of 'black listening'. As Camus has reminded us, in his brilliant study of the psychology of an occupied country, *The Plague*, it is almost impossible for a writer or broadcaster to 'tune in' to the mood of the 'black listener'. A direct emotional appeal may offend even the staunchest ally, while an enemy audience reacts against it as obvious propaganda.

By the end of the war, even the Russians had begun to realise that impersonal and unemotional news must be the main vehicle of psychological warfare, and that news selection is the discipline in which the propagandist must be trained, including the 'layout' of a leaflet and the ordering of the items in a newscast.

In this respect, the technique of propaganda is the same as that of popular journalism, with the difference that the public addressed is considerably more sceptical and critical in its attitude. Paradoxically, the propagandist must achieve a considerably higher standard of objectivity and conform more strictly to the canons of 'straight news' than the journalist in a democracy. There is little doubt, for instance, that throughout the war our German newscasts were more objective and sober in their treatment of news than any British or American newspaper. They had to be, since the listener was comparing them day by day with the German version, eager to catch us in attempts to deceive him.

Emotional appeals, therefore, and exhortations had to be introduced indirectly by apparently accidental juxtaposition of contrasting news items, and by the systematic *weighting* of newscasts and news sheets with items illustrating certain themes. 'News creation' was an important part of our task. This did not, of course, involve the invention of news items, but the collection of facts to sustain certain themes and the rewriting of them so that they sounded or read like 'hot news'. The art of the news editor was to build his bulletin or lay out his news sheet so that these 'propaganda nuggets' merged into the neutral items. Day by day he had to judge his public, and in particular its ability to digest propaganda without ill effects. The more hostile the audience, the smaller the dose and the more carefully he had to administer it. His art was to conceal the fact that any artifice had been employed.

Once 'objectivity' has been established by the predominance of 'straight' news, a certain amount of 'views' can be added. Here we found that comment and exhortation became more palatable, the more personally they were presented. The B.B.C. built up a carefully balanced team of named 'personality' speakers in all its language services. In the German service, to avoid the hostility attaching to emigrés, we all had strong British or American accents, and gave individual comments on the news from varying political standpoints. Naturally, disagreements were calculated, not accidental. The inhabitant of a totalitarian state craves for individualism as well as objectivity, and this craving was met to some extent by the 'personality' commentator.

Our most difficult task was to insure that the B.B.C. as such, or the leaflet newspaper as a newspaper, did not appear to be addressing or cajoling its public. Even the speeches of Roosevelt and Churchill and the 'Voice of S.H.A.E.F.' were presented as impersonally as possible, as 'news of views', rather than as direct appeals to the listener. In this way he was given the feeling that he was being allowed to make up his own mind and feel his own emotions.

Another cover for propaganda is, of course, entertainment. But here the dangers of 'black listening' and 'black reading' must be borne in mind. The public in a totalitarian country listens through heavy jamming and with a constant sense of insecurity. This is strong even in the case of reading a leaflet. Any waste of words is infuriating, therefore, to anyone living in such conditions. But, with this proviso, entertainment is a valuable narcotic for dulling the sensibilities of a propaganda-conscious mind. A subversive thought can be instilled even into a Nazi mind, under the cover of laughter; and a news sheet which features the legs of a film star will be kept even by an S.S. man; sooner or later he may read some of the letterpress.

We found also, particularly in the case of soldiers on the Atlantic Wall, that radio programmes chiefly devoted to light music were not switched off when the bulletin began, so long as the first items did not sound like enemy propaganda. Even if the soldier tried not to listen, he often took in some of the information and retailed it next day, without remembering the source.

But such tricks were merely the embellishments of our craft; and there was always the danger that the craftsman's delight in virtuosity would divert him from his main function—to 'exdoctrinate' the peoples of the enemy and enemy-occupied countries. That purpose was achieved by the provision, day in, day out, of a news and information service so authoritative and candid that the listener or reader learned to rely on it and pass it on to his friends. By so doing, he committed an act of spiritual desertion, or confirmed his earlier apostasy from Totalitarianism. And that was the one enduring aim of Allied Psychological Warfare.

7. CONCLUSIONS

(1) The secret of success in propaganda against a totalitarian State is to achieve objectivity, in two senses of that word. In the first place, the output must appear objective, not to someone sitting in London and Washington, but to someone reading it or hearing it inside the enemy state. This demands the second sort of objectivity, the understanding of the ever-changing emotions of the audience to be addressed. Such an understanding is impossible without a large and well organised research staff, trained to think and feel itself into the enemy, or enemy-occupied, mind. The combination of integrity (that is, faithfully stating the Allied case) with empathy (that is, stating it in terms the audience can understand) is an ideal which must constantly be aimed at, but with the knowledge that perfection is impossible.

(2) Psychological warfare is an aggressive weapon, which can achieve positive results only when combined with a military or diplomatic offensive. The one fatal mistake is to attempt to use it as a substitute for military or diplomatic success, or in order to cover up military or diplomatic embarrassment. When used defensively in this way, it destroys good will and advertises weakness and divisions.

In a defensive period, therefore, or in a period of stalemate, psychological warfare must be strictly limited to the objective of building up good will by the truthful reporting even of embarrassing events and defeats. If such misfortunes are reported objectively—preferably before the enemy reports them—a rich fruit will be reaped later on. If they are concealed in a period of adversity, then the offensive use of psychological warfare in a later period of victory will be undermined.

(3) Psychological warfare must never be directed in a way to satisfy the home public. If it is to be effective inside enemy territory, its tone and manner of presentation will constantly appear 'soft' or 'appeasing' to a home public, which has a 'propaganda picture' of the enemy very far from reality. It may not be wise to do as the

British Government did during the war and treat leaflets distributed in enemy territory as secret documents. But the purpose behind this decision was sound enough—to insure that an ill-informed public opinion shall not maul and mutilate the weapon of psychological warfare. This is the most powerful reason for making the department which supervises psychological warfare a secret department, whose output is not subject to detailed scrutiny by elected representatives.

In the second world war, British psychological warfare was organised as an auxiliary division of the Foreign Office and as a secret department. In America, it was divided, very unfortunately, between two independent and rival agencies. All experience suggests that it would best be placed under the Chiefs of Staff or the Combined Chiefs of Staff, with, of course, the closest liaison with the Foreign Office and the State Department. In view of the fact that psychological warriors, by their very nature, tend to be prima donnas, they can be more easily disciplined if they are put into uniform and a severe military hierarchy is established. Moreover, by and large, whereas trained diplomats have an instinctive aversion to psychological warfare, Service officers find it far easier to treat it objectively as a weapon of war. Lastly, once the campaign begins, the most important psychological warfare activities have to be conducted, or at least directed, from Supreme Headquarters in the various areas of operations.

(4) Psychological warfare can be used fully and effectively only when it has become clear to the enemy that outright victory is impossible. From then on, it will become progressively more important as the weapon for imposing the Allied will on the mind of the enemy and of the peoples in enemy-occupied countries. In the course of a campaign, the main objective will be to insure the strictest coordination between psychological warfare strategy and the strategy of military commanders. To avoid 'stunting' and to ensure correct timing will be the main tasks of those in command. It is at this stage that the 'market research' into the enemy mind, built up in the earlier defensive period, will fully justify itself.

(5) The strict subordination of psychological warfare to high policy is a relatively easy business. To make certain that this conformity does not degenerate into a lifeless uniformity of output is far more difficult. For this purpose, overcentralisation should be carefully avoided. An apparently untidy organisation—with executive units

operating at Army, Army Group and Supreme Headquarters levels, as well as far back in the civilian rear—is preferable to one so tidy that it defeats its object, which is always to guarantee that the enemy feels he is listening, not to propaganda, but to honest men honestly and simply telling him the truth.

DEMOCRACY AND FOREIGN POLICY

I spoke on this subject in August 1955 to a formidable assembly of Western intelligentsia organised by the Congress of Cultural Freedom in Milan. Apart from Kenneth Galbraith, whom I met for the first time, everyone there dismissed my thesis as too perverse and paradoxical to merit serious consideration. This angered me so much that I took the trouble to write it up, but since I could find no one to print it, it appears here rather defiantly for the first time!

i

How far can and how far should the foreign policy of a democracy be controlled by public opinion?
In his recent book, *The Public Philosophy*,[1] Walter Lippmann has stated the case against democratic control of foreign policy so succinctly and with such grave emotional force that I propose merely to summarise his arguments. In his view the decline of the West—which he dates from the first World War—has been due to the poisonous influence of a mass electorate on foreign policy. Philosophically, he derives this corruption of democratic freedom from the Jacobin heresy, which taught men to believe that freedom can be achieved by one violent act of revolution. The Communists and revolutionary socialists hold that this must be a class revolution. The national liberals and the democratic socialists, on the other hand, maintained that the single revolutionary change required was the establishment of an independent State, with representative instituitions based on universal suffrage. It is, of course, this second belief with which Mr. Lippmann is chiefly concerned. He believes that it is based on a heretical assumption that the electorate can be relied on to represent the people.

[1] Hamish Hamilton, London, 1955.

'It is often assumed, but without warrant, that the opinions of
The People as voters can be treated as the expression of the
interests of *The People* as an historic community. The crucial problem of modern democracy arises from the fact that this assumption
is false. The voters cannot be relied upon to represent *The People*.
The opinions of voters in elections are not to be accepted unquestioningly as true judgments of the vital interests of the
community.'

Mr. Lippmann gives two reasons why the electorate is incapable
of making the decisions on grave issues of State which were previously the responsibility of the Executive. In the first place, he uses
the argument, so familiar from Plato's *Republic*, that ruling is an
art calling for a special kind of knowledge and, even more important,
for a special kind of intellectual and moral training, that subdues
the baser passions and instincts to a reasoning faculty which understands natural law. In the second place, he maintains that the electorate, even if it were capable of deciding rightly, cannot do so
because it is denied access to the whole truth on which wise judgment must be based. 'There is an inherent tendency in public
opinion,' he observes, 'to feed upon rumours excited by our own
wishes and fears.' In wartime an electorate 'must be incited to paro-
xysms of hatred and to Utopian dreams in order to wage war
energetically' and refuses to 'tolerate the calculated compromises that
durable settlements demand'. In peacetime, when tension is relaxed,
it will veto unpopular measures necessary to preserve peace.

'At the critical junctures, when the stakes are high, the prevailing mass opinion will impose what amounts to a veto upon changing the course on which the government is at the time proceeding.
Prepare for war in time of peace? No. It is bad to raise taxes, to
unbalance the budget, to take men away from their schools or
their jobs, to provoke the enemy. Intervene in a developing conflict? No. Avoid the risk of war. Withdraw from the area of the
conflict? No. The adversary must not be appeased. Reduce your
claims on the area. No. Righteousness cannot be compromised.'

And he concludes:

'The unhappy truth is that the prevailing public opinion has been
destructively wrong at the critical junctures. The people have im-

posed a veto upon the judgments of informed and responsible officials. They have compelled the governments, which usually knew what would have been wiser, or was necessary, or was more expedient, to be too late with too little, or too long with too much, too pacifist in peace and too bellicose in war, too neutralist or appeasing in negotiation or too intransigent.'

There is plenty of evidence that a very large number of intellectuals in the West share Mr. Lippmann's doubts, even if they do not accept all his conclusions. It is therefore worth asking ourselves the question whether the history of our nations since 1914 provides any justification for the view that mistakes in foreign policy have been due to the extension of the franchise and to the doctrine that the electorate should have the last word not only in domestic but also in foreign affairs. Is it a fact, for instance, to take three of his own examples, that the Versailles Treaty, Munich and Unconditional Surrender were forced upon the politicians and their expert advisors by the masses?

I do not think it is. Indeed, I cannot recall an instance between the wars in which a British or American or French statesman tried to conduct the kind of policy we now think should have been adopted and was repudiated by the electorate for doing so. Surely it is truer to say that it was the traditional political leadership—backed nearly always by a large section of the educated élite—which led us in the wrong direction. There is no evidence, for instance, that the British people would have rejected Baldwin in the 1935 election or forced Chamberlain to resign in 1938 if either of them had repudiated appeasement and shown the courage demanded by Winston Churchill. Nor was it the mass electorate which saddled Britain and America with the Unconditional Surrender policy in 1942 or the Morgenthau Plan in 1944.

Since 1945 the record seems to me to be even more strongly against Mr. Lippmann's thesis. Time after time, when a British or American leader has screwed himself up to disregard his well-informed experts, forget party repercussions and take an unpopular decision which he knows to be right, he has been surprised to find that the people are not behind him but in front of him and waiting for him to catch up. Mr. Attlee's liberation of India was too extreme for the experts in Whitehall, but the British people were ready for it; and his two most 'unpopular' decisions—to introduce national service in peacetime, and to impose bread rationing in order to prevent famine in Bengal—lost him no votes among an electorate which Mr. Lippmann accuses of always seeking its creature comforts and saying 'no' to changes of policy. Mr. Truman—a much braver leader than Mr. Roosevelt—had the same experience. The Marshall Plan, the Berlin air lift, and the decision to resist aggression in Korea, were opposed either by experts or by a section of educated opinion, or by both. Yet the American people as soon as they were given the chance, responded to his lead.

Even if I win acceptance for the view that the electorate is not to blame, it still remains true that the Western democracies have made disastrous mistakes in foreign policy, and we must next proceed to discover the causes of this weakness. At one point in *The Public Philosophy* Mr. Lippmann observes:

'The powers which were ceded by the Executive passed through the assemblies, which could not exercise them, to the mass of the voters who, though unable also to exercise them, passed them on to the party bosses, the agents of pressure groups, and the magnates of the new media of mass communication.'

This seems to me to be much nearer the mark than Mr. Lippmann's sweeping indictment of public opinion. Indeed, had he followed up this line of thought, he might have reached a very different and much less pessimistic conclusion. The evidence of the last thirty years seems to me to show that the failures of democratic foreign policy are due not to the sovereignty theoretically accorded to the electorate, but to the frustration of that sovereignty by power groups and élites, greedy to retain their privileged status. To whom does the weak politician surrender when he funks an unpopular decision? Not to the electorate but to a press campaign, to a lobby, to a party caucus, to a financial backer, or even to the Foreign Office or the Chiefs of Staff.

Mr. Lippmann himself provides confirmation for this view when he compares British and American democracy. He remarks that the British system is the healthier of the two and praises it for 'enfranchising the masses into the government class, as distinguished from enfranchising them through the overthrow of the government class'. Surely this suggests that if, as Mr. Lippmann believes, democratic control of foreign policy has worked fairly well in Britain, badly in

America and very badly in France, one reason for this may be found to lie in the difference between the constitutional framework within which popular sovereignty operates in the three countries.

French democracy is based on an electoral system which encourages a multiplicity of parties. This in its turn makes for weak, coalition cabinets, unable to dominate the groups and interests represented in Parliament. Continuity of policy is therefore maintained by a powerful central bureaucracy, which continues largely unaffected by the ins and outs of the politicians. The variety of interests and views of the French voters is faithfully reflected in the Chamber, but for that very reason the French electorate finds it far easier to say 'no' than to say 'yes', and positive decision remains with the bureaucracy.

Like the French system, American democracy was designed to prevent the abuse of power by a despotic government. It does so, however, not by encouraging a multiplicity of political parties but through a carefully planned division of powers, first between Executive, Legislature and Judiciary at the centre and, secondly, between Federal and State government. The cohesion necessary to evolve a national policy is provided not, as in France, by a strong central bureaucracy but by a strong Presidential Executive and by the two-party electoral system under which the President is elected. But the American party is weak. It is not united by an ideology nor subject to strong central discipline. It is, in fact a coalition of groups of interests. Thus, the Constitution and the Party system of the United States and France look to an Englishman as though they were designated to frustrate positive action, to encourage surrenders by Government to special interests and to disintegrate popular sovereignty into the splintered voices of selfish groups.

In fact, British democracy in comparison with French and American, is authoritarian. It can, not unfairly, be described as a system of alternating party dictatorship (using 'dictatorship' in the Roman sense of the word). Enormous powers are concentrated in the hands of the central government, which is sustained in the Legislature by a highly disciplined party machine and faced by another party machine which constantly presents to the electorate an alternative Government. Ultimately the electorate is sovereign, but the only occasion on which it exercises that sovereignty is in a General Election, and even there its decision is limited to a choice between a Cabinet selected by the Conservative Leader and a Cabinet selected by the Socialist Leader. The British two-party system, simplifies every decision into a simple 'yes' or 'no'. It is grossly unfair to minority parties and minority views, but it has the single overriding advantage that the elector and the Member of Parliament alike are prevented from ever 'judging an issue on its merits'. They are constantly driven back to the one question, 'Whatever you think about this particular issue, do you want this Government to continue or do you wish to see the Opposition in power?' If Mr. Lippmann is right in his belief that the British have created a responsible electorate, that success is due (i) to the absence of a written constitution, pitting Executive against Legislature, (ii) to the transfer of an *undivided* sovereignty to the people as voters, and (iii) to the severe limitation imposed on the exercise of that sovereignty by a disciplined and strongly centralised two-party system, which encourages strong leadership and compels both the Member of Parliament and the electorate either to support it with an unambiguous 'yes' or to reject it with an unambiguous 'no'.

In each of these three systems public opinion plays a different role and popular sovereignty is exerted in a different way. The American pattern of freedom encourages social democracy in the literal sense of those words. Since there is little stratification of social class and only a weak civil service, the great decisions of State are the resultant of a public polygon of pressures. Government—and Government expenditure—are continuously subjected to the most searching investigation by the Legislature and by a press which has established itself as the fourth estate. If we mean by 'the defence of freedom' making sure that every decision is preceded by investigation and debate and followed by inquest, then the United States is the freest and most democratic country in the world. Its obvious weakness, however, is that an excess of investigation can frustrate action, and the absence of a respected bureaucracy can prevent the issues being properly presented either to the Government or to the people.

The French tradition carries the American suspicion of central government one stage further by substituting a multiple for a two-party system and a weak Cabinet for the strong Presidential Executive. But it compensates for this weakness by a civil service manned by a traditional intellectual élite, which is even more powerful than the British. Contrary to the popular view, this produces a remarkable continuity of policy both in the domestic and in the foreign field. The chief deficiency of French democracy is not volatility but an inability either to actualise the popular demand for social change or to adapt traditional foreign and colonial policies to changing circumstances.

Finally, the British system, though it has the one overriding advantage I have mentioned, is far too oligarchic for the taste of any democrat except an Englishman. By American standards, both Parliament and the press are inadequate watch-dogs; and the absence of a spoil system gives to the higher civil service, who survive all Government changes, a quite excessive power. Moreover, British party discipline is so illiberal that any Frenchman or American would regard it as nearer to Lenin's democratic centralism than to the standards of a free society. This is why public opinion, which in France and America operates on government directly as an independent and unpredictable force, is normally much less active in Britain. Only occasionally does it initiate policy: usually it is content to consent to a decision already taken at the top.

If, with Mr. Lippmann, I prefer this British system, that does not mean that I am suggesting that it should or could be imitated in France and in the United States. As each individual human being develops a unique personality, so each free people creates for itself over generations institutions which suit its character and environment. You can prefabricate a totalitarian system, export it and impose it on a satellite people. But Western democracy is not for export: it must grow. That is why the particular way in which democratic control of foreign policy is exercised must vary in accordance with the constitution and the traditions of each democracy. Bi-partisanship, for instance, may well be a sign of political health in the United States, where the constitutional inability of the Executive to control the Legislature could easily frustrate a strong foreign policy and must therefore be counter-balanced by intra-party collaboration. But in Britain, where the Cabinet controls Parliament by means of its disciplined party majority, a similar bi-partisanship could endanger freedom. True, a fundamental cleavage between the two parties on any basic issue would cause a break-down in British democracy. But if, on the other hand, they come to agree too closely and to work too comfortably together, then the only check on the powers of the Executive—the constant challenge of an alternative Government with an alternative policy—is removed, and with it the Great Debate across the floor of the Chamber, which is the main vehicle for educating British public opinion.

This example indicates the danger of trying to judge the procedures of one democracy by the standards of another. There may be one Communist way of life, though I doubt it. Thank heavens, there is no democratic way of life, but a number of individual democracies. If there is to be successful co-operation between us, then we should realise that the way each of the free nations takes its decisions is bound to seem absurd, or even undemocratic, to its neighbours. That is why the proposal to develop the military alliance of N.A.T.O. into an Atlantic Union, under some overall political organisation, would probably produce not an increase but a decrease of Western unity.

ii

Let us see where the argument has led us. In order to examine Mr. Lippmann's contention that the abuse of popular sovereignty, particularly in relation to foreign policy, has caused a catastrophic decline of the West, we first took a look at recent history and found that, where grave mistakes have been made, there is no good reason to believe that the electorate is to blame. When politicians have failed to carry out unpopular but necessary policies, the surrender appears to have been not to the people but to special interests and professional élites.

Next we examined the constitutions of France, the United States and Britain and found that the role of the electorate in the control of foreign policy varies in the three great democracies. Broadly speaking, it is very much easier for a British than for a French or American statesman to initiate a new unpopular foreign policy. But in all three countries it is the articulate élites, rather than the electorate, with which the statesman has to contend. It is they who settle the terms and the climate of the debate which precedes the decision—and often take the decision itself.

If this analysis is correct, we must conclude that the prime responsibility for the failures of Western diplomacy must fall on what we call 'enlightened public opinion', the educated minority who dominate the higher ranks of the civil service, the media of mass communications and the political parties. It is they who are responsible for the formulation of the decisions which must be taken by the government on the one side and by the electorate on the other. It is they who determine the quality of the secret discussions in the Cabinet and of the public debates in the Legislature and in the press.

It is Mr. Lippmann's contention that this debate tends to be so vulgarised and emotionalised that the electorate is bound to come to wrong conclusions. Instead of judging international affairs in the civilised and well-informed manner adopted by the élite which managed diplomacy in the nineteenth century, the sovereign people, he tells us, are captivated by stereotypes, seduced by slogans, and oscillate between the self-indulgence of appeasement and the totalitarian demand for unconditional surrender.

It is, of course, true that the terms in which a democratic public opinion discusses foreign policy are different from those to be found in a Foreign Office memorandum. The man in the street demands clear-cut solutions to problems which the diplomat often believes to be insoluble. Particularly in Britain and America, he tries to moralise into a decision between right and wrong what the expert sceptically regards as a choice between many varying shades of grey, and he demands an explanation of world politics in terms of a few simple concepts. Both among academics and among officials, there is a tendency, therefore, to write off public discussion of foreign affairs as journalistic vulgarisation or party propaganda, necessary, no doubt, for an ill-informed electorate but hopelessly removed from the real issues, which are discussed by officials and presented to the Foreign Secretary in their State Papers.

This theory of the gap between informed and uninformed discussion of public affairs was first formulated by Plato in *The Republic*. Only an élite, he said, is capable of a serious discussion which reaches the objective truth. The masses must be fed on vulgarisations and 'noble lies', which induce them to accept the right decision— if necessary, for the wrong reasons. In my view, it is the prevalence of this doctrine among the educated classes which is the main obstacle to the successful working of democracy. Wherever it is accepted, either consciously or unconsciously, it transforms the politician, the civil servant, the academic or the editor into a managerial oligarch and a secret enemy of freedom. But it is not only an immoral doctrine: it is also a foolish one based on a quite fallacious distinction between the enlightened and rational discussion of the educated élite, on the one side, and the unenlightened, irrational discussion of the masses on the other.

It is, of course, true that the electorate can very easily be bemused by stereotypes and myths and the kind of journalism and demagogy which deliberately distorts the facts. We have only to recall the success of National Socialist propaganda to realise that. But is it correct to assume that only the masses are duped. On the contrary, the Nazi leaders, including Hitler, were as deeply deceived by their own propaganda as the German people, and there is no evidence to suggest that Germans with university or secondary education were more successful than the working class in steeling their minds against it. Indeed, it was in the universities and among the middle classes that Hitler recruited his most fanatical followers. Education and expertise do not make those who acquire them proof against self-deception or political prejudice. Very often, by blunting natural common sense and inducing arrogance, they actually increase gullibility. The simple man in the street may know much less about China or Germany than the university don, the leader-writer and the diplomat. But that does not necessarily mean that, when he is faced with the decision whether to defend the off-shore islands or to rearm the Federal Republic, his answer is more likely to be wrong than theirs.

Moreover, it is a delusion to believe that thinking in stereotypes and clichés and an acceptance of myths and ideologies is only to be found among the unenlightened masses. Everyone, whatever his degree of education, must form habits of thought, prejudices and partisan loyalties: no one approaches a problem with an open mind, unless that mind is also completely empty. Objectivity, in so far as we can achieve it, means not an absence but a consciousness of prejudice and a willingness to consider the facts which contradict it. This unusual quality is by no means necessarily enhanced either by first-hand knowledge of a subject through book-reading or by the writing of official memoranda. Having spent my life before the war as an academic, during the war as an expert and since then as a politician and a journalist, I have come to two conclusions: first, that political wisdom has very little to do with formal education and that character is a much more important element in it than either knowledge or quickness of wit; and, secondly, that the quality of political discussion does not noticeably improve as you ascend the pyramid from its broad base in the mass electorate through the local party and local newspaper to Westminster and Fleet Street. Every group of human beings is a mixture of types, but the mixture of foibles, weakness and strength is much the same at the top as it is at the bottom. I am glad to have confirmed this by experience, since the faith that it is so seems to me to be the basic tenet of democracy. Certainly the experts and the élite who form enlightened public opinion *know* a lot more than the general public, and this makes many of them believe that they must also be wiser. That belief is an arrogant illusion: and that is why the educated élite must always be compelled to subject any conclusions they reach to the acid test of inexpert common sense, as represented first by the elected politicians, to whom they are responsible between elections, and then to the masses, whenever they reassert their sovereignty in the polling booth.

iii

But how on earth can such a test be successful? Because the great decisions which face free nations are all of them moral decisions which face free men in their daily lives. Anyone who worked during the war in a big headquarters will remember that, if a problem had to go right up to the Supreme Command, then it had to be boiled down to a form which could be presented on half a sheet of paper. Much the same is true of the problems presented to a Prime Minister or a President. He cannot possibly immerse himself in detail or pore over Blue Books and statistics. He too must have the ability to select the right expert advisers and then trust them to extract the essential issues and present them to him as a few precise questions, which preferably can be answered with a 'yes' or 'no'. It is the responsibility of the expert and the official to ensure that these questions are the relevant questions. If they fail to do so, the Government blunders.

The kind of questions which a democracy can be fairly expected to answer are precisely the kind of questions which Prime Ministers and Presidents answer; and, just as they will make terrible mistakes if their officials fail to distil the essential issues out of a mass of information, so the electorate will go wrong if the press, the radio, the Parliamentary debate and all the other means of public education have fallen down on their jobs of paring the problem down to its bare essentials, where a quite simple moral decision is all that is required. Those self-conscious members of the informed élite, therefore, who blame the democratic masses for the troubles which have befallen the Western Powers since 1914 should turn their criticism on themselves. Democracy is like a law court. If the jury errs, blame is laid on the lawyers and the judge, who have failed to present the issues in a form in which twelve men and women, inexpert in the law, can come to a sensible decision. If the electorate errs, then those who are its self-appointed advisers, whether as editors, pastors, teachers or officials, are almost certainly at fault.

'Knowledge is power,' said Marx, and Acton added that power corrupts. The fact is that the practice of democracy does not come naturally to those who feel that they belong to an élite. Education and enlightenment normally instil either (i) an apolitical indifference or (ii) a jealously defensive sense of status or (iii) an aggressive ambition to reshape society in accordance with a bold, rationalistic design.

Motive (i) is tacitly and motives (ii) and (iii) are actively totalitarian. If unchecked, they will transform democracy into a managerial oligarchy or explode in a Fascist or Communist revolution. Yet the administration of the modern state and of modern industry alike depend increasingly on educated élites, and democracy cannot function unless these élites sustain it with their technical skill and play their political role by formulating the decisions it has to take in simple, ethical terms. This new aristocracy of knowledge, in fact, is the engine which drives the modern state either forwards towards the enlargement of human freedom or backwards towards dictatorship and oligarchy. It is my contention that, wherever Western democracy has failed, either in external or internal policy, that failure is intimately connected with the abuse by this educated élite of the power which it wields.

Instead of talking about the incompetence of the people to come to wise decisions, we should realise that, in the brief period since universal suffrage was introduced, very little effort has been made by the educated élite to make democracy work. Of course the people will remain incompetent until those élites recognise that it is just as much their job to expound political problems to the electorate as it is the job of the advocate to expound legal problems to a jury. What is required to halt the decline of the West is a moral and mental revolution among the educated classes. And the first stage of that revolution would be to assume as a working hypothesis that, whenever wrong decisions have been taken, the blame lies with the experts, whose job it was to advise governments, and with the editors and educators, whose job it was to enlighten the people. If knowledge is power, it is also a privilege and, unless enlightened public opinion ceases to abuse that privilege, democracy will be destroyed before any serious and sustained effort has been made to work it.

EASTERN KOLKHOZ AND
WESTERN CO-OPERATION:

This essay, which I wrote in the American monthly *Commentary* in March 1963, incorporated parts of 'The Good Farmer Schweik', a contribution to the *New Statesman* in which twelve months previously I described a tour of Czechoslovakia.

i

NOTHING is of more central importance in Communist dogma than the *kolkhoz*—and nothing has provided such a spectacular failure in Communist practice. In stating this, I do not mean to suggest that the *kolkhoz* belonged to the original Marxist-Leninist doctrine which inspired the Bolshevik revolutionaries. Marx himself had very little to say about either the methods or the institutions to be employed in transforming capitalism into socialism. Anyway he confidently assumed that the dictatorship of the proletariat would first be established, not in a backward country with a primitive peasant economy, but in a highly developed Western nation such as France or Germany where capitalism would already largely have fulfilled the tasks in the countryside which the Kremlin has been forced to allot to the *kolkhoz*—namely: (1) the elimination of small-scale peasant production; (2) the driving into the towns of most of the peasants; and (3) the transformation of agriculture into a highly mechanised industry, organised in large units and relying on organised wage-earners whose skills and conditions had been assimilated to those of industry.

The countryside Marx envisaged, in fact, when he thought about agriculture under socialism was not that of Russia in 1917 nor even of Poland in 1945, but of 20th-century North America and Britain where capitalism had already eliminated not merely the peasant economy but the peasant mentality as well, and where ultra-efficient farms constantly break new records in production per acre and production per worker.

The revolution, however, took place not in an industrialised Western democracy but in Russia, with the result that agriculture suddenly became not only the biggest but also the most intractable problem that the revolutionaries faced. Lenin 'solved' it by giving the land outright to the peasants and so buying their political support. But this 'solution' has faced every Communist government since then with a painful dilemma. Unless they were prepared to accept an extremely slow evolution from peasant to industrial economy, the Communists had to find methods of modernising agriculture more effective than those prevalent in Western Europe. For after Marx published *Das Kapital*, it became clear that the elimination of the peasantry by modern capitalism was being slowed down if not stopped altogether by the working of representative institutions. Parliaments selected by universal suffrage were dominated by a right-wing alliance of peasant parties and large land-owners, sufficiently powerful to extract from the state the protection of inefficient home agriculture against competition from cheap overseas foodstuffs.

Although they needed the support of the peasants in order to achieve power, the Communists were not prepared to protect them after the revolution, since they felt that such policies would fatally retard the rapid industrialisation on which they had set their hearts. They assumed without question that in order to achieve 'Socialism in one country', the private land-owner, whether a big landlord or a small peasant, must be eliminated; and both the manpower and the capital for rapid industrialisation must be extracted from agriculture. The peasants must be compelled to deliver sufficient food to the towns to ensure a steadily improved standard of urban living, without themselves obtaining a fair return for their labour. Hence the need for an institution which, while purporting to protect and improve the independent peasants' way of life, would in fact destroy their independence and impose urban priorities on the countryside.

Almost by accident, the institution adopted for this purpose was the *kolkhoz* or collective village. As long as Lenin was in control, no decision was reached to impose a standard pattern on Russian agriculture. Instead, a number of experiments in cooperation and socialised farming were launched. It was only during Stalin's first Five-Year Plan that the *kolkhoz* became the chosen instrument of collectivisation. But the very fact that it aroused such fierce opposition among the peasants and had to be imposed on them by force, elevated the *kolkhoz* into a dogma and made any criticism of it heresy of the gravest kind.

It was almost inevitable therefore that in 1945 the satellite governments of Eastern Europe, instead of developing their own national experiments in agrarian socialism, accepted the Russian *kolkhoz* as their model. Completely slavishly, they proceeded to repeat all the brutal miscalculations and mistakes of Soviet collectivisation, deceiving their peasants with the promise that they should henceforward own their own land, and then bullying them into giving up their fields, their machinery, and finally their livestock to the *kolkhoz* established in each district by a handful of party agitators. By the early 1950s, mass collectivisation was well under way in every country in Eastern Europe—with the single exception of Yugoslavia, where a peasant revolt had been narrowly averted by Tito's hasty disavowal of the *kolkhoz*, along with the rest of Stalinism. And in the Far East as well, the Russian pattern was being faithfully repeated by the Chinese Communists despite their peasant origin and their practical understanding of rural problems.

ii

It is a great pity that so few Westerners have bothered to see for themselves how the *kolkhoz* works. Most travellers behind the Iron Curtain concentrate their attention on urban and industrial life, and are content to see the factories, crèches, schools, hospitals, and theatres which the Communists in all cases are anxious to show them. All these visitors see of agriculture, which is still by far the largest activity, and of the countryside where from forty per cent to seventy per cent of the population still live, are a few carefully selected tourist beauty spots. Yet, as I have now proved for myself in no less than five countries—Russia, China, Czechoslovakia, Poland, and East Germany—a request to make a detailed study of life in the *kolkhoz* is enthusiastically welcomed. Elaborate arrangements are made to enable the visitor to travel extensively, to see everything on his list, and to talk at length with all kinds of people, from the bureaucrats at the Ministry of Agriculture to disgruntled peasants in the collectives.

Unfortunately, in Russia as well as in China—which I visited just when the communes were being established—I was travelling alone; and I could not check against the considered judgments of real professional farmers the amateur impression of a socialist politician who has married into a farm, and who now spends his weekends trying to supervise it. In 1961 and 1962 I took care to make good this defect by suggesting to the Czechoslovak and Polish governments that I should bring a group of British agriculturists to see their countryside at harvest time. Both governments agreed and as a result I was able to make these two tours in the company of three members of the Labour Party's Agricultural Advisory Committee—all of them farmers on a scale that would cause them to be denounced in the Communist world not as mere *kulaks* but as landlords.

The division of labour on which we agreed was that I should listen to the official speeches, question the bureaucrats, and cross-examine our hosts on the collective farms, while my three farmer friends looked round for themselves and then put their supplementary questions based on what they had seen. Of course, travelling with Communist guides and talking through Communist interpreters, we were looking down on the peasant from the top floor of Communist society, and we could not expect to make much personal contact with him, even in Poland. But no Communist guide, however clever, can divert you from seeing whether crops are good, whether fields are clean, whether machinery is well looked after and livestock intelligently handled. And though we could not hope to discover what the peasants really were thinking, we could certainly see how they were living.

The one overwhelming impression I got from these tours was of the utterly mechanical way in which each of the non-Russian Communist governments had imposed the Stalinite pattern on its own countryside. Once one understands how a Russian state farm and a Russian *kolkhoz* works, one knows exactly what to expect in every other Communist country—even down to the smallest detail. What a contrast, I could not help feeling, with Israel—a tiny country but one that contains within it an astonishing variety of collectivist patterns. There is not only the difference between *moshavis* and *kibbutzim* but within each there are numbers of important variations in the form of cultivation and the methods of keeping livestock.

East of the Iron Curtain, this variety ceases and is replaced by set rules and standard practices, extending as I saw for myself even to such details as the number of cows per worker on a dairy farm. In 1958, I visited within a month, first a state farm on a *kolkhoz* in White Russia, and then a state farm on a people's commune near Peking—each with a dairy herd. In both I asked the same questions about the labour force and received exactly the same answers. Although the size of the dairy herd and conditions varied enormously, there was always one full-time worker to twelve cows when they were milked by hand, and one to sixteen cows when they were milked by machine. I should add perhaps that the Chinese are fond of neither butter nor milk, and there is therefore only a limited amount of dairy farming in China. But what there is of it seemed to conform precisely to the Russian pattern, just as the Chinese and Russian cowmen gave almost identical answers. And when I said that in the Western world a cowman will milk up to fifty cows without difficulty and without assistance except on his day off, I was met with that look of incredulity which blanks out all Communist faces when they are confronted with a fact that does not fit into their intellectual pattern—a look which combines a loyal conviction that you are a capitalist liar, with a disloyal suspicion that there may be something in what you say.

The kolkhoz, in fact, is a monstrous straightjacket, strapped by Stalin on to the back of Russian agriculture with a disastrous effect that has been repeated outside Russia since 1945. Quite recently, as a result of Krushchev's liberalisation policy, some local variants of the pattern have been emerging, even in such ultra-orthodox states as East Germany and Czechoslovakia. But these minor departures are insignificant compared with the uniformity that has been imposed on the peasant throughout the Communist world in the sacred name of progress.

The fairest way to judge the kolkhoz—which the Poles have so dramatically abandoned—is to examine it in the country where it is most efficiently managed. Along with the East Germans, the Czechs are the most Westernised and most highly industrialised people in the Communist world; and their peasants, before the Communist coup in 1948, were known as good farmers with excellent Cooperatives. Here, if anywhere, the kolkhoz could be made to work. And the Czechs have certainly tried. The countryside is 100 per cent collectivized—as one can see from the air. Flying over the mountains which divide West Germany from Czechoslovakia, one suddenly notices that the patchwork quilt of Bavarian peasant strips has been replaced by the huge fields of the Bohemian plain. If you look carefully, you can tell whether you are passing over a state farm or a kolkhoz, by noticing whether there is still a patch of strip farming close to the village. If there is not, it is a state farm since these are worked by salaried managers and employ agricultural workers who cultivate no land of their own. On the other hand, in most of the collectives the members still possess the famous 'private half hectare' as well as a private cow and a couple of pigs.

Motoring through the villages—particularly in Slovakia, which, before the war, was an agricultural slum—we could see the achievements of the kolkhoz at close range. In each village, all the old farmyards are being left to crumble away. On the leeward side, where the smell blows away, magnificent new buildings are being erected—the collective cowsheds, pig-sties, broiler factories, silos, and shelters for the new collectively-owned wheat, maize, and potato harvesters. All these new buildings—as well as the thirty or forty new homes we saw going up in each village—are a demonstration of the Communist determination to industrialise peasant production and bring rural life up to the standards of the towns.

I doubt if there is a peasant in the world more efficient than the Czech, or more independent-minded. He used to be his own master working his own land in his own time. Now he is a member of a work brigade, awakened at 5.30 each morning by the voice of the kolkhoz manager, barking the day's orders through the loudspeakers. He used to have an independent income. Now he is paid for piecework, partly in money and partly in kind.

How efficient is the Czech kolkhoz? The state of both the fields and the farm equipment, as we saw it during harvest, was as good as in any Western European country; and if the livestock was unimpressive, it is only fair to remember that many of the cows are the progeny of draft animals which the individual peasants brought with them less than ten years ago, when they joined the kolkhoz.

There are just two snags about Czech collectivisation. In the first place, the average age of the kolkhoz member is now well over fifty. Only the peasant too old and too rooted to escape stays on the land. Most of the boys and girls have either fled into the towns or live in the villages, travelling miles by bus to a job in industry or the public services. If one of the objects of collectivisation was to reduce rural over-population, this is a target which in Czechoslovakia has been over-achieved.

The second snag is the obstinate reluctance of the Czech collective farmers to sell their products at the low prices obtainable. Of course, the compulsory deliveries must be fulfilled; but beyond that point the Czech peasantry is showing that the kolkhoz can be used, not to serve but to frustrate the demands of the government. The Five-Year Plan dominates the life of the peasant. Already in 1962, he knows the extra tons of wheat and extra head of cattle which each acre must carry in 1967. He acquiesces—and when consulted about the plan makes sure that his target is nice and low! In Communist Czechoslovakia, the Good Soldier Schweik is now the Good Farmer Schweik; and in the countryside there is a gigantic grey market where the collective farms get together to defeat the demands of the state. Even ten years after collectivisation, the stubborn peasant mentality, which the *kolkhoz* was specifically designed to eradicate, is still strong. It is just possible that the huge amounts of capital invested in Czech collective farming have been justified in terms of food production: it is quite certain that it has not been justified in terms of food delivery.

iii

Next year I saw the other side of the shield. Poland is the only country in the Communist world which combines plenty of food for all its inhabitants with the role of food exporter to Western Europe. The Poles are now eating better than any of their Communist neighbours; and they are also providing the British consumer with bacon as good as anything the Danes provide, eggs, and best quality butter. Sales of foodstuffs abroad now comprise eighteen per cent of Poland's total exports.

What gives this agricultural revival such enormous political importance is the fact that it has been achieved as a direct result of Gomulka's decision six years ago, after the Posnan riots, to abandon collectivisation and permit the Polish peasant to walk out of the *kolkhoz*.

Today, eighty-seven per cent of Poland's arable land is privately farmed by the peasants, twelve per cent by state farms, and only one per cent by collective farms. And this movement away from the *kolkhoz* is still proceeding: last year sixty-four new collectives were established, but 231 were wound up. And the reaction from collective to private ownership has recently been strengthened by the restoration of a completely free market in agricultural land. The Polish peasant is now free either to sell off his land to a private buyer or, if he is elderly, to let the state have it and receive a pension instead. He is also free, once he has fulfilled his compulsory deliveries, to sell the rest of his produce in the completely free markets which exist all over the country. Yet despite this freedom of choice, he prefers to market eighty per cent of his produce through the socialist sector. It is this willingness of the peasant to deliver his produce to the state which distinguishes Poland from all her Communist neighbours.

How has this miracle been achieved? The answer is delightfully obvious to a Westerner, if not to a Communist. Once Gomulka had thrown away the stick of collectivisation, he was compelled to rely on the carrot of a price system favourable to the peasant. Only thirty per cent of total food production is now taken from the peasant in compulsory deliveries. Another thirty per cent, including all milk, is marketed by the peasants through their own central co-operatives. Another forty per cent, including bacon, sugar beet, oil-seeds, and eggs, is sold under long-term contracts to state factories. This contract production is a very important factor in the Polish Miracle. But it is not a Communist invention. Before the war, bacon factories, for example, concentrating exclusively on the British market, had been established in many parts of the country, catering for peasants in a radius of twenty to thirty miles. Because the peasants were primitive and incapable of doing it for themselves, the bacon factories laid down the precise animal they required, controlled the breeding, and even provided much of the foodstuffs. In return they guaranteed to accept every pig the peasants produced at a fixed price, provided it passed the standard laid down by the factory. In 1945, the contract system was resumed—the only change being that the factories were now state owned. Collectivisation, however, threatened to destroy it altogether, and it is only since the retreat from the *kolkhoz* that the state factory has come into its own, providing by far the most effective incentive to modernisation that we saw in Poland. Our Communist guides, when pressed, did not deny that the relationship between the peasant and the state factory to which he delivered his bacon is very similar to that between the individual farmer and the co-operative bacon factory in Denmark.

Of course the peasants complained that they were over-taxed. In fact, though rent has been officially abolished, each peasant pays a land tax graded according to the quality of his soil, which comes to exactly the same thing. In addition they make their compulsory deliveries—a harsher form of taxation, which is all the more irritating because they are excluded from every kind of social service except education. The Health Service, for example, is available only to the agricultural worker on a state farm: the peasant, as well as any worker he employs, must find a private doctor—and usually there aren't any in the countryside.

But though the peasant has his legitimate grievances, the fact remains that it is industry and the urban population that are paying the bill for the failure of collectivisation. Last year, for example, real wages in industry only advanced by 2·7 per cent, but the figure for the peasants was no less than eleven per cent. In recent years, the number of peasant houses with electricity has doubled. Four hundred thousand young peasants now own motor-cycles. And on every road and lane in the countryside you meet the parents of these young people, sitting in their traps and surreys behind those magnificent silky grain-fed horses of which they are so proud. It would be very nearly true to say that Gomulka has turned Marxism on its head by making the socialised sector of the economy pay for the improvement of the peasants' lot.

The problem set by the decision to abandon collectivisation was that it enabled the peasants not merely to regain their own land but to revert to their primitive peasant methods. The size of the plots is ludicrous. Two million peasants each farm twelve acres or less. To make matters worse, these tiny peasant farms usually consist of half-a-dozen strips scattered around the village, and on the death of the owner they are divided up among his children. We visited one village in Silesia which, to judge by its noble red-brick farm houses and farm buildings, had been the home before 1945 of prosperous German *kulaks* or middle peasants. Now it has been taken over by Galicians who have divided up the big houses into one-room flats.

Here was a chance to break with the medieval strip system and give the primitive peasants a new start by dividing up the ample land available into decent-sized plots. But the Communists had found it impossible to do this. After one unsuccessful attempt at collectivisation, the peasants had distributed the fields around the village once again into strips. One owner of some twenty acres proudly showed me where his five plots lay all around the village. 'But wouldn't you save labour by having them all in one place?' I asked him. 'Maybe', he replied, smiling craftily, 'but what would happen if a thunderstorm hit one side of the village? We have to share the risk.'

Parcelisation gets worse and worse; and with the unit of production so ridiculously uneconomic, mechanisation is almost impossible.

Combines, which are universal in Czechoslovakia, are not to be found except on the state farms. The total number of tractors in Poland is only 30,000—16,000 communally owned and 14,000 in private hands. As I saw for myself, much of the corn is still cut with sickles, and a farmer considers himself go-ahead if he uses his fine horse to pull a kind of flail reaper, which I had previously seen only in Victorian pictures.

What chances are there, since compulsion is now out of the question, to persuade the peasants voluntarily to abandon their primitive methods and accept modernised farming? Alas! Nearly all the peasants we talked to in the villages, on the fields, and by the roadside, during a tour which took us three-quarters of the way round Poland, were as reactionary as they were prosperous, consumed by a burning hatred of two things—Russia and Communism, which are associated in their minds with modernisation and improvement. Under pressure from a foreign visitor, most of them would agree that since Gomulka came to power they have been free to say what they like. Gomulka himself is popular. But I scarcely heard a favourable opinion expressed about the bureaucrats in Warsaw during the whole time of my tour.

Every peasant, of course, wants to make more money. Most of them would like to cultivate more land, if they can be sure of keeping the profits they earn. But even such an obvious reform as a change in the law which permits parcelisation is viewed with suspicion. In three of the villages we visited, there was only one Communist —the hard-working secretary of everything. And he obviously felt himself a gallant member of a small persecuted minority! The officials from the Ministries who accompanied us on our visits were not much better off. While our interpreters tried in their translation to water down the violence of the peasants' language, they stood uncomfortably in a bunch, obviously anxious lest the proceedings should get out of hand.

iv

I certainly did not envy these officials their main job, the establishment in each village of an Agricultural Circle—the primitive form of Co-operative on which the government is relying to introduce modern farming techniques. The name 'Agricultural Circle' has been chosen because any reference to 'co-operation' would arouse memories of the detested *kolkhoz*, and the organisation is an ingenious gimmick for bribing non-co-operative peasants into *de facto* co-operation without any theoretical recognition that this is what they are doing. The precise method of working is as follows: every year a calculation is made for all of Poland's 40,000 villages in order to assess the exact difference between the price the villagers receive from the state for compulsory deliveries and the price they could have got for those same deliveries if they had sold them on the free market. When this sum has been assessed, the amount is duly banked to each village's account.

But there it stays in the bank until the village establishes a Circle. For the fund may only be used where a Circle has been actually started, and where, furthermore, the members of the Circle have contributed a sum equivalent to twenty-five per cent of the village fund out of their own pockets. At this point permission is given to use the fund for a limited number of purposes. The Circle can drain or improve land; or it can buy machines and hire mechanics to drive and maintain them, so that any villager can go to the secretary of the Circle and arrange to have his field ploughed, his grain harvested, or his potatoes transported.

We visited some five of these Circles, and since on each occasion it was necessary to drive some fifty or sixty miles, I suspect that those worth showing to a foreigner were very few in number. Even the Ministry of Agriculture does not claim that more than 5,000 of them actually own a tractor. Moreover, in each of the carefully selected Circles to which we were taken the peasants we met—although they were desperately anxious to modernise their methods and improve their own earnings—were still suspicious of cooperation.

In one village, the Circle had begun to farm communally some of the large areas of land left derelict since the Germans fled in 1945. The fields were a long way off and when we reached them it was obvious that they were deplorably farmed. Our Ministry guides looked very embarrassed when the peasants eagerly pointed out the contrast between the poorly kept communal fields, and their own beautifully tended strips on the other side of the path. 'I suppose this experiment in co-operative farming by your Circle is a first step on the return road to the *kolkhoz*,' I said to the village chairman, rather naughtily. My words must have been faithfully translated, for there was a moment of horrified silence and then uproar as the chairman denounced the *kolkhoz* and told us how the attempt to introduce it was defeated ten years ago.

It is important to remember that, even at the height of the collectivisation campaign, only ten per cent of Poland's arable land was collectively farmed. Yet in every village we visited, the peasants had seen enough of the system to abominate the *kolkhoz*; and they remained deeply and I think quite unreasonably suspicious that the bureaucrats in Warsaw might one day feel tempted, if too little progress is being made by voluntary methods, to revert to compulsion once more. Collectivisation has never been formally abandoned by the government, and the threat of it hangs like a thunder-cloud over the countryside.

Throughout our tour, our dedicated Communist guide continued to assert to me, in the course of a long series of heated arguments, that the reversion to private ownership was only temporary, and that the final aim still remained a fully collectivised agriculture. But these assertions had a strangely hollow ring, and in this case I feel pretty sure that the hard facts of life will defeat this aim. By his silence, Krushchev has given his consent to Gomulka's decision to abandon the breakneck revolutionary methods of collectivisation, and to try the experiment of changing the peasant by a slow process of voluntary persuasion and passive evolution. Even more recently, by coming to terms with Tito, he has once again made it clear that the *kolkhoz* is no longer regarded in the Kremlin as the sole chosen instrument for socialising agriculture. And that is why he is now prepared to turn to the West to find other ways to achieve his ends.

v

In no field of economic activity is there a larger range of choice. Ever since the great slump of 1929, the idea that classical free enterprise could ever be applied to agriculture has been abandoned by the Western democracies. In its place, we have evolved a wide variety of devices designed to maintain prosperity in the countryside, while at the same time reducing the numbers employed in agriculture and encouraging improvement and modernisation. Today we all recognise the need to combine centralised state planning of agriculture with voluntary co-operation, not only in the marketing of produce but in the provision of seed, machinery, etc. In North

America, France, and Germany, these schemes are described as democratic; in Scandinavia, as socialist. The semantics do not matter. What is important is the discovery that the modernisation of agriculture requires the most skilled combination of central direction and grass-roots co-operation for success. In Western Germany, to take only one example, more than 1,300,000 peasants were transferred from agriculture into industry between 1951 and 1961, without any of the appalling political and economic consequences which Communist ruthlessness creates. And by 1970, when the transitional Seven-Year period ends and the E.E.C. agricultural policy really begins to function, another 750,000 will have been moved. The main method employed by the government in Bonn is a regulation of agricultural prices skilfully designed to eliminate the small peasant while providing his sons plenty of opportunities in an expanding industry under conditions of full employment.

But what are the chances that the Communists can learn the lesson and apply it? Certainly their bureaucrats are not trained to do the kind of tactful 'extension' work which the British, American, or Danish farmer has come to expect as a matter of course from government experts or co-operative representatives. Nevertheless, the Polish government really has no choice in the matter. With the Catholic Church still immensely powerful and eager to exploit any crisis, Gomulka cannot risk open conflict with peasants who still form no less than thirty-eight per cent of the population, and whose stubbornness was enormously increased by the victory they achieved after the Posnan riots. Thus it looks inevitable that Polish Communism, like Yugoslav Communism, will be forced in the foreseeable future to plan for a completely nationalised industrial sector existing alongside a privately owned agriculture, conforming to state requirements not by compulsion but by consent.

But when they see this new attitude adopted in dealing with the peasants, the workers in industry are bound to insist that they too shall be led by carrots instead of being driven by sticks. So it is not only the future of Polish agriculture that is at stake, but the whole concept of totalitarian planning as a short cut to industrialisation. For once a Communist government admits that in one section of the economy, a planned free market and voluntary co-operation work better than centrally imposed discipline, the freedom is bound to spread to other sectors of the economy. Poland under Gomulka cannot remain half slave and half free. And the two most powerful national emotions—Catholicism and hatred of Russia—are on the side of the free peasant.

And what is true of the different sectors of the Polish economy is also true of the different national economies within Eastern Europe. The abandonment by both Poland and Yugoslavia of collectivisation is having its effect on their neighbours. Everywhere—even in Czechoslovakia where Communism is most monolithic—there is a loosening up and a readiness to permit in the countryside minor departures from the Russian model of collectivisation. It is clear enough from impatient speeches and from official articles in the Russian press, that Krushchev now recognises agriculture as far the weakest link in the Communist chain.

I suspect that the turning point was his trip to the U.S. and in particular the days he spent with the corn farmers of the Middle West. Krushchev has eyes to see and he was obviously overwhelmed by the success story of American agriculture since the New Deal. The soil of Illinois is very good, but it is no better than the black earth of the Ukraine. Yet Krushchev could see for himself the deadly contrast between the miraculous improvement in both rural production and rural prosperity since the 1930s, and the sullen failure of Russian collectivisation. Of course, in speeches he is careful not to compare the two systems, but to urge his own collective farmers to learn what they can from American applied science and technology. But he now knows very well that the *kolkhoz* is not a short cut but a dead end. The best way to maximise food production is to allow your farmers to go on owning their own land, encourage them to work together in genuinely free co-operatives, and when you have earned their good will, subject them to central state directives in return for guaranteed prices.

But how are these lessons to be applied east of the Iron Curtain? In Poland and Yugoslavia, the retreat from collectivisation took place early enough to permit a return to a peasant economy. But in Russia, after thirty years of Stalinite *kolkhoz* and state farm, the recreation of an independent peasantry seems completely out of the question. A vast amount of capital has been invested in machinery and buildings, quite unsuitable for small independent farmers. Even in Czechoslovakia where collectivisation has only just been completed, its abandonment could precipitate a counter-revolution.

Nevertheless, I am convinced that, now that the inefficiency of the *kolkhoz* has been demonstrated in terms of production per acre and—even more important—in terms of production per man employed in agriculture, the Kremlin will be compelled to follow Gomulka's example in one respect at least. It will have to relax its pressure on the countryside and permit the collective farmers to retain far more of the product of their labours.

Of course this will mean a far slower rate of industrialisation and the end of the spectacular annual figures of economic growth which are the pride of the Communist world. In order to relax the centrally imposed discipline, reduce the compulsory deliveries, and raise peasant living standards, the Communists will be compelled to make available far more of the consumer goods which the people in the country passionately desire. That can only be done by cutting capital investment and arms expenditure back to the kind of level which the free electorates of the Western democracies are prepared to tolerate.

In their peaceful competition with the West, the Communists have only been able to keep their rate of growth ahead of ours by dragooning the countryside into submission by means of the kolkhoz and deliberately retarding its rate of improvement. Once this artificial unbalance between industry and agriculture, town and country, begins to be reduced, Communism will begin to lose its totalitarian features, and the main gap which now sunders it from Western democracy will be narrowed. For the peaceful competition between democratic and Communist planning will then be taking place on something approaching fair terms; and co-existence which up to now has been merely a political abstraction could begin to become a social and human reality. So far agriculture has been the Achilles' heel of the Communist system. But its very failure could well provide a breach in total planning through which freedom could percolate throughout the Communist world.

GROTIUS ON ATOMIC WAR

In the Labour Party there was more passionate feeling about nuclear weapons than about any other issue with the exception of Clause IV. Unable to agree either with the nuclear warriors or with the nuclear pacifists, I contributed a series of joint articles in collaboration with George Wigg to the *New Statesman* in 1957.

It was our contention that defence problems could not be settled in terms of abstract principles; and we urged that the Labour Party, instead of tearing itself apart, should unite in denouncing the new nuclear strategy proclaimed in 1957 on the ground that it would sacrifice our real conventional defences to the illusions of nuclear defence.

This review of a forgotten work by Henry Kissinger was published in the *New Statesman* when the controversy was at its height. I reprint it as a reminder how fleeting fashions are in the world of military gamesmanship.

WHEN an intelligent man makes a convincing analysis and then proceeds to draw a ridiculous conclusion, you can be pretty sure that some political or moral obstacle has blocked the main channel of his argument and forced it to issue in an absurdity. The sad case of Henry A. Kissinger is a perfect example of this kind of subconscious *reductio ad absurdum*. Here is a young man with a penetrating mind, who has had access to all the relevant facts about nuclear weapons and American foreign policy. Yet the conclusion of his long and absorbing study is the proposal that the Soviet Union should be induced to accept an unwritten convention for limiting nuclear warfare and so permitting the Americans to wage it safely!

This is all the more depressing in that *Nuclear Weapons and Foreign Policy*[1] is the quintessence of U.S. high-level thinking on this subject. Seldom can there have been a more 'select'

[1] Oxford: Harper, 1957.

committee than the bunch of soldiers, scientists and administrators who were invited by the American Council on Foreign Affairs to collate the facts about nuclear strategy. The committee sat for 18 months, and then very sensibly decided that, instead of drafting a futile compromise document, it would encourage its able young secretary, Mr. Kissinger, to summarise its findings in a book, for which he would assume personal responsibility. The result is the most authoritative study of American strategic thinking since the Oppenheimer transcript.

To start with, Mr. Kissinger describes to us how the Pentagon has given military reality to the Dulles doctrine of massive retaliation. Its reaction to the Korean episode was—never again. Since then, the only kind of war for which the U.S. has been preparing is an all-out war, to be won in the first twenty-four hours by an all-out nuclear attack on the Soviet Union. This attack—which, of course, is always assumed to be a retaliation for a Communist Pearl Harbour—would at present take place from the ring of overseas bases which now run from Iceland, Canada and Alaska through Okinawa and the Philippines to Saudi Arabia, Morocco and Spain, and finally to the main atomic base in Great Britain. American thought and money have all been concentrated on ensuring that this all-out attack would succeed. Training in the Strategic Air Force, Mr. Kissinger reveals, is now so specialised that each crew only knows how to reach its own special target in the Soviet Union. And he adds:

> There will not even be the moral consolation that a Soviet surprise attack will appear unambiguous to world opinion. Given the distribution of the base system, our retaliatory blow is likely to reach Soviet territory before the first Soviet planes have reached their targets after crossing the Distant Early Warning Line.

One result of the Pentagon's concentration on massive retaliation is that Congress is unwilling to appropriate dollars for limited war preparations. As a result, there has been a crazy competition between the three services, with each trying to get the job of delivering the all-out blow and so make sure of the biggest appropriation. This has left the U.S. with virtually no power, either offensive or defensive, in anything less than an all-out war. The Eisenhower Doctrine, for instance, might require the movement by air of an American division to the Middle East. Mr. Kissinger tells us that, owing to the refusal of Congress to vote the money for an Army Transport Command, this would involve at present the mobilisation of every aeroplane in the United States for thirty days, including the civil air reserve.

Mr. Kissinger clinches his analysis with an analogy. The role of the nuclear deterrent in nuclear war corresponds, he says, to the role of the fleet-in-being in traditional naval strategy. The Grand Fleet was vital to British sea power; but what would one have thought of the Admiralty if it had concentrated on battleships—and nothing else? Moreover, whereas there was a balance of naval power, which could be altered if one side outbuilt the other, what we face now is a nuclear stalemate. That stalemate is not a product of nuclear parity: indeed, it will not be altered by a decisive technological break-through (the Russian construction of the inter-continental missile, for instance), provided that the other side still retains sufficient nuclear power to destroy the possessor of the new weapon. This is why the American determination at all costs to keep ahead of the Russians in the nuclear arms race is so wasteful and debilitating. As for our little stockpile of British H-bombs and hundred odd British H-bombers—strategically all these assets are a total loss.

I believe that this demolition of the all-out strategy is unanswerable; and it applies just as devastatingly to the Duncan Sandys defence policy. But what does Mr. Kissinger put in its place? His proposal is that, while America should maintain a Great Deterrent, equal priority should now be given to the provision of forces capable of fighting limited nuclear wars. The grand nuclear striking force should be kept out of sight, like the Grand Fleet, while all over the world American diplomacy is backed by mobile forces, equipped with tactical nuclear weapons.

Two reasons are given why the western world should adopt this strategy. First, the wide range of nuclear weapons required by a limited war is beyond the capacity of any but a highly industrialised nation. Secondly, the mobile and dispersed forces with which it will be fought require of the soldier the essentially democratic qualities of individual initiative, self-reliance and spontaneity. From this Mr. Kissinger concludes that, so far from seeking to limit membership of the nuclear club to the super-powers, Washington should welcome the prospect that nuclear weapons will soon be available to every nation—in the confidence that only the U.S. and its western allies are fully capable of using them.

But what is to prevent limited nuclear war developing into all-out nuclear war? Unless he can solve this problem, Mr. Kissinger's whole argument collapses. He solves it by the assertion that, while the Pentagon develops a spectrum of nuclear tactical weapons, the State Department must persuade the Russians to accept an unwritten convention for the conduct of limited war. Adopting the role of a 20th century Grotius, Mr. Kissinger proclaims the rules of nuclear war:

> We might propose that neither bases of the opposing strategic air forces nor towns above a certain size would be attacked, provided these bases would not be used to support tactical operations and that the towns would not contain military installations useful against armed forces.

There are pages more of this kind of absurdity—all based on the assumption that, whereas the Russians will not agree to any control or limitation of armaments, they will agree to fight limited wars under rules drawn up in order to ensure an American victory! In one passage Mr. Kissinger honestly admits that this proposal is not the only possibility, and that there is another strategy available to the West:

> If limited nuclear war is, as some say, a contradiction in terms, then the whole thrust of our military policy towards developing a diversified nuclear establishment is meaningless and dangerous. *We should then place our reliance on the most fearful application of our power to deter all-out war and on preparing conventional forces for limited wars.*

Of course, this was the obvious conclusion, to which Mr. Kissinger's analysis irresistibly pointed. The obstacle which prevented him from reaching it was, I think, an amalgam of a deep-seated instinct and a political decision. Instinctively, the American people revolts against the idea of waging war with any but the most modern weapons; and it will always feel that American boys should not be asked to risk their lives in close combat against the enemy, if he can be destroyed at a distance by a weapon of mass destruction. It was in response to this national instinct that the Administration committed itself to equipping its forces with nuclear tactical weapons. Mr. Kissinger is certain that we shall never again

see an American army or an American fleet which relies exclusively
on conventional weapons. And that is why the Kremlin will retain
its capacity to fight non-nuclear wars and use that capacity when it
chooses to call our nuclear bluff.

There is one way out of the impasse. Just because the Americans
are committed to nuclear weapons, there is no reason whatsoever
why America's allies should go the same way. Indeed, there is every
reason why Britain and the other European members of Nato should
draw the opposite conclusion from Mr. Kissinger's analysis. I am
arguing, in fact, that, in view of the inherent American inability to dispense with nuclear weapons, it is essential that
America's allies should concentrate their efforts on building up
conventional defences. This is the natural and obvious division of
labour inside Nato. For, if it is against the American national instinct and national interest to renounce nuclear weapons, the renun-
ciation of their production and use is something to which every
European would instinctively respond and which would also increase
our national security.

No one will deny that such a proposal, coming from Britain,
would have an immense response, not only in France but, even more,
in West Germany, where the aversion to nuclear arms is still
immense. What Mr. Kissinger's remarkable book has done is to provide an authoritative demonstration that the proposal would also
be acceptable to the Pentagon and the State Department. At present
they are reluctantly permitting us to indulge in nuclear *folies de
grandeur* and forcing the Germans to become a nuclear menace. But,
if only Britain were voluntarily to give the lead in renouncing nuclear
weapons, how relieved the Americans would be! In that case they
could give up this ridiculous idea that limited nuclear warfare is
possible and rely on their old-fashioned defence forces which are so
repugnant to their own national tradition.

WESTERN DEFENCE IN THE 1960s

The Royal United Services Institution ran a series of lectures in 1961 on the general problem of Western defence. By accepting its invitation I compelled myself to work out, more fully than was possible either in an article or in a back bench speech, my objections to the current theories of nuclear strategy.

i

LET me at once confess the qualifications I lack for talking about Western defence in the 1960s. I was a civilian throughout the second World War. I have not even the book training of having studied strategy or read military history. I am, however, what is called an intellectual; and, ironically enough, this means that, by modern American standards, I am fully qualified to write a long book on the theory of nuclear warfare.

One of the strangest features of American life in the 1950s—which no doubt will continue throughout the 1960s—is that many of the experts who lead the discussion on the nature of war have no experience or training. Since the weapons which it is assumed will be decisive in the next world war have never been used, except on two occasions, and then against an enemy without means of retaliation; since the strategy to be employed has never been tested, and since the whole character of the next war is assumed (I shall query this assumption later) to be totally unlike that of any preceding war, all three American Services now employ pure—or impure—intellectuals to discuss its nature. Indeed, things have gone so far, I gather, that anyone with experience of previous wars or previous fighting is written off, owing to that experience, as out of date, biased, or prejudiced.

I was very struck the other day when I was talking to one of the most famous strategic pundits of America just before he went to the White House to join Mr. Kennedy's staff. I said to him in conversation, 'Did you ever in your life go near the Army or hear a shot fired in anger?' 'Of course not', he said, 'one would hardly get to my position if one had'. I know he was joking. But it's a remarkable fact that a new profession had been created in the United States, the profession of war gamester. His job is, by the severest and most abstract kind of hypothetical logic, to work out the possible moves and counter-moves of nuclear war and on this basis to suggest to the politician and the practical soldier what strategic decisions they should take. The qualifications of a war gamester combine those of a chess player and a soothsayer. He needs a clear mathematical mind, which can abstract itself from all human considerations, assimilate facts like an adding machine, and then, with absolute predictability and accuracy, produce the logical conclusions from the particular sets of facts which have been fed into his thinking machine. The war gamester, in fact, is a human computer.

I am frankly horrified by the thought that possibly the strategy and the foreign policy of our strongest ally is being decided by the kind of books and papers to which I am referring. Moreover, although I have admitted that I am an intellectual, I must now add that I have two disqualifications which would always have prevented me from becoming a war gamester. The first is that I am a practical politician and I now know something about the way political decisions are arrived at. The second is that, in the second World War, I spent some three years attached first to A.F.H.Q. Algiers and then to S.H.A.E.F., and in these two Headquarters I learned at first hand a little about the way that military decisions are reached. So I know something about the stuff of human nature in politics and in war.

I hope that this experience, which disqualifies me from joining the American war games, may qualify me, in your eyes, for discussing the relations between politics and strategy. In this country we still believe that no war gamester, thinking in the abstract, can teach us much about the decisions which Presidents, Premiers, and Chiefs of Staff have to take. For those solemn decisions are often neither technical nor complex. At least, that was my experience in that no-man's-land between strategy and policy, between the soldiers and the politicians, where I lived during the war and which I have revisited from time to time since 1945. Most of the decisions which have proved to be real turning points in modern history were neither purely military nor purely political. They were a mixture of both— and this applies not only to the topmost decisions but also lower down; on the level, for example, of the Commander-in-Chief of an expeditionary force or the British representative on an international commission. To be a successful commander, a soldier has to understand the nature of the politician's problem, and vice versa.

ii

Let me start, therefore, with a politician's reflections on the title of this lecture. Would I be right in assuming that implicit in this title is the assumption that Western defence includes the defence of Britain and of British interests; that when one says 'Western defence in the 1960s', one includes in that concept not only the defence of these islands but of British interests throughout the world? Now that was not an assumption which would have been accepted without question even as recently as 1945. When Lord Attlee took over from Sir Winston, there was a powerful stream of public opinion in this country, particularly on the Left, which believed that Britain's role in the post-war world should be to lead a 'Third Force', which would stand between Russia and America, mediating between East and West and, if possible, preventing the world being riven into rival blocs. Indeed, it would not be unfair to say that, in so far as foreign affairs was an issue in the 1945 election, the mandate on which the Attlee Government was elected was against the integration of Britain into a Western alliance.

When, therefore, Ernest Bevin rebuilt the Anglo-American alliance, he did it against the natural inclinations of a large number of the back-benchers behind him in Parliament and a great section of public opinion outside. As a trade union leader, he had learned always to see where the real power was and to make sure that, in any fight he had on, the big battalions were on his side. As soon as he came to the Foreign Office he saw something which I, as an ex-member of General Eisenhower's staff, knew well. When the war ended, one of the few stable factors in Europe were the armies organised under Anglo-American integrated command.

There was some whisper in Anglo-American circles about the possibility of 'finishing the job', and there is little doubt that, at the time, the Anglo-American alliance had the military power to 'liberate' Eastern Europe had the decision been taken. Of course, I am not suggesting it would have been a wise decision or politically practicable. But the physical power was at our disposal. 1945 was not a year when the West was inferior to the East in conventional strength. It was probably the last moment in history, indeed, when the West had the capacity to enforce its will by a superiority in conventional weapons. And behind that military strength was the enormous, co-ordinated war economy that had been established not only in the North Atlantic but in the Mediterranean and the Middle East as well.

On the other side of the world there was an equal and opposite reality, whose nature Mr. Bevin was quick to realise—the implacable hostility towards the British Empire developed by the Soviet Union. At the time, I was one of those who believed passionately in the Third Force, but our difficulty in persuading the Labour Government to take our views seriously was the lack of evidence to support our belief that, if Britain tried to act as leader of a Third Force and mediator in world affairs, either Russia or the United States would accept her. I say 'either Russia or America' because it is sometimes forgotten that, during that first dreary post-war winter, there were strong forces in Washington (though they did not include President Truman) who favoured the achievement of co-existence with the Soviet Union at the cost of the old 'colonial Powers', including Britain. During the war there had been plenty of evidence that Mr. Roosevelt and his Chiefs of Staff were constantly suspecting Sir Winston's motives in urging a Mediterranean strategy. They thought his aim was not to win the war but to promote Britain's imperial interests after the war, an objective in which they had no interest. Indeed, at Yalta Mr. Roosevelt seemed on occasion to regard himself and Stalin as the two progressive statesmen whose job it was to share world leadership and put the old colonialists in their place.

True enough, even Mr. Roosevelt, just before he died, was shaken in these assumptions, particularly by Russian behaviour in Poland. But Mr. Truman's decision abruptly to terminate Lend-Lease in August, 1945, suggested that, though his suspicions of Stalin were strong, he still regarded Britain as a strong and dangerous rival and not as a partner in urgent need of assistance. It was Ernest Bevin who changed this atmosphere in Washington. Deliberately he shattered any chances that remained of an American-Soviet *rapprochement* and sowed the mustard seed of suspicion in the American mind which grew up into the great tree of the cold war. The Persian crisis gave him an ideal opportunity to swing an America, only too anxious to retreat into disarmed neutrality, into acceptance of its responsibility as the leader of the Western alliance. From that *ad hoc* Anglo-American alliance, with its limited objective of forcing the Russians to withdraw from Azerbaijan, there grew the Truman doctrine, under which Greece and Turkey were taken over as responsibilities by the U.S.A. Out of the Truman doctrine of 1947 grew the Anglo-American airlift of 1948 and the N.A.T.O. alliance of 1949.

iii

In the conditions of 1949, Ernest Bevin was right in regarding the construction of N.A.T.O. as essential to the defence of these islands and of Western Europe. But is, there any case for revising this assumption in the new conditions of the 1960s? One answer to this question is to reflect for a moment on the Suez venture, which showed the difficulty for Britain of trying to 'go it alone' in military terms. We now know that it was only three days before the American Treasury was able to bring Sir Anthony to heel by a direct threat to the pound, combined with the prospect of something approaching oil sanctions. From this point of view, Suez was a painfully unsuccessful experiment in military independence, which is not likely to be repeated by Britain. And the fact that the bitter ill-will engendered on both sides of the Atlantic by this episode was so rapidly dissipated demonstrates what a profound common interest Britain and America both have in maintaining the alliance.

Yet it cannot be denied that, during the 1950s, this conviction that N.A.T.O. is a good bargain for Britain has been undermined. And the chief reason for this deterioration is nuclear strategy. For, if I am to be convinced that the defence of these islands should be based upon the Western alliance, then I must be able to assure myself that the strategy on which the defence of the whole alliance is based, (a), does not commit this country in peacetime to nuclear threats, whose fulfilment would mean national suicide, and (b), gives us a reasonable chance of survival in case of actual war. Any sane man who could not be sure on both these points would at least have to ask himself whether N.A.T.O. should continue to be the basis of our British defence policy. But, provided we can be reassured that the Western alliance does not fail on these two tests, it is difficult to deny that the terms on which America is committed to the defence of Western Europe under the N.A.T.O. alliance are a good bargain for this country.

But what about the rest of our defence interests? One of the things which strikes me when I listen to the defence debates in the Commons each year is the way in which they tend to concentrate on N.A.T.O. and Europe, as though this country's defence policy was predominantly concerned with Europe and the Mediterranean.

Yet Great Britain is something more important than two islands off the coast of Europe, and obviously we do have other defence problems. Indeed, this was made very clear by Ernest Bevin in 1946. For, at the self-same moment that he made it his major objective to commit the Americans to the defence of Europe (he defined this to include Greece and Turkey), he was taking endless trouble to exclude America from any political influence in the Middle East. If there was a motive in Mr. Bevin's mind as strong as his will to get the Americans into Europe as the senior partner in the Western alliance, it was his determination to keep British predominance in the Middle East and persuade America to play the role there of our junior partner. Of course, he would have liked to have American troops, but only on condition that they were there to assist him in enforcing his own Palestine or Egyptian policies, and his own ideas for securing our oil supplies. And when it became clear that no American President could ever play this humble role, Ernest Bevin decided that Britain, out of her own resources, must at all costs hold the Middle East. 'Out there I am fighting for the British workers' standard of life', he used to say to us in the Parliamentary Labour Party. 'Unless we are prepared to see a cut in that standard, we just cannot afford to lose Persia'.

So, even in those difficult post-war years, when we were desperately weak and desperately in need of an alliance which firmly committed America to our defence, there were still areas in which we were prepared, if necessary, to act on our own and to maintain an independent imperial strategy, distinct from and, if necessary, in conflict with that of the Western alliance. This applied not only to the Middle East. Bevin envisaged Britain as a great military power in the Far East as well, operating from a naval base at Singapore and still playing a role in the defence of Australia and New Zealand. And he also accepted heavy defence obligations in many parts of Africa.

Any attempt, therefore, to define Bevin's defence policy simply in terms of N.A.T.O. or the Western alliance leaves out a vital element of it. He at least was too canny to assume that either the Americans or N.A.T.O. would feel an unlimited obligation to look after British interests in the Persian Gulf, in Africa, or in the South Pacific.

Of course, much of the Empire the Labour Government inherited has since been given up, and with it the strategic commitments it involved. But the defence of the scattered remains of a great Empire may be more burdensome than the defence of its earlier unity. Certainly today we cannot reckon that any of our allies are vitally concerned to preserve what British interests remain in our areas of previous suzerainty. So we have to postulate that there are two disparate and conflicting elements in British defence policy, (a), the defence of Western Europe and the British Isles, which takes place within the Western alliance, and (b), the defence of purely British overseas interests which must be covered by British forces and a British defence policy outside S.E.A.T.O. and C.E.N.T.O.

iv

If I have been labouring the obvious, it is because of something very puzzling which seems to follow from it. Here on these islands we have a people with limited manpower and limited resources, who have inherited the task of defending what are still vast British interests outside Europe, on which our influence and prosperity depend. One would have thought, therefore, that our strategy would be designed to ensure that, while we made a fair and full contribution to N.A.T.O., we should make sure that the fulfilment of this European commitment did not prevent us from looking after our non-N.A.T.O. commitments. In particular, it would seem obvious common sense that our contribution to N.A.T.O. should, if possible, be made in terms of equipment and trained manpower that can be used both for European and for Imperial defence.

Yet in the 1950s exactly the opposite decision was taken. A few months after Suez—possibly in reaction against it—the decision was taken to run down a large part of our conventional forces and to give top priority to the effort to maintain Britain as the third nuclear power with its own independent nuclear deterrent and, as a backing to this strategic threat, to build up 'nuclear streamlined forces' in place of the conscript army that we had kept in being since the war.

In this essay I am not asking what value the independent British deterrent has for the defence of the West in its role as an addition to the American deterrent; that is a separate subject. I am asking a much simpler question. What value has the British independent deterrent for the second of our two defence objectives, the defence of British overseas interests throughout the world? In the Persian Gulf, in Singapore, in Hongkong, in the crisis which may blow up at any moment in Central Africa or Kenya—will our V-bombers, with their H-bombs, be of any assistance whatsoever? Where in the world can we find one point at which the Sandys defence policy strengthens our Commonwealth position? Ironically enough, a strategy designed chiefly to maintain Britain as the third Great Power has made us a minor nuclear satellite of the United States and finally destroyed whatever capacity we still retained to remain a Great Power in terms of military defence.

What were the motives which prompted this extraordinary decision? I shall have one or two tentative answers to this question when I deal with nuclear weapons at the end. Now, however, I want to indicate the second part of this unresolved puzzle. We have concentrated since 1957 on making ourselves the second nuclear power of the Western alliance. In view of the political necessity to prevent a sharp growth in the annual defence budget, this decision was accompanied by drastic economies in conventional weapons and conventional manpower: the Government decided to abolish National Service and to build up a purely Regular Army. Again, I do not question here the long-term goal. My puzzle is this. How could a responsible Government announce its decision to end National Service when the nuclear tactical weapons which were to be the substitute for conventional forces were not yet in production? How could the Minister of Defence, in 1957, make the security of these islands depend on weapons, many of which have not yet gone into production four years later?

Moreover, once the decision had been taken, it faced the country with a dilemma. If there is to be no National Service; if the size of each Service is to be limited to the number we can afford to persuade to become Regulars; if, on the other hand, it is out of the question to go back on our commitment to maintain four divisions or their equivalent in Western Europe; if all this is true, it is surely clear that the only alternative to reintroducing conscription will be a ruthless cut-back of our Commonwealth commitments. I am not, of course, saying that this cut-back will take place. I am merely saying that it may be forced upon us by the decision to rely on all-Regular forces of limited size.

I am aware that one or two of my colleagues, on both sides of the Commons, have suggested as an alternative a further withdrawal of our forces from Germany and the maintenance of what would in that case be merely a token contribution to the S.H.A.P.E. Army. I find it difficult to believe that any British Government, whether of the Left or the Right, could take this action. After all, the French decision to permit German rearmament was only extracted from them by Sir Anthony Eden's solemn pledge to keep four British divisions in Europe for 99 years. And if there are some people who say we need not be too conscientious about keeping our pledges, since so many of our European allies have defaulted on theirs, I would remind them of an even stronger argument. The West German Army is already some eight divisions strong and within the next year or two will achieve its full strength of twelve divisions. Compared with this, our contribution, whittled away by successive reductions, is now dangerously small. To reduce it still further would be to surrender to the Germans any influence we may still possess over the strategy and defence policy of the S.H.A.P.E. armies.

So there it is. Since we must not and dare not whittle away our N.A.T.O. commitment any further, the dilemma which faces us is extremely acute. Either we are determined, at all costs, to maintain what is left of our Commonwealth defence obligations. In that case we must be prepared to pay the price by raising the minimum manpower required to cover them, even in ways which are intensely unpopular. The only alternative is to do something equally unpopular and admit that, since we haven't got the men, we must cancel the commitments. Perhaps I should add that there is a third possibility— to continue carrying the commitments in the hope that we shall never have to honour them, and then find ourselves unable to do so when the moment of crisis comes. No one is shameless enough openly to recommend that we should adopt this third possibility, that we assume the obligations of a Great Power without willing the means to honour our bond. But that something uncommonly like this is actually happening today.

v

I now turn to the other half of our problem, the defence of these islands within the Western alliance, and I want to start by asking why it is that N.A.T.O. is disintegrating before our eyes? The precise figures of the targets agreed at Lisbon are disputed. But it will not be denied that the firm goal for 1952 established at that conference was fifty divisions. Why are there only some twenty or so divisions under S.A.C.E.U.R., many of them under-manned and under-equipped? Why, to make it worse, do we find, combined with this failure to provide the physical strength the alliance requires, an increasing moral disintegration? First we can summarily dismiss all the physical excuses for these failures. It is sometimes said that we cannot provide fifty divisions because we in Western Europe are outnumbered by the Russians. The actual figures belie this excuse. The population of Britain and Western Europe is larger than that of the Soviet Union, considerably better educated, and enriched with traditional skills. There is no numerical limitation which prevents us raising the manpower required.

I conclude, therefore, that the basic problem of N.A.T.O. today is a moral problem, a problem of will power. Unless the politicians tackle this moral problem, the soldiers can do nothing at all. An authoritarian nation can conscript its people and even maintain the fighting morale of its army, although the ordinary man in the street, when left to his own thoughts, feels morally uncommitted. But you cannot raise armies in a democracy unless you convince the people that what you are doing is sensible, just, and necessary. One of the things which most gladdened me about the election of President Kennedy is that he is a young man who recognises the importance of will power and morale, who has stopped talking only in terms of statistics and weapon systems, and admits that what has been lacking with us during the 1950s is will power and a good conscience. And what saps that will power is the uncertainty of our aim. We all say we want to defend freedom. But if we dare to start discussing with each other exactly what we feel about freedom, the nations start quarrelling with each other, and within each nation we fall apart into warring groups.

I will mention only two of the uncertainties which have recently demoralised the Western alliance. The first is the assumption which often underlies the concept of interdependence. Many supporters of N.A.T.O. wish to transform it into an Atlantic confederation, thinking of it as a kind of modern Roman Empire, whose frontiers are coterminous with the limits of civilisation. Here, within these frontiers they say, is contained the 'free world', which we must defend against the modern barbarians who are threatening it from outside.

I can best comment on this concept of Western defence by means of an anecdote. In 1929 I went to Germany for a year and lived for some months in Frankfurt-am-Main. My host was a distinguished Jewish judge, who committed suicide when Hitler came to power because he was the kind of German Jew who could not bear to leave his own country. On Sundays we used to walk on the Taunus mountains. Along the great bare saddle at the top there still runs the line of the Roman *limes*, a barrow and a ditch, with a magnificent view towards the Rhine valley. I remember standing there one Sunday morning, as the old man said to me, 'Things haven't changed much since the Romans left. This side, my dear Dick, civilisation. The other side, barbarism. It was true then. It is still true today.' This German judge had a clear and precise notion of Western defence. The job was to defend the *limes* of civilisation, the place where the West ends and slavery begins. It was the simplicity of their strategic concept which maintained Roman morale for so many hundreds of years. The Roman legionaries knew what they had to do and why they were doing it.

Would a similar concept give a similar morale to N.A.T.O.'s soldiers today? The belief that it would was, I think, at the core of what we may call the Dulles doctrine. John Foster Dulles saw the world in terms of a simple conflict between good and evil, along a line that divided the 'free world' from its enemies. Lack of success made the Dulles doctrine unpopular. Yet a number of people, here as well as in America, still profoundly believe in this basic assumption.

The trouble about this idea of a frontier of freedom is that it divides far more than it unites. Within the Western world there are many millions who do not believe either that all freedom and civilisation is contained within the Atlantic alliance or that Communist Russia and China can be intelligently compared with the barbarian hordes outside the Roman *limes*. The concept which gave morale to the Roman armies divides and demoralises those of N.A.T.O. In our modern circumstances, it is a defeatist doctrine, because the forces it condemns as barbarism are so patently capable of outpacing our rate of technological progress and adding superiority in science to their already overwhelming superiority in numbers.

At least for two hundred years the Romans had the strength required to hold the *limes* against the barbarians, whereas we know that, if we define as barbarism everything outside N.A.T.O., then barbarism is bound to win. That is why, when I hear talk about the 'free world', as contrasted with the Communist world, two doubts arise in my mind. First I ask myself whether all freedom is in fact contained within N.A.T.O.; and, secondly, I wonder whether, even if it were, it would be wise to declare permanent war on those outside.

Let us assume, however, for a moment that the concept is sound. If one accepts it, it seems to me clearly to follow that the only rational thing for the West to do is to integrate our nations into a single super-state. If we are to defend this small part of the world against a rapidly growing and rapidly developing Communist bloc, it is surely clear that we cannot afford the waste of divided sovereignty and the disastrous military and economic weakness that it brings. Theoretically, it is possible to conceive that an Atlantic Union, organised as a single confederation dominated by the United States, could survive for some generations at least. What is not conceivable is that an Atlantic community, divided into a number of independent nations, each producing its own weapons, each with its own strategy, can be militarily viable. If Rome had permitted thirty different Emperors, each with his own army, inside its frontiers, the Empire would have disintegrated hundreds of years earlier. It was the strength of Rome to realise that, against the barbarians pressing on the *limes*, defence must be under highly centralised control.

This logic, however, is unacceptable not only to the White House and the Pentagon but to the other members of N.A.T.O., including ourselves. I have not met any prominent soldier or politician willing to accept the view that we are the Greeks in an American Empire and that we must become members of an Atlantic super-state in order to defend ourselves in the cold war.

vi

Then what is the alternative? I suggest that our strategy should be based on a very different concept. We should assume that the era during which the world was dominated first by the European Powers and, more recently, by the North Atlantic community, is drawing to a close. By the end of this century the balance of power will have shifted from the old, industrialized Western Powers to the new Powers grouped round Russia and China. On that assumption the major objective of our defence policy would be to ensure that this transition occurs without a world war which blows us all to pieces.

It is clear that such an outlook will lead us to develop quite a different kind of strategy. Instead of trying to contain a barbarian threat along a *limes* that runs right across the world, it should be our object to break up the power blocs that have been formed since 1945 and to create buffer areas of independence or neutrality between the two super-Powers, and so gradually produce new terms of co-existence.

I realize that the assumptions which underlie this concept of Western defence policy will be profoundly distasteful to many. But I am sure you will agree with me on one thing at least. We cannot have a successful N.A.T.O. defence policy without deciding between these rival concepts and making up our minds what it is that we are basically trying to do. For, if we try to confuse both concepts and do two things simultaneously—to man the frontiers of freedom and to achieve terms of co-existence—then we are not likely to come off very well against some very formidable opponents.

A good illustration of the defeats we inflict on ourselves by this uncertainty of purpose is to be found in Germany. Suppose for a moment our strategy is based on the concept of the *limes* of civilisation. In that case we should be wholly content with the present *status quo* and it should be regarded as fortunate that the frontier of civilisation has been drawn so as to put most of the Prussians outside, whereas we have the South and West Germans inside the Atlantic community. On this assumption, indeed, it should be our policy deliberately to keep Germany divided and to integrate our Germans into the Atlantic confederation. At least that is a policy. It makes sense, militarily as well as politically. But it is not the policy of N.A.T.O. today. On the contrary, every N.A.T.O. Government is committed to the objective of German reunification and denounces as intolerable a partition which keeps eighteen million Germans under Russian control. Our strategy, in fact, is based on two contradictory assumptions: (1) that we should keep Germany and Europe divided and be content to defend the frontier of civilisation established in 1945; (2) that we should seek a reunification of Germany as part of the pacification of Europe and the reduction of tension that can only be achieved on the basis of peaceful co-existence with the Soviet Union.

No wonder N.A.T.O. is in trouble. For the soldier requires from the politician a clear directive. He must be told what the mission of the N.A.T.O. armies is. And if the politicians do not know the answer or give contradictory answers, it is not surprising that morale is undermined.

The second uncertainty in N.A.T.O. policy relates to the use of nuclear weapons, both strategic and tactical. Nothing has demoralised the Western world more than the ambiguity of the attitude adopted by our Governments to these new weapon systems. It is as though our politicians and our soldiers had both refused to think clearly, for fear of facing the facts.

What is it that has prompted this prolonged exhibition of intellectual cowardice? In studying this problem, we should first observe that our uncertainties and ambiguities do not seem to occur in the Communist States. The Russians have had no difficulty in assimilating nuclear strategy into their military system—nor have the Chinese! When I was in Peking a few years ago, I did not meet a single Chinese Communist who felt the faintest moral compunction at the prospect that his country might some day rely on nuclear threats. On the contrary, they were all looking forward to it with eager anticipation. Why is it that the Communists have avoided the agonising moral reappraisals which have racked the Western World?

Some people will say that it is because they are uncivilised or because Marxism is fundamentally immoral. I do not agree. The explanation, I think, must be found in the fact that the Communists do not welcome nuclear weapons as an epoch-making innovation, which renders all previous weapons and strategies obsolete. They see them merely as another phase in the development of warfare and try quite coolly to assess their objective utility as a means of imposing one's will on the enemy.

Looked at from this point of view, nuclear weapons, at least in their present stage of development, have grave disadvantages. Like gas, they work both ways and that is one reason why, to the Russians, they are not particularly attractive. Of course, if the potential enemy has them, they must have them too. But we have plenty of evidence that the Russians did not rush into the nuclear arms race with any great enthusiasm or expectations. They followed us into it because they could not afford to permit a Western monopoly in this respect.

What a contrast with the attitude of the Western democracies! In our countries the nuclear weapon was welcomed because it seemed to provide a method of containing Communism without the trouble either of waging conventional war or raising and equipping large fighting armies. This conviction that the nuclear bomb could provide a substitute for the fighting soldier was already in evidence as early as 1945. There is now little doubt about the motives that prompted the American administration to sanction the use of the atom bomb at Hiroshima and Nagasaki. One reason why the President was urged to drop the bomb was undoubtedly the desire of those responsible for its production to test its effect before peace made the test impossible. But Mr. Truman's main concern was to shorten the war and save casualties. It is absurd to attribute to the President Machiavellian calculations about keeping Russia out. In sober fact, although Japan was broken and desperately seeking to negotiate an armistice via the Russians, Mr. Truman was still trying to make Stalin honour his promise to come into the war against Japan. What moved him and his closest advisers was the thought that the war could be ended by a nice clean act of annihilation, in which hundreds of thousands of American lives could be saved at the cost of a few thousand remote and unknown Japanese civilians.

vii

Anyone who is shocked at a leader of a Western democracy thinking in this way should remember that Hiroshima and Nagasaki were not the first acts of this kind. The nuclear weapon—the final instrument of annihilation—was only the logical fulfilment of the strategy of area bombing evolved by our own Bomber Command and employed by the Americans in their fire-bomb raids against Japanese cities. Already in the 1930s the possibility of substituting aerial annihilation of the enemy home front for old-fashioned warfare in the field had been discussed in a number of theoretical strategic treatises. It is interesting to note that this concept of annihilation by remote control was not the brain-child either of Hitler's Germany or of Stalin's Russia. It was evolved after the first World War by the theorists of air warfare in Paris, Washington, and London, and it was accepted uncritically by the politicians because we

Westerners detest war and are always searching for a substitute for it.

What evidence was there to suggest that, with bombs of the strength then available, an enemy home front could be broken from the air? Careful German experimentation during the Spanish war had shown that Republican morale was actually stiffened by aerial bombing. Later this was confirmed during the second World War. During 1941 and 1942, one of my jobs as Director of Psychological Warfare against Germany was to study German home morale and, in particular, to assess the effects, both on war production and on the spirit of the German people, of our bomber raids. I remember my Department put forward paper after paper indicating that there was no evidence that Germany would surrender even if she were subjected to a far higher level of bombing than that which Britain had suffered. Indeed, all our evidence about the moral effect of the blitz on Britain suggested that so far from breaking morale, it actually strengthened it. Unless the effectiveness of the bombing, therefore, was raised far beyond even the biggest claims of Bomber Command, we predicted that its effect would be to stiffen German resistance. Our expert predictions had no effect on the War Cabinet. Among its members, particularly Sir Winston and Lord Attlee, there was a will to believe that a substitute for Passchendaele and the Somme must be found, and our soldiers and sailors spared the casualty rates of the first World War. If that could be achieved only by annihilating the German home front, well, the Germans had brought their fate on themselves.

As Sir Charles Snow pointed out in his recent *Science and Government*,[1] the priority given to bombing was not justified in terms of the destruction caused; indeed, it probably delayed the invasion of Europe for a year. Yet the same prejudices were revealed and the same mistakes made when we were confronted with the issues of nuclear warfare after 1945. But now there was added to those prejudices a new and even more dangerously arrogant assumption of technological superiority. Even if the Russians tried to compete, it was assumed that we should always remain well ahead in this particular arms race and never be called on to make good the threat of annihilation on which our new nuclear strategy was based. With these new weapons, in fact, we could do what the Romans were never able to do—defeat the barbarians without fighting them. The

[1] Oxford University Press, London. 1961.

Roman Empire failed when the manpower for the legions failed. It was no good maintaining the Roman Wall unless there were sufficient men to garrison it. Armed with nuclear weapons, our leaders had the wonderful feeling that they could keep the peace and preserve Western freedom without the burden of using mass armies.

Not unnaturally, this nuclear strategy was particularly popular among the politicians, who realised the unpopularity in a democracy of maintaining large armed forces in peacetime. For the soldiers, too, the strategy had its temptations. One reason at least which prompted our Service Chiefs to accept the Sandys defence policy in 1957 was the unpopularity of National Service in the affluent society and the difficulty of turning the citizen of a modern democracy into a fighting soldier. In Korea, it became only too clear that most Western soldiers are unwilling to fight on level terms with a Communist enemy. Indeed, one of the moral problems of Western defence is our reluctance to be killed, compared with the stoic fatalism of a Chinese or a Russian soldier. That is why no Western army can sustain a casualty rate such as the Russians sustained in the second World War and the Chinese in Korea. Western soldiers expect their commanders to provide them with overwhelming superiority in both long-range and short-range weapons of annihilation. Where this superiority is denied them and they have to fight on level terms, then morale becomes questionable. The truth is that the nuclear weapon was developed in the West as a substitute for the fighting soldier, and nuclear annihilation came to be regarded as a means of avoiding the long, evenly matched slaughter of battles of position.

In the critical years when this nuclear strategy was adopted, a number of voices were raised against it. In Washington, for example, as we know from the transcript of the Oppenheimer hearings, George Kennan, then head of policy planning at the State Department, and a number of leading scientists foresaw clearly what has actually happened and warned the President against it. Mr. Kennan, in particular, was able to predict with uncanny accuracy the effect of reliance on the H-bomb on Western morale and Western diplomatic strength. The result has been a crisis of conscience, combined with a growing impotence. A false assumption of the West's nuclear strength has been used to justify a failure either to raise the necessary manpower or to provide that manpower with adequate equipment. As a result, our leaders have had to tell S.A.C.E.U.R. that his armies must rely, from the very first stage of a war, on nuclear tactical weapons. This nuclear strategy was adopted and our conventional forces were permitted to run down some years before the nuclear tactical weapons existed. Now that they are beginning to come into production, S.A.C.E.U.R. has been compelled to dispose of them at battalion level by the fact that he does not have sufficient conventional strength to hold positions on level terms against Russia's fighting strength. This reliance on the nuclear armoury as an *ersatz* for fire power saps morale and makes it very difficult to train a fighting soldier. After all, our men know perfectly well that the Russians also possess nuclear tactical weapons, which cancel out any advantage ours may give us. They also know that, once ours are employed, the chances of the Russians failing to blot out the bases in N.A.T.O. countries are small indeed. So the strategy of N.A.T.O. becomes a threat by the N.A.T.O. countries to commit national suicide if the Red Army moves in Europe. That is hardly an encouragement to fighting morale. If you tell a soldier that his job is to stand on guard while the button is pressed and his home is destroyed, he is not likely to exude self-confidence.

We could tell them something very different. 'We know that the Russians have more men and better equipment,' we could say 'and we are determined to remedy this as soon as possible. But meanwhile, if trouble comes, it will be your duty to put up the best resistance you can with conventional weapons alone. If you fight to the death, the crisis may be averted. If you fail, nuclear weapons are bound to be employed, and your homeland will be destroyed.' A strategy of this kind would, I believe, restore to the soldier his fighting spirit, because it would give him a cause and restore his importance to his country.

I conclude with this thought. The blame for our plight does not lie with the soldiers but with the politicians and so-called leaders of public opinion. N.A.T.O.'s morale is being destroyed by two factors: (1) an arrogant assumption that the Westerner, as the defender of civilisation, must always be able to rely on superior equipment in the field and superior economic strength and scientific skill at home; and (2) a morality, or lack of morality, that justifies the democracies in relying on weapons of annihilation as a substitute for the will to sacrifice for the cause of peace. It is the combination of this intellectual fallacy with this moral decadence that has blinded us in the last decade and a half, so that we have permitted ourselves to become almost completely impotent to defend ourselves. The beginning of wisdom for N.A.T.O. is the recognition that, whether in peaceful competition or in cold or in hot war, the West must now compete on level terms with the Communists or go under.

R. H. S. CROSSMAN

R. H. S. Crossman was born in 1907, the son of the late Mr. Justice Crossman. He was educated at Winchester and New College, Oxford, where, between 1931 and 1938, he was Tutor in Philosophy. During this time he was active in local politics and led the Labour Group on Oxford City Council. During the war he was Director of Propaganda to Enemy Countries in the Political Intelligence Department of the Foreign Office, and between 1943 and 1945 served on General Eisenhower's staff with S.H.A.E.F. Between 1938 and 1945 he was Assistant Editor of *The New Statesman and Nation*. In 1945 he was elected M.P. for Coventry East. On the return of the Labour Party to power in October 1964 he was appointed Minister of Housing and Local Government. His publications include: *Plato Today*, (1937); *Socrates*, (1938); *Government and the Governed*, (1939); *How We Are Governed*, (1939); *Palestine Mission*, (1947); *The Charm of Politics*, (1958); *A Nation Reborn*, (1960), and in 1949 he edited the famous examination of Communism, *The God That Failed*.